T0313876

DEALING WITH PEACE

The Guatemalan Campesino Movement and the Post-Conflict Neoliberal State

Dealing with Peace

The Guatemalan Campesino Movement and the Post-Conflict Neoliberal State

SIMON GRANOVSKY-LARSEN

UNIVERSITY OF TORONTO PRESS
Toronto Buffalo London

ISBN 978-1-4875-0143-3

Library and Archives Canada Cataloguing in Publication

Title: Dealing with peace : the Guatemalan campesino movement
 and the post-conflict neoliberal state / Simon Granovsky-Larsen.
Names: Granovsky-Larsen, Simon, author.
Description: Includes bibliographical references and index.
Identifiers: Canadiana 20189067543 | ISBN 9781487501433 (hardcover)
Subjects: LCSH: Agricultural laborers – Political activity – Guatemala. | LCSH:
 Peasants – Political activity – Guatemala. | LCSH: Social movements –
 Guatemala. | LCSH: Neoliberalism – Guatemala. | LCSH: Agricultural
 development projects – Guatemala. | LCSH: Land reform – Guatemala.
Classification: LCC HD1531.G9 G73 2019 | DDC 305.5/63097281—dc23

This book has been published with the help of a grant from the Federation
for the Humanities and Social Sciences, through the Awards to Scholarly
Publications Program, using funds provided by the Social Sciences and
Humanities Research Council of Canada.

University of Toronto Press acknowledges the financial assistance to its
publishing program of the Canada Council for the Arts and the Ontario Arts
Council, an agency of the Government of Ontario.

 Canada Council **Conseil des Arts**
for the Arts **du Canada**

 ONTARIO ARTS COUNCIL
CONSEIL DES ARTS DE L'ONTARIO
an Ontario government agency
un organisme du gouvernement de l'Ontario

Funded by the Financé par le
Government gouvernement
of Canada du Canada

Contents

List of Tables, Figures, and Illustrations   vii

Map: Location of Main Research Sites   xi

Acronyms Used in the Text   xiii

Acknowledgments   xvii

Introduction   3

1 Strategic Engagements with Neoliberalism   21

2 The Guatemalan Campesino Movement: Organizing through War and Peace   42

3 Between the Bullet and the Bank: Campesino Access to Land   66

4 CONIC: A Campesino Organization Apart   98

5 CCDA: A Revolutionary Enterprise   139

6 Beyond the Post-Conflict Period   184

Glossary   215

List of Interview Participants and Research Sites   217

Notes   225

References   241

Index   265

Tables, Figures, and Illustrations

Tables

2.1 Campesino Umbrella Groups, 2010   54

2.2 Campesino Organizations Discussed in the Text   55

3.1 World Bank Support for State Agrarian Projects, 2000–2007   68

3.2 Government Land Distribution, 1954–1989   68

3.3 Farms Purchased through *Fondo de Tierras* Land Access Program   70

3.4 Debt Payment Status of FONTIERRAS Farms, through 2008   73

3.5 FONTIERRAS Land Title Regularization, 2000–2009   75

3.6 Land Disputed in Agrarian Conflicts, 1997–2015   82

3.7 Land Provided through MAGA and SAA Conflict Resolution, 2006–2010   86

3.8 Land Access Strategies Employed by Campesino Organizations in 2010   91

4.1 CONIC Communities, by Method of Land Access   103

4.2 Projects Funded in Victorias III, 1999–2010   112

4.3 Crop Production in Victorias III, 2009–2010   119

4.4 Corn and Black Bean Production in San José La Pasión, 2009–2010   133

5.1 Community Land Accessed through the CCDA, 1998–2009   143

5.2 CCDA Coffee Producers by Municipality, 2008–2009   149

Figures

3.1   Hectares of land distributed by INTA and FONTIERRAS, 1962–2008   71
3.2   Farms purchased through *Fondo de Tierras*, by agrarian region   72
3.3   Agrarian conflicts by SAA category, 1997–2015   79
3.4   New agrarian conflicts registered annually by the SAA, 1997–2015   85

Illustrations

3.1   A community in La Tinta, Alta Verapaz   88
4.1   CONIC municipal council meeting in Chahal, Alta Verapaz   106
4.2   A house under construction in Victorias III   109
4.3   A house in Victorias III   114
4.4   The building used by the Victorias III *alcaldes auxiliares*   115
4.5   A composting outhouse built by Doctors without Borders   115
4.6   A communal well in Victorias III   115
4.7   Victorias III community leaders and CONIC promoter Juventina López Vásquez at a communal fish tank   116
4.8   Map of Victorias III   117
4.9   Sesame plants grow among drying corn   120
4.10   A map of development projects under way with *Oxlajuj Tz'ikin*   123
4.11   A strategy session for infrastructure projects in Victorias III   124
4.12   A typical house at San José La Pasión   127
4.13   San José La Pasión   131
5.1   Don Bonifacio dries coffee from his trees in Salvador Xolhuitz   155
5.2   Map of Salvador Xolhuitz   158
5.3   Harvesting coffee from an old tree   159
5.4   A plantation house turned community day-care centre   160
5.5   Drying coffee beans by hand at the Salvador Xolhuitz processing plant   161
5.6   The entrance to Salvador Xolhuitz, a site of conflict   163
5.7   Don Efraín tends to corn and coffee in his forest plot in Don Pancho   167

5.8   A house provided by FONTIERRAS "basic roof" program   173

5.9   A FOGUAVI house   173

5.10 Waterwheel pumping water to a cattle field   174

5.11 Pipes carrying water through the forest for irrigation   174

5.12 Map of Don Pancho   175

5.13 A chipilín patch   176

5.14 Corn, coffee, and pacaya grown in the forest at Don Pancho   177

5.15 A day-care centre built by the CCDA   179

5.16 Digging the foundation for a CCDA house at Don Pancho   180

Location of Main Research Sites

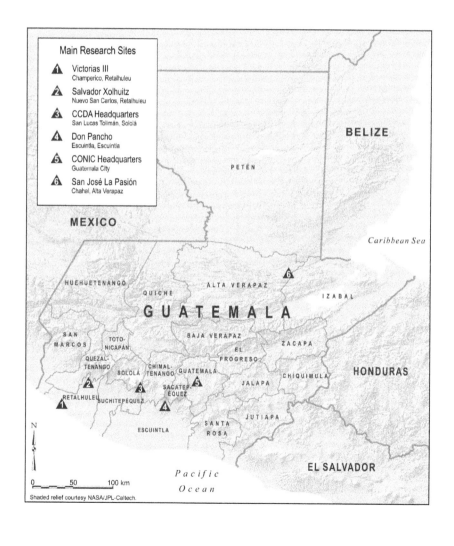

Main Research Sites

1. Victorias III
   Champerico, Retalhuleu
2. Salvador Xolhuitz
   Nuevo San Carlos, Retalhuleu
3. CCDA Headquarters
   San Lucas Tolimán, Sololá
4. Don Pancho
   Escuintla, Escuintla
5. CONIC Headquarters
   Guatemala City
6. San José La Pasión
   Chahal, Alta Verapaz

BELIZE

MEXICO

Caribbean Sea

PETÉN

HUEHUETENANGO

QUICHÉ

ALTA VERAPAZ

IZABAL

GUATEMALA

SAN MARCOS

TOTO-NICAPÁN

BAJA VERAPAZ

ZACAPA

QUEZAL-TENANGO

SOLOLÁ

CHIMAL-TENANGO

GUATEMALA

EL PROGRESO

CHIQUIMULA

HONDURAS

SACATEP-ÉQUEZ

JALAPA

RETALHULEU

SUCHITEPÉQUEZ

JUTIAPA

N

ESCUINTLA

SANTA ROSA

EL SALVADOR

0   50   100 km

Pacific
Ocean

Shaded relief courtesy NASA/JPL-Caltech.

Acronyms Used in the Text

ACDIP	*Asociación Campesina del Departamento del Petén* Petén Campesino Association
ACROX	*Asociación Campesina Rosario Xolhuitz* Rosario Xolhuitz Campesino Association
ACSUR	*Asociación para la Cooperación con el Sur* Association for Cooperation with the South
ADISC	*Asociación de Desarrollo Integral Santa Cruz* Santa Cruz Association for Comprehensive Development
ADRI	*Alianza de Desarrollo Rural Integral* Alliance for Comprehensive Rural Development
AMR	*Alianza de Mujeres Rurales* Alliance of Rural Women
ANC	*Asociación Nacional Campesina* National Campesino Association
ANN	*Alianza Nueva Nación / Alternativa Nueva Nación* Alliance for a New Nation / Alternative for a New Nation
ASC	*Asamblea de Sociedad Civil* Civil Society Assembly
ASOCODE	*Asociación Centroamericana de Organizaciones* *Campesinas para la Cooperación y el Desarrollo* Central American Association of Campesino Organizations for Cooperation and Development
AVANCSO	*Asociación para el Avance de las Ciencias Sociales en* *Guatemala* Association for the Advancement of the Social Sciences in Guatemala

CACIF	*Comité Coordinador de Asociaciones Agrícolas, Comerciales, Industriales, y Financieras* Coordinating Committee of Agricultural, Commercial, Industrial, and Financial Associations
CAFTA-DR	Dominican Republic–Central America Free Trade Agreement
CCDA	*Comité Campesino del Altiplano* Campesino Committee of the Highlands
CEH	*Comisión para el Esclarecimiento Histórico* Historical Clarification Commission
CDN	*Consejo de Dirección Nacional* National Directive Council
CICIG	*Comisión Internacional Contra la Impunidad en Guatemala* International Commission against Impunity in Guatemala
CLOC	*Coordinadora Latinoamericana de Organizaciones del Campo* Latin American Coordinator of Rural Organizations
CNAIC-P	*Consejo Nacional Indígena-Campesina y Popular* National Indigenous-Campesino and Popular Council
CNCG	*Confederación Nacional Campesina de Guatemala* National Campesino Confederation of Guatemala
CNOC	*Coordinadora Nacional de Organizaciones Campesinas* National Coordinator of Campesino Organizations
CNP-T	*Coordinación Nacional Permanente sobre Derechos Relativos a la Tierra de los Pueblos Indígenas* Permanent National Coordinator on Rights Related to Land and Indigenous Peoples
CNUS	*Comité Nacional de Unidad Sindical* National Committee on Labour Union Unity
COCODE	*Consejo Comunitario de Desarrollo* Community Development Council
CODECA	*Comité de Desarrollo Campesino* Campesino Development Committee
CONAMPRO	*Coordinadora Nacional de Pequeños y Medianos Productores*

	National Coordinator of Small and Medium Producers
CONAP	*Consejo Nacional de Áreas Protegidas*
	National Council for Protected Areas
CONATIERRA	*Comisión Nacional de Tierras*
	National Land Commission
CONDEG	*Comité Nacional de los Desplazados de Guatemala*
	Guatemalan National Committee of the Displaced
CONGCOOP	*Coordinación de ONG y Cooperativas*
	Coordinator of NGOs and Cooperatives
CONIC	*Coordinadora Nacional Indígena y Campesina*
	National Indigenous and Campesino Coordinator
CONTIERRA	*Dependencia Presidencial de Asistencia Legal y Resolución de Conflictos sobre la Tierra*
	Presidential Office for Land Conflict Legal Assistance and Resolution
CRD	*Convergencia para la Revolución Democrática*
	Convergence for the Democratic Revolution
CTG	*Confederación de Trabajadores de Guatemala*
	Confederation of Guatemalan Workers
CUC	*Comité de Unidad Campesina*
	Committee for Campesino Unity
DED	*Deutscher Entwicklungsdienst*
	German Development Service
EGP	*Ejército Guerrillero de los Pobres*
	Guerrilla Army of the Poor
FAR	*Fuerzas Armadas Rebeldes*
	Rebel Armed Forces
FDYEP	*Empresa de Fomento y Desarrollo del Petén*
	Petén Promotion and Development Agency
FEDECOCAGUA	*Federación de Cooperativas Cafetaleras de Guatemala*
	Guatemalan Federation of Coffee Cooperatives
FLACSO	*Facultad Latinoamericana de Ciencias Sociales*
	Latin American Faculty of Social Sciences
FNL	*Frente Nacional de Lucha*
	National Struggle Front
FOGUAVI	*Fondo Guatemalteco para la Vivienda*
	Guatemalan Housing Fund
FONAPAZ	*Fondo Nacional para la Paz*
	National Peace Fund

FONTIERRAS   *Fondo de Tierras*
Land Trust Fund
FUNDAECO   *Fundación para el Ecodesarrollo y la Conservación*
Foundation for Ecodevelopment and
Conservation
IBRD   International Bank for Reconstruction and
Development
INE   *Instituto Nacional de Estadística*
National Statistics Institute
INTA   *Instituto Nacional de Transformación Agraria*
National Institution for Agrarian Transformation
MAGA   *Ministerio de Agricultura, Ganadería, y Alimentación*
Ministry of Agriculture, Cattle, and Food
MLAR   Market-led agrarian reform
MSICG   *Movimiento Sindical, Indígena y Campesina
Guatemalteco*
Guatemalan Labour, Indigenous, and Campesino
Movement
MST   *Movimento Dos Trabalhadores Rurais Sem Terra*
Landless Workers' Movement
ORPA   *Organización Revolucionaria del Pueblo en Armas*
Revolutionary Organization of the People in Arms
PTI   *Pastoral de la Tierra Interdiocesana*
Interdiocesan Land Pastoral
PTSM   *Pastoral de la Tierra Interdiocesana de San Marcos*
Interdiocesan Land Pastoral of San Marcos
RIC   *Registro de Información Catastral*
Cadastral Information Registry
SAA   *Secretaría de Asuntos Agrarios*
Secretariat of Agrarian Affairs
UASP   *Unidad de Acción Sindical y Popular*
Union for Labour and Popular Action
UNAGRO   *Unión Nacional de Agricultores*
National Farmers Union
URNG   *Unidad Revolucionaria Nacional Guatemalteca*
Guatemalan National Revolutionary Unity
USAID   United States Agency for International
Development
UVOC   *Unión Verapacense de Organizaciones Campesinas*
Verapaz Union of Campesino Organizations

Acknowledgments

This book is a collaborative project. Hundreds of people were involved in its creation: people who opened their doors to me, who fed me and gave me a place to sleep, who took time to talk to me and help me understand, who went out of their way to show me what they consider important, whose ideas and words helped me to find my own.

The collaboration began with campesino activist and now Guatemalan Congressperson Leocadio Juracán, and I owe him the greatest debt of gratitude. Leocadio brought me into the campesino world, changed my perspective on Guatemala, set the groundwork for my research, and became a close friend. The Juracán and Morales family also became close friends of mine, and much of my time in Guatemala over the years has been spent with them. I thank them for their friendship and insight.

The greatest number of people involved in this project live in the rural communities that I visited as research sites. To the many people who went out of their way to help my research, thank you for welcoming me into your communities and your homes.

In addition to those in the communities, many people in the campesino movement and other grassroots groups provided indispensable support for the project. Friends in the Campesino Committee of the Highlands (*Comité Campesino del Altiplano,* CCDA) welcomed me into the group's offices, took me to visit communities, and passed many hours talking politics. I especially thank Marcelo Sabuc, Lesbia Morales, Cristina Ardón, Marco Tulio, and Teodoro Juracán for their support. Activists from the Territorial Collectives network of the National Indigenous and Campesino Coordinator (*Coordinadora Nacional Indígena y Campesina,* CONIC) used their deep knowledge of regional issues to help me understand agrarian dynamics in Alta Verapaz, Izabal, and Retalhuleu.

I thank César Bol for introducing me to many helpful people and for talking over all my questions throughout the year; Hermelindo Chub Icó for allowing me to follow him to agrarian conflicts across Alta Verapaz and for accompanying me and providing translation in the community of San José La Pasión; Juventina López for bringing me to Victorias III and remaining my supporter on the South Coast; Candelaria Beb and Celso Caal for taking me to various land occupations; and Rigoberto Monteros for discussing at length all of my questions about CONIC's agrarian strategy. Carlos Morales of CNOC and UVOC wouldn't let our interaction end with interviews, insisting that I accompany him on a day-long trip to a recent land occupation victory in Baja Verapaz, an experience that proved important for my work. Eugenio Incer and Luis Galicia of AVANCSO encouraged and supported my research from the beginning and engaged me in conversations that helped form my understanding of the movement. Discussions with other activists, including especially Hélmer Velásquez of CONGCOOP, Sergio Funes of CNP-T, and Ingrid Urízar of PTSM, were also vital to this research and I thank them all for their time. Finally, people working in the offices of the *Fondo de Tierras* and the Secretariat of Agrarian Affairs helped me to find the documentation necessary to back up my case studies.

I also owe thanks to a dear friend, Caren Weisbart. Over the years, Caren first introduced me to Leocadio Juracán and the Guatemalan campesino movement, then became a close friend and sometimes roommate, and provided endless encouragement and feedback on my work, reading drafts and talking over problems on countless occasions. Thank you, Caren, for your friendship and for being a part of this project from before it even began.

My doctoral supervisor Nicola Short, a model of encouragement and patience, nudged me gently in various directions to help bring out the best from my research. The strength of the final product is a result of her support, and I cannot thank her enough. Another committee member, Liisa North, has been my closest academic ally since I began graduate school in 2004. I owe much of my own perspective on Guatemala to Liisa, whose friendship and dedication have served as a launch pad for many of my projects and as a filter for their coherence and final presentation.

Research in Guatemala, and the writing that followed, would not have been possible without generous grants provided by the Social Science and Humanities Research Council, the Ontario Graduate Scholarship, the Canadian Union of Public Employees (CUPE) 3903, and the York

University Faculty of Graduate Studies, and later by funding from the University of Regina Faculty of Arts. I am extremely grateful for their assistance. Invaluable support was also provided by the Centre for Research on Latin America and the Caribbean at York University.

Finally, this book is dedicated to my partner, Rebecca, in eternal thanks for her collaboration and encouragement. She has been my closest partner in all my work in Guatemala, from our time as human rights accompaniers through the year we spent engaged in this research. Rebecca, this book wouldn't have existed without you: thank you for your role in its creation and for sharing with me a world of fun and love beyond academia.

DEALING WITH PEACE

The Guatemalan Campesino Movement and
the Post-Conflict Neoliberal State

Introduction

The contrast between injustice and hope in Guatemala is such a stark and foundational characteristic of the country that a number of books have alluded to this tension in their titles: *A Beauty That Hurts* (Lovell 2000), *Gift of the Devil* (Handy 1984), *Guatemala: Eternal Spring, Eternal Tyranny* (Simon 1987), *My Painful Guatemala* (Aragón 2006). Across these and other works, Guatemala is depicted as a country of beauty, resilience, inequality, and unimaginable violence. Nowhere is this tension stronger than in the struggle over land that has lasted for more than five hundred years. The legacy of colonialism is engraved in the racialized and wildly uneven distribution of land, concentrated heavily among an oligarchy of European descendants who view the earth as a resource for extracting profit. But it is also present in the unrelenting insistence of Guatemala's twenty-three Maya, Xinca, and Garifuna Indigenous peoples that land forms a part of territory, to be respected and protected (Resistencia de los Pueblos 2014).

The subject of this book, the Guatemalan campesino social movement, has organized with rural communities in the pursuit of justice for forty years now, accompanying struggles to access or defend land and territory, and fighting for political reform in favour of the majority population. Following the end of armed conflict in 1996, the movement entered a new stage, with land made available for collective purchase through a state institution that ultimately sought to pacify the radical movement and transform communal land into a market commodity. As such, in this study that charts and assesses the work of the contemporary campesino movement, I focus largely on the relationship between the movement and neoliberal agrarian institutions. While Guatemalan campesino organizations are clearly anti-neoliberal in their outlook and have visions of alternatives to neoliberalism that look beyond capitalist production and social relations, they have also relied heavily on the agrarian institutions and official policies that make up part of the country's post-conflict neoliberal transition. Does engagement with neoliberal institutions thus limit the ability of campesinos (small-scale or landless rural farmers, often translated as "peasants") to resist neoliberalism and to launch socio-economic alternatives? Across the six case studies presented in this book – two campesino organizations and four recently landed rural communities – I found that this is not necessarily the case and that social movement organizations are capable of subverting resources intended to co-opt them. This argument is expanded upon throughout the book, while the case studies also seek to present the workings of the movement in the post-conflict period, highlighting its considerable achievements while exploring the factors that have prevented the movement from flourishing further.

The stage upon which campesino politics plays out in Guatemala is immensely complex, and the campesino movement itself is today a product of centuries of a national history of violence, dispossession, exclusion, and inequality. The details of agrarian politics in the twentieth century are explained further throughout the book, as are the conditions of wartime and post-conflict violence that further influence these. Before proceeding, however, this introduction offers a brief overview of the *longue durée* in Guatemala (Braudel 1980) and its continuing influence on life conditions for the majority population. This is followed by a personal and methodological narrative of the events that brought me into a relationship with the movement and allowed me to produce this text.

Dispossession, Violence, and Poverty

Throughout the nearly five hundred years since the Spanish conquest of the Maya began in 1524, power in Guatemala has remained deeply tied to land. What makes the question of land so contentious and so lasting is not only its importance for economic and political position – the immense wealth and power of the landed oligarchy; the hunger, poverty, and exploitation of those who work the land but own none or very little of it – but the fact that the claim to resistance and autonomy by Guatemala's Indigenous peoples rests on the connection of these to control over territory. This divide is most visible in conflicts over extractive projects, where hundreds of primarily Indigenous communities across the country oppose the construction and operation of mines, hydroelectric dams, agro-fuel plantations, oilfields, and more. The related conflicts – which involve a range of pacific opposition tactics from community consultations to blockades and are met with waves of repressive violence – are not fought over the benefits of "development," as the projects' proponents would have it. They are evidence of the insistence of the rural and Indigenous majority that, despite centuries of colonization, they retain the right to determine access to resources where they live. As this book explores the current chapter in struggles over access to land, it is important to view these responses within a longer, overarching history of dispossession and resistance.

The current distribution of land ownership in Guatemala, including large plantations as well as areas allocated to or claimed by Indigenous communities, has deep roots in a series of colonial institutions (Cambranes 1992a; Grandin 2013; McCreery 1994; C.A. Smith 1990b). Right from the first days of conquest in the sixteenth century, Europeans arriving in Maya territory were concerned with dividing land and labour in order to generate profit. The *Requerimiento*, a document demanding that Indigenous peoples across the Americas submit to Christianity or face war and enslavement, was read aloud, in Spanish, to the Maya, not in order to convert them, according to Guatemalan historian Severo Martínez Peláez (2009, 39), but "[counting] on the fact that Indians would reject the *requerimiento* and offer resistance; this would then afford conquerors a legal basis to justify war and destruction." Conquest was followed by the Spanish Crown's distribution of land, and by the institutionalization of forced labour through colonial systems including the *repartimiento de indios* and the *encomienda*, which served to secure a steady stream of coerced plantation labour. During the Liberal era of expanding coffee production beginning in 1871, these colonial labour systems would be updated with debt-based forced labour, vagrancy laws, obligatory participation in the construction of public works, and the *colonato* system of live-in plantation workers (Grandin 2013; McCreery 1994).

Systems implemented to acquire land and free or cheap labour during centuries of colonial control helped to lay a map of land ownership in the country that has largely survived – large plantations of export crops along the South Coast, mixed Maya and European political control (until the late 1800s) of villages across the Western Highlands, and surviving communal land management in the north and east of the country. Where this map has been altered over the centuries, it has been through the fall of many areas of Indigenous control to plantations through successive waves of dispossession, especially through the expansion of coffee *fincas* in the late nineteenth and early twentieth centuries.

Describing the experience of the Maya Q'eqchi' people of eastern Guatemala, Grandia (2012, 30–48) suggests three periods of enclosure of traditional territory. First, the Q'eqchi' faced "conquest by Christianity" during three centuries of colonialism. Next came "conquest by commerce" after 1821, as the Liberal governments of independent Guatemala attempted to expand plantations into communal Q'eqchi' lands. Finally, "conquest by colonization" beginning in the 1940s saw a series of attempts to bring Q'eqchi' territory into the formal private property system through state-led land distribution programs. The specific experience of the Q'eqchi' differs from that of Maya groups in the Western Highlands and elsewhere, in that the Q'eqchi' maintained relatively strong autonomy from the state across all of these periods. Nevertheless, Maya groups across Guatemala have faced a similar succession of forms of dispossession. Following the colonial institutions mentioned above, the establishment of the Liberal coffee state after 1871 saw a reconfiguration of these dynamics in a way that further pushed Maya communities off land desired for coffee plantations, and that transformed institutions of forced labour through vagrancy laws and the establishment of the *colonato* system of live-in plantation labourers. Knowlton (2017), Abbott (n.d.), and others have suggested that a fourth period of conquest and enclosure is represented by the period since the end of the armed conflict – the current violent expansion of extractive industries and the creation of agrarian institutions, described in this book, that aim to control and reconfigure the rural economy.

Struggles over land ownership and political power in Guatemala came to a head in the mid- to late twentieth century. A short-lived agrarian reform saw 364,000 hectares of land distributed to small farmers in nearly 800 communities under the government of Jacobo Arbenz between 1952 and 1954, the final years of Guatemala's decade of "democratic spring" (Handy 1994b, 90–2). In 1954, however, the Arbenz government was overthrown in a CIA-designed coup d'état, and land distributed to campesinos was quickly returned to large landowners. Violent repression of campesinos, unions, and other organized sectors followed the coup, and by 1960 the country was at war. Despite being a period of guerrilla attempts to seize the Guatemalan state, the internal armed conflict that lasted until 1996 is not best characterized by clashes between rebels and government forces, but by systematic state terror that culminated in genocide against the Maya in the late 1970s and early 1980s. The inequality of land distribution was the most important cause of the war, but the severity of its violence was driven by another of Guatemala's dark qualities: racism. The violence of the land-owning class, which had been exercised against the Indigenous rural majority for centuries, reached a fever pitch of racist fear in its attempt to suppress the guerrilla threat and maintain the structure of the country's political economy. Land is connected in many ways to these four decades of war: land distribution as the spark for conflict; agrarian reform as a central guerrilla demand; land as the power base that the dominant elite fought to maintain; and land as the location of violence, the dispossession wrought by massacres, threats, and fear as the armed forces reconfigured the demographic makeup of the country-side and advanced their own economic and political standing (Huet 2008; Manz 1988; Schirmer 1998; C.A. Smith 1990c).

More than twenty years have passed since the Guatemalan government and URNG guerrillas signed "firm and lasting" peace accords. As agreements intended ostensibly to address the root causes of war, land featured heavily in the final agreements. However, as explained in chapter 1 and supported by data throughout this book, the approach to land adopted in the peace accords betrayed an intention of the Guatemalan elite to move the country towards a neoliberal economic model. Distributive agrarian reform was excluded from the agreements, and a transition to a rural economy based in transnationally oriented extractive industries was facilitated by a combination of market-based solutions to agrarian problems and an invitation for civil society participation intended to dampen resistance and alternative models.

Whether civil society incorporation into the neoliberal model was successful is the central concern of this book, and I will show that some campesino organizations managed to participate without losing their strength as grassroots movements. The solidification of the new rural economic model, however, has been successful despite ongoing community-based resistance. The share of the economy derived from traditional agricultural exports has shrunk steadily since the 1980s, as the rural economy has shifted to include more non-traditional agricultural exports and extractive industries such as mining, oil, and hydro-electricity (Schneider 2014). Coffee, sugar cane, and bananas still topped Guatemala's list of exports in 2012, but minerals had climbed to fourth place (World Bank 2017d), and sugar is now destined in large part for the agro-fuel industry. To reach this status, extractives and other nontraditional exports have been driven to trample over the little land and water remaining under the control of rural and Indigenous communities. The long-standing *latifundio* approach based in large plantations, while still present, has now been supplemented by a fervour for the acquisition of community lands for resource extraction. This is often accomplished through state-sanctioned violence, as in the cases of Canlún and Xya'al K'obe' discussed in chapter 3.

Instead of easing unequal distribution in the post-conflict period, land ownership has in fact become more concentrated. National agrarian surveys show that overall concentration has remained untouched: 2 per cent of landowners held 60 per cent of all agricultural land in 1950; in 1979, 2.6 per cent controlled 65 per cent; and in 2003, 3.2 per cent of landowners controlled 66 per cent of land in the country (Grandia 2012, 118). Studies conducted in areas undergoing major rural transition in the post-conflict period, however, demonstrate a widespread acquisition of small parcels by companies, large landowners, and narcotics-trafficking groups (Gould 2014; Hernández 2016; Hurtado Paz y Paz 2008; Solano 2016). In the northern department of El Petén, for example, Milian and Grandia (2013) found that between 31 and 46 per cent of campesinos whose land had been granted title under peace accord–based programs had since sold their land. Hurtado Paz y Paz (2008) found similar results in a study of one municipality in Alta Verapaz. These figures point to a widely recognized regional re-concentration of land occurring alongside a relatively constant scenario at the national level. Social conflict over the use of natural resources has accompanied this new wave of expansion, acquisition, and extraction, and the Guatemalan agency responsible for tracking agrarian conflicts registered over seven thousand cases of conflict between 1997 and early 2016 (SAA 2016).

Within this historical and contemporary context, it should come as no surprise that the majority of Guatemalans face deplorable living conditions. Poverty in Guatemala may present itself as especially unjust, given the immense national wealth that accompanies it. Guatemala as a whole is becoming richer, with gross national income per capita rising steadily, from $930 in 1990 (measured in 2017 U.S. dollars) to $1,600 in 2010, to $3,590 in 2015. The distribution of this wealth has remained largely stagnant, however, with the national Gini index of income distribution shifting from 54.8 in 2000 to 48.7 in 2014. In fact, the number of Guatemalans living in poverty has grown in recent years, with nine million people, or 59 per cent of the population, living below the national poverty line in 2015, as compared to seven million and 56 per cent in 2000. Contained within these figures is an immense racial discrimination, with over 90 per cent of the Indigenous population living in poverty (World Bank 2016; 2017a; 2017c).

A lack of income is, of course, not the only way in which such extreme poverty is experienced. With the majority population living in poverty and the Guatemalan state dedicating a paltry 8 per cent of GDP to social spending in 2011 (as compared to 12 per cent in neighbouring Honduras and 22 per cent in Costa Rica), Guatemalans are for the most part left to fend for themselves. Many communities raise funds collectively to install basic infrastructure such as paved roads and electricity, and the combination of state neglect, resource theft, and climate change leaves many people across the country thirsty and hungry (Granovsky-Larsen 2017; Murphy 2004). According to the World Food Programme (2017), the rate of chronic malnutrition in Guatemala – a staggering 47 per cent in 2016 – is among the worst in the world. Some important health indicators have improved in recent years – most dramatically infant mortality, which fell from thirty-nine deaths per 1,000 live births in 2000 to twenty-four in 2015 (World Bank 2017b) – but overall the majority population in Guatemala can add heightened exposure to disease and a lack of access to health services to the long list of conditions of structural violence (Farmer 1996).

Episodic violence is also endemic in post-war Guatemala, and here the poor are again more vulnerable, with women and urban youth affected with extra disproportionality. Crime and violence have overwhelmed the country, the fallout from decades of war followed by a hollowing out of state institutions by organized criminal and other interests. A murder rate of between 30 and 45 per 100,000 over the last ten years – comparable to many war zones – is met by a rate of conviction for homicide of only 3 per cent (CIIDH and El Observador 2014; Handy 2017; *Prensa* Libre 2017). The ever-present possibility of violent death caps an overall scenario of tragedy and injustice faced by most Guatemalans today.

Poverty, discrimination, violence, and landlessness are all intertwined, products of centuries of exploitation, racism, patriarchy, and state neglect that have carried forward into the post-conflict period in updated but historically consistent ways. This is the backdrop against which the Guatemalan campesino-based social movement organizes. The movement focuses primarily on accessing and defending land for mainly Indigenous rural communities and pressuring the government to better support campesinos, but ultimately this is a movement that seeks to transform Guatemalan state and society so as to reverse the national power imbalance.

The history and current activities of the movement are detailed at length throughout this book, with a focus on interactions between campesino organizations and the Guatemalan state during the post-conflict period of neoliberal consolidation. Before beginning this task, however, I want to position myself within the narrative. What follows for the remainder of the chapter is a personal and methodological over-view of my time spent with the Guatemalan campesino movement and the work that went into producing this text.

Positioning the Case Studies: CCDA and CONIC

The argument presented in this book draws primarily from my obser-vation of two campesino organizations: the Campesino Committee of the Highlands (*Comité Campesino del Altiplano*, CCDA) and the National Indigenous and Campesino Coordinator (*Coordinadora Nacional Indí-gena y Campesina*, CONIC). Out of the dozens of campesino organiza-tions active in the country when the research began in 2009, the CCDA and CONIC were selected not for their satisfaction of any particular cri-teria but simply because they were the two that presented themselves to the project. As I explain in the methodological section of this intro-duction, I had already established a relationship with the CCDA more than five years before the outset of this project; the group's perspective on campesino politics had greatly shaped my own, and it made sense to me to carry on with this established relationship. CONIC, on the other hand, was suggested to me by members of the CCDA as well as by Guatemalan researchers as an appropriate second case for the project, and I was grateful when the national council of this very large organi-zation agreed to work with me.

If the selection of cases was less than deliberate, however, I could not have been more fortunate for the degree to which these two orga-nizations would present differing aspects of, and contrasting positions within, the campesino movement. At the time of the main round of fieldwork in 2009–10 – shortly before conflicts over resource extrac-tion began to dominate rural social movement organizing in the coun-try – both the CCDA and CONIC focused largely on supporting rural communities in their quest to access land and engage in appropriate community development. The two represented different moments in Guatemalan social movement organizing, and their approach to campesino politics reflected their roots.

The CCDA formed in 1982, at the genocidal peak of the armed conflict. It began as a civilian organization that was allied with the guerrilla movement, with deep connections to campesino communities in the highlands departments of Chimaltenango and Sololá, and with a political perspective characterized primarily by class analysis. Until recently the CCDA has been mostly regionally focused, working within the area of its traditional strength, and it has shied away from the national political spotlight, even when engaging in pan-campesino organizing, partly as a protection against repressive violence. CONIC, on the other hand, formed from a split within the Committee for Campesino Unity (CUC), another Marxist-informed campesino organization. Those who left the CUC to form CONIC were mainly Indigenous, and they maintained a focus on resolving the many agrarian conflicts plaguing rural communities. CONIC has always been characterized by an embrace of Indigenous identity, and spiritual practices stemming from the Maya cosmovision often shape the group's work. Dedication to resolution of community conflicts has also shaped CONIC, and at the time of my fieldwork I found that the strength of CONIC lay in its long-standing will to negotiate directly with state institutions in order to settle agrarian conflicts and secure community land access. By contrast the CCDA, while active in community land access, had its particular strength in economic projects with rural communities, through the management of a coffee-exporting cooperative and alternative agriculture carried out in allied communities.

In the years since the first round of research for this project, however, the two organizations began to drift farther apart (a divide explored in detail in chapter 6). CONIC's willingness to engage the state directly began to influence the group's formerly radical political position, and the group forged ties with state institutions and even the executive, ties that ultimately weakened the group's ability to fight for campesino and Indigenous rights. The CCDA, on the other hand, underwent rejuvenation and expansion – as well as indigenization, in that the already Indigenous leadership of the group began to incorporate that identity into its policies and analysis. These changes saw the once regionally focused CCDA acquire substantial national influence and popularity within the campesino movement and other grassroots sectors. What is revealed by this divergence, as I explain in chapter 6, is the potential within social movements to utilize neoliberal resources intentionally to their advantage – both CONIC and the CCDA accepted support from neoliberal agrarian institutions – building the strength to resist and to propose alternatives precisely through the use of resources intended to pacify them.

Methodology: Activist Research amid Violence

This book is over fifteen years in the making. In a sense it began in a Halifax coffee shop in 2002, at my first meeting with the Guatemalan campesino activist Leocadio Juracán. In Canada to promote the *Café Justicia* direct trade coffee produced by the Campesino Committee of the Highlands, Juracán presented me with a perspective on Guatemalan politics grounded in the daily struggles of social movements and rural communities, one that immediately altered my understanding of the country. Although I had spent three months travelling and volunteering in Guatemala three years earlier, I knew that I hadn't even scratched the surface of the country's rich and complicated reality. Less than a year after meeting Juracán, my partner Rebecca and I began work as human rights accompaniers with the CCDA in Guatemala, and deep bonds formed with activists there that would tie me to the campesino struggle. Over the next twelve years I returned six more times to Guatemala as a human rights accompanier and researcher, accompanying the CCDA and the left-wing *Alianza Nueva Nación* political party in the 2003 and 2007 elections, living as an observer at a land occupation in 2004, and conducting first MA fieldwork on human rights defenders in 2005 and then PhD and follow-up research in 2009–10, 2013, and 2015.

By the time I embarked upon the doctoral fieldwork that would produce this book, then, I was already deeply involved with the movement that I set out to study. Traditional approaches to methodology tell us that such involvement weakens or invalidates research by sullying the objectivity of the researcher. Recently, however, researchers who work closely with people in struggle for social justice have articulated methodologies that celebrate the impact of forms of collaboration that disregard attempts at objectivity. Working closely with people in struggle allows them to participate in the research rather than merely having their actions studied. That involvement, it is argued, brings analytical and theoretical insights that would not be possible through attempts to study a social movement at arm's length (Hale 2006a, 98). This perspective is present in methodological schools including participatory action research, political activist ethnography, emancipatory research, and Indigenous methodologies (Hale 2006a; Humphries, Mertens, and Truman 2000; Hussey 2012; L.T. Smith 1999).

I had read widely on involving participants in the research process before beginning my fieldwork, and I adopted for this project the approach outlined by the anthropologist Charles R. Hale (2006a, 2008a; 2008b) in his work on "activist research" or "activist scholarship." Hale's work spoke to me particularly because of its emphasis on embracing any existing relationships with social movements, collaborating with movements in every step of the research process, and producing research products that are accessible and useful for movement participants. "By *activist research*," Hale writes (2006a, 97), "I mean a method through which we affirm a political alignment with an organized group of people in struggle and allow dialogue with them to shape each phase of the process, from conception of the research topic to data collection to verification and dissemination of the results."

My close ties to the CCDA had already shaped my perspective on events in Guatemala, and Hale's work encouraged me to acknowledge this and to allow further collaboration to shape the project. In designing my research, I spoke in person with CCDA activists at the Americas Social Forum in Guatemala in 2008, and then in more detail when I arrived in the country to begin the research in 2009. Discussions with both participating campesino organizations – the CCDA and CONIC – early in the first year of research helped me to refine my understanding of communities that had accessed land and their role in the broader campesino movement, and both campesino organizations played a strong role in adjusting my plans to fit the existing panorama of agrarian dynamics in Guatemala. Case study communities were also chosen in collaboration with the organizations and, as I explain below, the collection of data for this book took place largely through participant observation in settings including daily work tasks in rural communities and discussion in internal strategic meetings.

The activist research methodology also encourages researchers to disseminate findings in a way that participants within social movements "can recognize as their own, value in their terms, and use as they see fit" (Hale 2008b, 4). To this end, my research process involved first a presentation of preliminary findings to the CCDA and CONIC leadership councils before leaving the country, then follow-up trips to Guatemala in 2013 and 2015 in order to present findings and deliver translated case studies. When writing, I tried to use the data collected in Guatemala in a way that would document the efforts of the movement and remain true to campesino perspectives, while also being critical of the movement where appropriate. Activist research is necessarily conflictive, as we researchers first become involved in very real, messy political movements and later grapple with balancing the positions of research participants and our own interpretation of events. As Hale (2006a, 98) puts it, "When we position ourselves in such spaces, we are also inevitably drawn into the compromised conditions of the political process. The resulting contradictions make the research more difficult to carry out, but they also generate insight that otherwise would be impossible to achieve. This insight, in turn, provides an often unacknowledged basis for analytical understanding and theoretical innovation."

The majority of the primary data for this book were gathered in Guatemala between April 2009 and April 2010, with additional material collected in 2015. As such – and with the exception of the final chapter, which considers the movement in 2015 – the discussion of the campesino movement here focuses on a snapshot representing one year of detailed observation. Where updated information is available or essential, the chapters also mention changes to the movement during the period of 2010–15. Six case studies covering two campesino organizations and four rural communities were at the centre of that year of research in 2009–10, and these were complemented by supporting interviews as well as document collection through archival research and access-to-information requests. Research with the CCDA and CONIC campesino organizations lies at the heart of this study, and it was carried out through a combination of participant observation and interview.

My experience with each of the two organizations was slightly different. Since I had already established ties with the CCDA, and since that group counts with a central leadership that is involved with most participating communities and projects, my research with the CCDA was focused on the core activists of the group's National Coordination Council. Over the course of the year I spent time in the CCDA central office in the village of Quixayá in San Lucas Tolimán, Sololá, and at the nearby property where they process coffee, I sat in on strategic meetings, attended protests, and visited rural communities allied with the group. While researching with the CCDA I also interviewed members of the council and was given access to internal documents and plans, such as the group's annual operating plans and the business plans for their coffee exports.

Participant observation with the other organization, CONIC, took place at the level of two regional groups: the CONIC Territorial Collectives in the departments of Retalhuleu and Alta Verapaz. There I spent a good deal of time with one local CONIC activist in each region – Juventina López Vásquez in Retalhuleu and Hermelindo Chub Icó in Alta Verapaz and Izabal – who introduced me to my case study communities and also brought me around to see other communities in their respective regions. My research with CONIC in Alta Verapaz was especially important for this study, as I was taken to numerous land occupations and other agrarian struggles that provided me with first-hand observation of important dynamics in agrarian organizing. In addition to interviews with Juventina López, Hermelindo Chub Icó , and three other CONIC Territorial Collective organizers, I interviewed members of CONIC's national leadership and, as with the CCDA, was given access to a number of internal and strategic documents.

The four case studies of rural communities – two associated with CONIC and two with the CCDA – consisted of groups of campesinos that had recently accessed land, either through a loan for its purchase or as the result of land occupations. The cases were spread out across the country in order to cover a variety of changing agrarian dynamics: in the northern lowlands of Alta Verapaz, the southern piedmont coffee region of Escuintla and Retalhuleu, and the coastal plantations of Retalhuleu. Data were collected in each case through participant observation and interviews. Except for the case of the CCDA community Don Pancho, where I stayed for a single five-day visit, I visited each community a number of times over the year, staying for between one and four days per visit. While in the communities I would stay with a family, accompany people in work tasks, talk to community leaders, and conduct survey interviews. I was conscious of gender dynamics and attempted to balance the number of female and male participants in survey interviews, often by interviewing house-to-house at a time when men would typically be working in their agricultural plots. My goal was to interview half the households in each community; I was able to do this with the two CONIC communities, but a violent internal conflict in the CCDA community of Salvador Xolhuitz stopped me from completing the research there, and replacement research in the community of Don Pancho fell short of reaching half of all households. In addition to the survey interviews, I also recorded conversations with the elected community leadership of two of the four groups, in the form of group interviews and two testimonies on the communities' experiences with agrarian conflict.

I gathered a wealth of data and experiences for the case studies, through 99 community survey interviews, 7 recorded group interviews and testimonies in case study and other communities visited, and 19 interviews with CONIC and CCDA organizers, along with the considerable time spent with the two organizations and four communities. In order to compare those detailed accounts with a broader picture of campesino activism across the country, in the main year of fieldwork I also interviewed representatives of ten other campesino organizations, people from five grassroots or research organizations working with the topics at hand, and four people representing the *Fondo de Tierras* and Secretariat of Agrarian Affairs (*Secretaría de Asuntos Agrarios*, SAA) government institutions. The accounts from those 18 interviews confirmed, and sometimes contradicted, what I had seen with CONIC and the CCDA, enriching my account of the campesino movement and its agrarian struggles. I visited thirteen rural communities for the study and collected 143 interviews, survey interviews, and testimonies in those communities and other settings.

The identity of participants has been revealed or concealed in this study according to a number of factors. First, all research participants were asked whether or not they wanted their names to be included in the research results. The overwhelming majority asked for their names to be used. Second, some participants asked for their names not to be attached to particular parts of our interview, and their wishes were respected. Third, I decided to include only the first names of research participants in the community case studies. Finally, I took the liberty to remove names from passages or topics that I deemed to be particularly sensitive. The result is a combination of named and anonymous sources, depending on the wishes of the participant and my own interpretation of the topic. Where names appear, however, they have not been changed. The names and locations of communities mentioned in the study are also real.

In addition to the interviews and participant observation, I also collected data through access-to-information requests and from various archives. When I began my research in 2009, Guatemala had just passed a law requiring all public institutions to set up an office to accommodate requests for information (Gobierno de Guatemala 2008). The *Fondo de Tierras*, the Secretariat of Agrarian Affairs, and other institutions were accommodating and prompt in their replies, providing me with invaluable information in response to ten requests. These yielded databases on land sales and agrarian conflicts, as well as files produced on each of the four case study communities. The primary data were further complemented by rare or unpublished material found through the archives and collections of the CCDA, CONIC, the National Coordinator of Campesino Organizations (*Coordinadora Nacional de Organizaciones Campesinas*, CNOC), the Association for the Advancement of the Social Sciences in Guatemala (*Asociación para el Avance de las Ciencias Sociales en Guatemala*, AVANCSO), the Latin American Faculty of Social Sciences (*Facultad Latinoamericana de Ciencias Sociales*, FLACSO), the National Statistics Institute (*Instituto Nacional de Estadística*, INE), and, back in Canada, the archives of the Latin American Working Group housed at York University's Centre for Research on Latin America and the Caribbean (CERLAC).

The year of fieldwork was exhilarating but also challenging, especially because of the repressive violence that hangs over the movement. My time in the community of Salvador Xolhuitz was laden with a fear of violence breaking out, and it was eventually cut short by an escalation of conflict, including a shooting and an attempted lynching. CCDA General Coordinator Leocadio Juracán and his family, my closest friends in Guatemala, were forced to leave the country in response to paramilitary threats towards the end of my time there. The five days that my partner and I spent helping them to leave was one of the hardest times I have ever faced. After I returned to Canada, violence in Salvador Xolhuitz claimed a life. The community of X'ya'al K'obe, where I had visited briefly, was evicted during two months of martial law in Alta Verapaz in 2011, and a community leader went missing for days after being abducted; photos reached me of the thatched-roof homes where I had slept, ablaze during the eviction. And the community of Canlún, where I had also spent a couple of days, was evicted along with thirteen others in the Polochic Valley; people from Canlún and other communities were killed over the following months as private security used terror to keep them away from their land. The taste of fear I experienced wasn't for my own safety, but for that of people I had become close to, whom I cared for, and who had taken me in as a guest. This is the reality of grassroots organizing in Guatemala, where any challenge to power can end violently and without warning. My proximity to violence was necessary in order to understand, from a limited perspective, the risks and suffering that go along with grassroots struggles, and to appreciate one aspect of the significance attached to land gained, fought for, or lost.

My closeness to many communities, organizations, and people involved in those struggles necessarily affected the ways in which

I collected and interpreted the information presented here. As mentioned above, much of this was intentional, as I set out to engage in an activist methodology that would involve participants in research design and attempt to produce material of value to the movement. The account presented here approximates perspectives held by Guatemalan campesino activists and communities, because of my own convictions learned while working in solidarity with them. Within those perspectives, the particular stances of CONIC and the CCDA at times prevail over other positions in my writing.

At the same time, this book is far from uncritical. Researchers such as Charles R. Hale (2006a, 2011), Marc Edelman (1999, 2009), and Wendy Wolford (2003, 2010b) have shown us that we can engage with social movements on the basis of solidarity while still exposing the shortcomings or failures of those movements. I do my best not only to avoid the "official narratives" (Edelman 2009, 249) of any organization but also to highlight the less savoury aspects of campesino organizing in order to show where the movement has been held back as the result of its own problems. In fact this book's central question on the relationship between the Guatemalan campesino movement and neoliberal agrarian institutions points to the difficult strategic debates that have at times prevented the movement from moving forward and at others, as shown in my case study of Salvador Xolhuitz, led to devastating results. This is a social movement attempting to navigate the onslaught of a neoliberal transition, the lingering elements of military rule and genocide, and a peace process intended to pacify grassroots opposition rather than to alter the inequalities that led to war. The discussion that follows highlights important advances forged by the movement. However, it also points to areas where campesino organizing has been unsuccessful as the result of both the context within which it operates and the imperfect structure and tactics of the movement itself.

There have been enormous changes to the campesino movement since my period of extended observation in 2009–10. Since that time, community-based grassroots movements against extractive projects have sprung up alongside formal social movement organizations like the CCDA and CONIC and have taken on the role of fighting for justice in the countryside with perhaps even more fervour than formal organizations. As discussed in chapter 6, those campesino organizations that survived the post-conflict attempt at incorporation and pacification – with the CCDA at the forefront – have adapted to this new reality and taken on a supportive role backing those communities, similar to their longstanding support for agrarian conflicts. The quest for land access, especially through state agrarian institutions, has now taken something of a backseat to the largely Indigenous defence of territory.

As a tragic result, violence against campesino organizations and community members defending territory has increased rapidly. Guatemalan state forces now engage in violent land evictions regularly, similar to those described in chapter 4, and in many instances police and military have murdered protesters and activists. Criminalization of the movement has increased at an even greater rate, with one recent study indicating that over 450 activists across the country were targeted with legal charges or arbitrary or illegal detention, between 2012 and 2017 (UDEFEGUA 2017b). The targeted assassination of movement leaders has also left hundreds of human rights defenders, including many campesino leaders, dead in recent years, often at the hands of hired assassins (Granovsky-Larsen 2018).

Conditions have undoubtedly worsened, but the dedication to fight for social justice has only increased. Many of the same campesino organizations whose efforts to assist in campesino land access I observed in 2009–10 have now thrown themselves fully into the defence of territory and the protection of activists within this scenario of intensified violent conflict. The following text has been updated to consider changes to the movement between 2010 and 2015, but I also am certain that my observations from 2009 to 2010 hold true today. It is my hope that the exploration of the roots of today's movement will help us to understand their work, shortcomings, and strengths in the future.

Overview of the Book

Dealing with Peace consists of six chapters, each of which examines one aspect of, or angle for considering, the Guatemalan campesino movement. The chapters progress from a theoretical and top-down examination of the movement, increasingly downwards to the grassroots work of campesino organizations and rural communities. Chapter 1 presents the context of the transition to neoliberalism that frames the current moment of campesino organizing in Guatemala. In doing so, the chapter surveys the involvement of social movements in neoliberal agrarian institutions in Guatemala's post-conflict context and introduces the central theoretical question of the study: does the acceptance of neoliberal concessions by a social movement suggest that the transformative potential of that movement has been dampened?

The following two chapters examine the work of the campesino movement and outline the extent of such involvement in neoliberal agrarian institutions. Chapter 2 details the history of the movement and presents an overview of contemporary organizational goals and strategies. Chapter 3 looks at strategies to access, hold onto, or reclaim communal land that have been used by the movement, organizing them into two categories of a market-based approach and agrarian conflict.

Chapters 4 and 5 each present an account of one campesino organization and two communities that have recently accessed land, presenting detailed examples of how campesino organizing – and its engagement with neoliberalism – plays out within the movement's constituent organizations and communities. And, where the first five chapters are based primarily in an assessment of the campesino movement during the main period of research (2009–10), chapter 6 tracks changes to the movement over the following five years and considers the ongoing practical and theoretical implications of its struggles, using a growing divergence between the case study organizations to reassess the impact of neoliberal resources on social movement organizing.

Overall the book explores how organizations within the contemporary Guatemalan campesino movement deal with peace, in both senses of the verb *to deal*: how they navigate the difficult context set by the post-conflict transition, but also how they negotiate directly with dominant institutions established by that transition in order to build alternatives. The results of this dealing, we will see, are complicated and contradictory but ultimately lead to much hope for a better Guatemala.

1 Strategic Engagements with Neoliberalism

This book explores the Guatemalan campesino social movement in the period since the end of armed conflict in 1996, and specifically the efforts of campesino organizations to access communal land together with organized rural communities. In doing so, it considers the nature of the relationship between this explicitly anti-neoliberal social movement and the neoliberal agrarian institutions upon which they have come to rely. Following a peace process dominated by an ascendant neoliberal faction of the Guatemalan elite, and peace accords that called for a distinctly neoliberal post-conflict order, state involvement in rural and agrarian affairs has been steeped in market-based solutions and the formation of political subjects as *Homo economicus* (Brown 2015, 80–7). Decades of grassroots struggles for agrarian reform were reduced, through the accords, to the creation of the *Fondo de Tierras*, a World Bank–funded institution that provides loans for land transactions and aims to strengthen private property in Guatemala.

Instead of resisting the new institutional order, however, many campesino and Indigenous organizations have participated in the neoliberal agrarian regime in order to make the most of the institutions founded through peace negotiations. But to what extent does campesino engagement with these neoliberal concessions suggest a dampening of the transformative potential of their movement? Charles R. Hale, an anthropologist and long-time observer of land struggles in Central America, suggests that the "rules set in advance" of neoliberal support for Indigenous territory include the realization of neoliberal subject formation and the cancellation of a movement's potential to affect significant change (Hale 2011). This study questions Hale's conclusions by exploring campesino organizations and communities that participate in neoliberal agrarian institutions while retaining an ability to oppose the neoliberal order and to construct socio-economic alternatives. In this chapter I draw out the meaning of neoliberalism and its role in the establishment and practice of the Guatemalan post-conflict state, in order to explore the significance of interactions between social movements and neoliberalism that may not always appear to be entirely oppositional.

Transitions to and through Neoliberalism

Social movements across Latin America have flourished during the neoliberal period, responding to harsh restructuring by launching radically new repertoires of contention that have pushed the boundaries of what is considered possible through collective action (Tarrow 2011). Workers occupied hundreds of factories in Argentina and turned them into cooperative, democratic workplaces that in some cases out-performed their previous capitalist enterprises. In Brazil thousands of communities were formed on occupied plantations as the Landless Workers' Movement (*Movimento Dos Trabalhadores Rurais Sem Terra*, MST) attempted to shift the nature of both agrarian politics and the Brazilian democratic transition. The *Vía Campesina* embarked upon the worldwide coordination of peasant activism through a transnational network of 149 organizations in fifty-six countries, including groups from seventeen Latin American countries. And Indigenous nations rose from political invisibility to force the transformation of national political systems, rewriting constitutions and creating hundreds of small-scale territories under the jurisdiction of Indigenous self-governance (Desmarais 2007; Martí i Puig 2010; Vieta and Ruggeri 2009; Wolford 2010b).

In each of these and many other cases, the contentious politics of ordinary people produced a change in material conditions for participants as well as a transformation in the political imagination of other grassroots actors. In countries including Bolivia, Ecuador, and Venezuela, social movements and states have combined forces, helping to shift the purpose of government to people-focused policies influenced by grassroots groups. In others, Indigenous groups have embarked on decolonial processes, using social movement tactics to create spaces of autonomous governance and to decolonize public institutions. Both processes have been imperfect and have yielded mixed results – such as the Bolivian government of President Evo Morales, which is increasingly distant from its Indigenous and social movement base – but social movements have nevertheless represented a powerful force for political and social change across the region over the last thirty years (Dinerstein 2015; Erazo 2013; Stahler-Sholk, Vanden, and Becker 2014; Webber and Carr 2013).

The recent innovations of Latin American social movements, which have collectively altered global perceptions of grassroots power and the relationship between states and societies, formed in large part in response to the prior attempt at restructuring represented by neoliberalism. The political-economic shift associated with the global adoption of neoliberalism represents the most universal and thorough top-down attempt at restructuring since the spread of colonialism and capitalism. At its core, neoliberalism is a political ideology, one that has risen to near-total acceptance by governments around the world since the late 1970s. In *A Brief History of Neoliberalism*, Harvey (2005, 2) introduces neoliberalism as "a theory of political economic practices that proposes that human well-being can best be advanced by liberating individual entrepreneurial freedoms and skills within an institutional framework characterized by strong private property rights, free markets, and free trade."

Neoliberal theory was accepted quickly around the world – through processes discussed below – at the expense not only of the regulatory, social welfare state encouraged by Keynesian economic thought earlier in the twentieth century, but also at the expense of a collectivist, rather than individualistic, view of society. The neoliberal perspective on human advancement has been adopted almost universally within approaches to governance, leading to the creation of what Harvey calls the neoliberal state (2005, 2): a state form characterized by the guidance of neoliberal principles that lead to the stripping of state participation in market regulation and social welfare while simultaneously bolstering state intervention in the creation of markets (where areas such as water or education had been considered public endeavours), and in the protection of those markets through legal and coercive systems. In the four decades since its rise to global prominence, analysts have shown that the implementation of neoliberalism has restored power and wealth to elite classes, undermined the ability of unions and other grassroots sectors to organize collectively, and replaced the political character of democracy with primarily economic functions (Brown 2015; Fraser 2009; Harvey 2005; McNally 2011; Wacquant 2012).

There is substantial disagreement on the character of neoliberalism, either as primarily material, aimed first and foremost at the ascendency of market rule in the pursuit of class-based interests (the Marxian perspective), or as primarily subjective, intended to expand governmentality, or the acceptance that individuals, rather than the state, are responsible for their own well-being (the Foucauldian stance) (Wacquant 2012). In my own view, and in the assessment of Guatemalan politics that follows, neoliberalism is both material and subjective, aimed simultaneously at the restoration of class power through restructured states and economies, and at the subjective reconstitution of society in a way that would perpetuate that power.

Material restructuring features heavily in neoliberal reform. The doctrine of neoliberalism, while vast in its economic, political, and social implications, includes a call for policy reform including liberalization of trade, privatization of state assets, and deregulation of industry. The role of states is thus altered, and transnational processes are increasingly involved in production, finance, and accumulation. For this approach to be adopted, a global sea change in economic policy was necessary. Embedded liberalism, or the active involvement of governments seeking economic growth to support full employment and social welfare systems, gave way, beginning in the late 1970s, to the pursuit of growth for individuals and corporations based in the freedom of capital. These changes were forced abruptly and violently in most settings, as neoliberal economic policy was adopted around the world through a series of interrelated economic shocks. In countries of the Global North, governments pushed through the first neoliberal economic and social reforms under the guise of recovery from an economic downturn. Through the U.S.-based Volker Shock, domestic and global interest rates were raised drastically in order to curb inflation and, by extension, to deal a blow to organized labour, whose demands were seen as driving inflation. Across the Global South, skyrocketing interest rates left many countries shackled with insurmountable debt overnight. Structural adjustment policies followed in the South, with neoliberal reform presented as a condition for bailout loans from the International Monetary Fund and private banks (Duménil and Lévy 2004; Gill 2003; Harvey 2005; McNally 2011; Saad-Filho and Johnston 2005).

In the Global North and South both, the lasting impact of the neoliberal transition was to return wealth and power to economic elites. Traditionally powerful classes around the world had felt the blow of multiple challenges to their hold on power in the years since the Second World War. Across the South, independence movements did away with most European colonialism, revolutionary movements threatened to overturn established national elites, and radical political leaders attempted sweeping change after being elected democratically (Prashad 2007). In the North the class compromise of embedded liberalism drove down significantly the share of profits held by elites (Harvey 2005, 15–19). Under neoliberalism these challenges were put to bay, at least initially.[1] By the late 1990s, when left parties and social movements in Latin America began to confront neoliberalism with viable alternatives, the neoliberal project had already accomplished its main political and economic goals. The welfare state and other challenges to concentrated wealth had been at least partially overturned, returning significant profit and power to the highest economic classes worldwide (Duménil and Lévy 2004; McNally 2011).

The material repercussions of restructuring were devastating, but the impact of the neoliberal turn did not stop there. As early theorists and the heads of state pushing the first rounds of neoliberal reforms understood, the lasting effects of neoliberalism would also include a reconfiguration of the meaning of citizenship and of the role of the individual in society. In the words of Margaret Thatcher, "Economics are the method, but the objective is to change the soul" (cited in Harvey 2005, 23). This change in the soul aimed at a shift in the perception of the role of individuals, who would no longer be seen as members of collective society but rather as rational economic actors subject to market forces. The roots of this attempted transformation lie with the intellectual founders of neoliberalism, the economic theorists who, beginning in the 1940s, laid the groundwork for eventual neoliberal policy. Foucault's lectures on governmentality argue that the work of the Chicago school "attempt[ed] to re-define the social sphere as a form of the economic domain" (Lemke 2001, 197). Whereas classical liberal economic thought recognized a separation of social matters from the economy and looked to the state for social regulation and welfare provisions, neoliberalism reimagined all human activity as subject to market forces.

Far from the "invisible hand" description of a naturally occurring market that appears in classical economics, however, neoliberals explained those market forces as relying on outside intervention (Lemke 2001, 193). Of course critical political economists have long understood that the founding of the capitalist market was anything but natural and could come about only through violent intervention (Marx 1976; Polanyi 2001). But with neoliberal theory, proponents of capitalism were themselves now writing into their own doctrine a recognition that the market is not natural and must be intentionally created and maintained. As a result, neoliberal thought not only analyses individual behaviour according to economic criteria, it perceives individuals to be manipulable through changes in economic variables (Lemke 2001, 200). If society is understood as a purely economic realm and individuals behave rationally according to their economic interests, then that behaviour can be altered through the very intervention that maintains the functioning of the market.

We can thus understand the rationale for neoliberal restructuring as at once material and subjective. Economic conditions are changed forcefully through austerity measures and structural adjustment in order to return power and wealth to national and global elites, and attempts are made to alter social behaviour to prioritize atomized economic concerns above all other considerations – and in place of collective identities and practices – as a disciplinary measure to sustain the power and wealth of those elites. This is a political project that is ongoing and cannot be completed through the imposition of a set of neoliberal reforms, no matter how severe. It is, however, also a project that is ripe with resistance, since it has failed to consolidate either political-economic hegemony or the form of subjectivity outlined in neoliberal theory.

In Latin America the contested consolidation of neoliberalism has driven politics for over thirty years. Following an initial wave of macroeconomic restructuring, political institutions have become battlegrounds, with economic and political reforms aimed at consolidating a neoliberal transition in state institutions and state-society relations, but with organized grassroots movements seeking either to block that transition or to shelter sectors of society from its effects. The nature of this struggle varies significantly by country, on the basis of particular experience of the neoliberal transition in each case. Nevertheless, general trends characterize the transition to neoliberalism across most of the region, some of which are pertinent to our discussion and are outlined below.

First, the impetus to adopt neoliberalism came from outside, but reform was welcomed and facilitated by some local sectors. Beginning in the 1980s the debt crisis provided the main vehicle for neoliberal structural adjustment, and restructuring rolled quickly across the continent in the form of liberalization, deregulation, and privatization (Green 2003; Thorp 1998; Williamson 1990). Democratization and peace processes also proved to be mechanisms for neoliberal restructuring, as political reform most often fit the neoliberal institutional prescription of the day (North 1998; Pearce 1998; Robinson 1996, 2003; Short 2007). In the case of both structural adjustment and democratization, however, local elites who stood to benefit from the reconfiguration of political and economic power participated willingly in neoliberalization, as did members of technocratic classes eager to see change to state bureaucracies (Margheritis and Pereira 2007; Potter 2007; Robinson 1996, 2003).

Second, even while the degree of neoliberal reform varies by country, the role of the state has changed across the region. Although historical processes had left many Latin American nations with weak state institutions and little commitment to the social welfare of their citizens (Kay 1989; Moore 1993; Rueschemeyer, Stephens, and Stephens 1992), the political-economic context of the twentieth century had led to a spike in the role of states as agents of development. Neoliberalism did away with this, and states and state institutions were repositioned as referees for capital accumulation first and foremost, and only as an afterthought as providers of occasional and unevenly applied development aid and social services (Kay 2006; Molyneux 2008; Mukherjee Reed 2008).

Finally, the shape of power, wealth, and inequality has shifted during the neoliberal period. Neoliberalism failed in most countries across the region to generate even the economic growth that was its supposed centrepiece (Weisbrot and Ray 2011), but the concentration of wealth has nevertheless shifted drastically in favour of the rich. Upper and middle classes have shrunk since the 1970s, but the amount of income concentrated among top earners has grown (Portes and Hoffman 2003). Poverty, meanwhile, has grown numbers and severity in many countries, pointing to increasing inequality within nations as well as across Latin America as a whole (Helwege and Birch 2007; Stiglitz 2003). Alongside changes to the distribution of national wealth, much economic power has also shifted to the transnational sphere, as trade liberalization and changing national economies have encouraged transnational corporations from sectors including finance and resource extraction to increase their activity across Latin America (Robinson 2008).

If the neoliberal project has altered the political, economic, and social landscape of Latin America, it remains an incomplete transition. States have been transformed significantly, with neoliberalism emerging as the prevailing form of political organization in order to enshrine the power of local elites and transnational capital. That transition relied on the *acceptance* of the new model by the majority, however, in order for either the hegemony of neoliberalism to solidify within national societies or the subjective shift to a market-based citizenship to occur. Both of these elements, necessary for a thorough transition to neoliberalism, fell flat. While the impact of neoliberalism has been real and severe, then, the consolidation and sustainability of the neoliberal project are less clear.

Peace, Land, and Neoliberalism

The resistance generated by neoliberal restructuring, as explained above, left its mark on many countries of Latin America, whose states and economies were altered by social movements contesting consolidation of the new political-economic paradigm. If this is true as a general trend across the region, however, there remain countries where circumstances have prevented movements from instigating the same degree of change. Unfortunately Guatemala provides one such case, and our discussion of the Guatemalan campesino movement also serves as an example of the inner workings of transitions to neoliberalism, and of the contradictory and ever incomplete nature of struggles to reshape states and societies.

Guatemala's experience with neoliberalism is unique in that the primary delivery tool for restructuring came not in the form of structural adjustment but in the contents of the negotiated accords that ended decades of war. Civil society was also included in accord negotiations, so the consolidation of neoliberalism through Guatemala's peace process is also distinct in that the basis for the neoliberal transition was established through the consent of the organized left. As a result, a framework has been established in post-conflict Guatemala under which little social movement can be understood as occurring outside the blueprint of neoliberal peace, and the energy of many social movements has been channelled into implementing the accords that ultimately fit the dominant order of transnational neoliberalism and local elite power. As we will see over the following chapters, there is still much potential for significant social movement activity within these constraints, but we must first explore the boundaries that have taken shape under Guatemala's neoliberal peace.

Neoliberalism crept slowly into Guatemala, in contrast to more dramatic, nearly overnight transitions such as those of Chile or the United States. The support base for neoliberalism formed during Guatemala's long internal armed conflict before taking hold of political and economic power in the mid-1980s. Following a CIA-orchestrated coup against the reformist president Jacobo Árbenz in 1954, the Guatemalan elite began to split in three: the traditional agricultural oligarchy, their military backers who branched off after a sustained run of political power, and a new right that was based in non-traditional economic activity (Dosal 1995; McCleary 1999; Robinson 2003; Schirmer 1998; Short 2007). This third faction, which would rise to power in tandem with neoliberalism in the 1980s and 1990s, was groomed in large part through support from the United States. Funding from the U.S. International Cooperation Agency (which would later become the US Agency for International Development, USAID), the World Bank, and private consulting firms such as Klein and Saks encouraged the "modernization" of the Guatemalan economy and an increased role for foreign investment (Short 2007, 45–6). As new sectors grew – especially those of banking, non-traditional agricultural exports, maquila production, and tourism – USAID provided support to strengthen the organizational and political capacity of the new right. Following the end of military rule in 1986, USAID began pumping hundreds of millions of dollars into the new right through the Private Enterprise Development program, which aimed to increase transnational economic activity in Guatemala and enhance the political importance of like-minded local elites (Robinson 2003, 109–13). By the early 1990s, as the Guatemalan government and guerrillas began negotiating an end to the armed conflict, the importance of new economic activities had surpassed that of traditional agricultural exports; non-traditional elites had gained control of the largest private sector organization in the country, the Coordinating Committee of Agricultural, Commercial, Industrial, and Financial Associations (*Comité Coordinador de Asociaciones Agrícolas, Comerciales, Industriales, y Financieras*, CACIF); and the new right had begun to exert considerable influence over political decision-making, including lobbying to pass early liberalization and deregulation measures (Robinson 2003, 109–13; Segovia 2005; Short 2007).

While the new right faction of the Guatemalan elite was on the rise in the 1980s, their domination of the political scene – and the transition to neoliberalism that this set in motion – would be secured in the 1990s through the Guatemalan peace process. The series of accords that ended the conflict in 1996 should be understood as signalling more than the end of hostilities between the government and the guerrillas. Rather the process of accord negotiation, the contents of the accords, and the selective implementation of those agreements all form part of a transition in state form in Guatemala, from the counter-insurgent state to the post-conflict neoliberal state (Cox 1981; Short 2007). And while the balance of power between elite factions shifted towards the new economic elite, the transition was conducted in such a way as to also preserve the power of the armed forces and include elements of the counter-insurgent state within the new, neoliberal state.

The preservation of military power was achieved when the armed forces themselves initiated a democratic transition, calling for a presidential election in 1984 and the rewriting of the national constitution the following year. The late stage of the armed conflict preceding this transition, beginning in 1978, was characterized by state terror and genocide. The armed forces, in power with few exceptions since 1954, had gradually subsumed all elements of the state within the counter-insurgent apparatus and had turned that system on the civilian population in an effort to eradicate the guerrilla threat. Death squads were institutionalized and coordinated under the military and police command, and they systematically targeted suspected "subversives" in urban centres. Meanwhile military troops and special forces coordinated the scorched earth massacre of hundreds of rural Indigenous villages in an attempt, steeped in racism, to deny support for the guerrillas (Barrios 2013; CEH 1999; Grandin 2011; Huet 2008; ODHA 1998; Schirmer 1998; Weld 2014). As the armed forces oversaw the violence, they also rose to economic importance through their own activities and through alliances with the new right. Military officers took hold of large tracts of land, mostly in the sparsely populated but resource-rich northern lowlands; they gained control of the nascent drug trade and other organized criminal activity; and both individual officers and the armed forces as an institution invested in banking and other legitimate activities (Kading 1999; Peacock and Beltrán 2003; Schirmer 1998; C.A. Smith 1990c; Solano 2005). As the Guatemalan economy sank under the debt crisis of the early 1980s, then, and as the military command began to regret its poor international reputation earned through counter-insurgency, the need for civilian transition and economic stability became clear.

The democratic transition and the peace process that followed were initiated by the armed forces and supported by the neoliberal faction of the Guatemalan elite. Since those same forces managed to dominate the long transition, the peace process also became the vehicle through which the post-conflict order was established. The Guatemalan accords in fact went beyond the technical agreements that are the standard fare of peace negotiations to present a series of accords aimed at the root causes of the conflict (Jonas 2000; Short 2007; Torres-Rivas 2012). Far-reaching accords, including the Agreement on the Strengthening of Civilian Power and the Role of the Armed Forces in a Democratic

Society, the Agreement on Identity and Rights of Indigenous Peoples, and the Agreement on Socio-Economic Aspects and the Agrarian Situation presented suggestions for the broad reform of political, economic, and social institutions that amounted to "proposals to change the nature of power" in post-conflict Guatemala (Torres-Rivas 2012, 129). Over eight years of negotiation, however, Guatemala's new right, along with international actors involved in the peace process, guided those proposals so that power would adopt a thoroughly neoliberal bias, turning the process into one of not just peace-building, but of neoliberal restructuring as well.

From the first moments of their adoption, the peace accords received mixed and cautious reaction. Guatemalan and international commentators alike heralded an end to armed conflict and the substantially progressive language of accords such as those addressing Indigenous and human rights (Jonas 1997; Short 2007, 1–3). What was equally clear, however, was that the results of the peace process would do little to address the broader violence ingrained within Guatemalan state and society or to correct the economic injustices that were, to a large degree, at the root of the armed conflict (Jonas 1998; Pearce 1998; C.A. Smith 1990c). As Jonas argues (1997, 9), the accords were "subordinated to the logic of neoliberal fundamentalism," an overarching economic regression that threatened to "be the Achilles' [sic] heel of the whole arrangement, and could eventually undermine democratic gains." Prompt criticism of the Socio-Economic Accord was especially harsh, with Guatemalan activists, academics, and politicians all pointing out that the approach to land contained within the accord would serve to "consolidate the present unequal system of land ownership" (Tiney referenced in Palma Murga 1997, 78).

As Nicola Short (2007) demonstrates in a Gramscian analysis of the Guatemalan peace process, the accords are best understood as representing the triumph of the new right and neoliberal ideology in the post-conflict order. Short (63) describes the peace process as a "passive revolution of certain elites, assisted by the international community, both through official channels and civil society." Gramsci explained power as operating through a combination of coercion and consent, where the dominant social group holds the means of coercion but must constantly construct its legitimacy across the rest of society. A passive revolution is one way in which that legitimacy can be constructed, when the dominant group responds to demands for social change by co-opting those demands and granting only enough concessions so as to satisfy society while maintaining its hold on power (15–16). The Guatemalan peace process, when viewed through a Gramscian lens, appears as a textbook example of a passive revolution, with the ascendant neoliberal faction of the Guatemalan elite, along with their international supporters, ensuring that neither the negotiations nor the content of the accords would challenge the dominant order.

Neoliberal elites in Guatemala managed this passive revolution by first positioning themselves as a pro-peace lobby group and gaining the support of the United Nations and other international bodies and then managing to defer the discussion of substantive issues until the end of the negotiations. Short (2007, chap. 4) explains the peace process as occurring in four phases, each of which further advanced the position of the dominant, neoliberal elite. The first phase set an agenda for peace negotiations that focused on the continuation of electoral democracy without institutional reform and highlighted the importance of economic development. The second phase occurred suddenly, when Guatemalan President Jorge Elías Serrano responded to political turbulence by attempting to hold onto power through a self-coup, suspending Congress and the constitution. The neoliberal right, coordinated through the private sector umbrella organization CACIF, stepped in to position itself as the representative of democratic civil society, hosting a broad-based forum (the *Foro Multisectorial*) that would prove instrumental in transferring the presidency to a civilian and ensuring the continuation of electoral politics. Following the *Serranazo*, as Serrano's attempted self-coup became known, the participation of civil society in the peace process gained international recognition and acquired formal status. In this third phase, the United Nations–sanctioned Civil Society Assembly (*Asamblea de Sociedad Civil*, ASC) held discussions to propose content for the accords under negotiation. CACIF did not join the ASC, preferring to lobby the negotiation process as a separate representative of the business sector – and one that had earned international respect through its role in ending the *Serranazo* (Brett 2008, 48–50; Short 2007, 72–6).

With the inclusion of civil society proposals in the negotiation process now institutionalized – and with the cohesion of perspectives between CACIF and international donor parties to the accords such as the United States, the World Bank, and the International Monetary Fund – the neoliberal elite represented in CACIF managed to defer discussion of substantive issues in the fourth, most strategic phase of the accords. The discussion of land and economic issues, most importantly, was pushed out of each accord until the final one. Although the question of land factors heavily into the discussion of Indigenous rights and the resettlement of refugees, for example, neither agreement addresses land in its text. Instead, the discussion of agrarian issues, which had formed the basis of URNG demands for reform prior to negotiation, was tabled until a final agreement. That accord, the Agreement on Social and Economic Aspects and the Agrarian Situation, or the Socio-Economic Accord, attempts to resolve all questions that challenge the structure of Guatemala's grossly unequal society in terms that are decidedly inoffensive to the neoliberal elite (Palma Murga 1997; Short 2007, 76–84). In fact, as we will see below and throughout the following study, the language used in the Socio-Economic Accord is so heavily neoliberal that the possibility for significant social change based in the peace accords was effectively cancelled in the final phase of the peace process. With the Socio-Economic Accord, the dominant sector of the Guatemalan elite had completed their passive revolution successfully, co-opting the call for reform and defining change in their own terms.

Guatemala thus entered the post-conflict era under a blueprint for peace-building that fit the perspective of neoliberal elites and neoliberal international donors and that defined all socio-economic concerns in market terms. In the years since the agreements were signed, accordingly, the Guatemalan state has taken on a neoliberal form, including elements of the previous counter-insurgent model. Neoliberal restructuring across Latin America focused on dismantling state institutions and policies aimed to protect national economies and vulnerable groups. Since the Guatemalan armed forces had already gutted all state institutions to serve the counter-insurgency, however, the neoliberal transition in Guatemala required only that post-conflict political and economic policy not stray from the neoliberal path set out in the peace accords. And while the six administrations elected since the end of the armed conflict have oscillated between the representation of various elite factions, they have all governed according to a neoliberal political rationale, as evident in successive social and economic policy.[2]

Social policy has not taken a substantive or even coherent form in the post-conflict era, consisting instead of haphazard programs to deliver resources to select groups, such as conditional cash transfers to mothers with children in school, chemical fertilizers for small farmers, and the installation of basic services such as electricity or running water, under much fanfare, in remote villages (Batres 2012; Gaia 2010). Economic policy, on the other hand, has consistently supported the deregulation and liberalization of increasingly transnational economic activity. Guatemala has signed multiple trade deals in recent years, most contentious among them the Central American Free Trade Agreement – Dominican Republic (CAFTA-DR) between the isthmus, the United States, and the Dominican Republic; the government rewrote the country's mining code to increase financial incentives to transnational companies, a move that has brought an influx of new mines and related social conflict; other transnational projects for resource extraction have likewise expanded, chief among them hydroelectric dams and oil; and the transnationally oriented service sector, including banking and other financial activities, has steadily increased its share of the Guatemalan economy (Nolin and Stephens 2010; Robinson 2008; Segovia 2005; Solano 2005).

Elements of the counter-insurgent state have also survived or been revived, and they have fused with processes of neoliberalization to form the post-conflict neoliberal state. Guatemalan sociologist Edelberto Torres-Rivas (2012) points to the continuation of counter-insurgent state power as a key factor in the failure to consolidate popular democracy in post-conflict Guatemala. For Torres-Rivas, that power is evident today in the fact that the national intelligence system remains under the control of the military, and in the weakness of the judiciary, which remains "the Achilles heel of Guatemalan democracy" following its key role in the counter-insurgent state (Torres-Rivas 2012, 110–16, 126–7). To these we can add two uses of repressive force. On the one hand, the armed forces have slowly increased their role in domestic security to the point that troops are now used to repress grassroots movements, such as in the frequent eviction of land occupations and in the military massacre of seven Indigenous protesters in Totonicapán in 2012 (Archibold 2012; Batres 2011). On the other hand, the continued use of paramilitary force has kept the counter-insurgent model alive and underscored the power of the military elite, through dozens of murders of social movement activists, human rights defenders, and individuals involved in legal cases that challenge military impunity (Granovsky-Larsen, forthcoming). There is much overlap between remilitarization and neoliberalization – in the importance of paramilitary forces in protecting mining projects, for example, and in the role of economic and military elites within the government of retired general Otto Pérez Molina (2012–15) – a confluence that underscores the role of both forces within the post-conflict neoliberal state (Pérez 2013; Solano 2012).

A look at state involvement in agrarian issues since the end of the armed conflict provides excellent insight into the process through which the Guatemalan state consolidated its neoliberal form. The current institutional framework for rural and agrarian policy was established through the contents of the Socio-Economic Accord as well as through its scant implementation. After the discussion of land was suspended until this final agreement through CACIF's deferral tactics, the consideration given to agrarian issues was presented in exclusively neoliberal language (Short 2007, 91–9). In place of the redistributive agrarian reform sought by the guerrillas, the accord defined the problem facing rural Guatemalans as one of a lack of productivity and efficiency, and proposed market-based solutions in response. In her analysis of the Socio-Economic Accord, Short highlights language that discusses Indigenous people, women, education, labour, and housing, as well as land access and distribution, in market terms. "The Socio-Economic Accord fundamentally prioritizes growth over everything else," writes Short. "The discourse of growth prefaces nearly every section of the agreements and growth precedes any mention of social development or justice every time either term appears in the accord" (95). Small campesino landholders are discussed as a hindrance to growth, for example, alongside the government's commitment to support their transformation into micro-entrepreneurs (97–8). Similarly the right of Indigenous and resettled peoples to make use of their landholdings is introduced in terms that make clear "their individual and collective obligations to society" (Socio-Economic Accord, cited in Short 2007, 96), presumably to participate in national economic growth rather than engaging in traditional subsistence practices. Ultimately, Short (95) notes, "the accords construct a situation where the country is invested in economic growth as a requirement for the social services promised in the agreements."

To make matters worse, those social services are themselves based in market relations, both in the commitments adopted and in the shift in state-society relations intended by the accord. The specific commitments set out to address unequal land distribution consisted of the creation of an internationally funded "market-led agrarian reform" scheme and legal reforms to improve land titling and registration. The cornerstone institution discussed in the Socio-Economic Accord, the Land Trust Fund (*Fondo de Tierras*, FONTIERRAS), has as its mandate the sale of land to groups of campesinos through the provision of loans at favourable interest rates, as well as the coordination of efforts to survey and register properties and provide land titles where they are lacking (Gobierno de Guatemala 1996). By replacing the possibility of agrarian reform with low-interest market access and the strengthening of the private property regime, the Socio-Economic Accord also aims to make neoliberal subjects of Guatemala's rural and Indigenous populations. Just as structural adjustment programs force changes to state economic activity, the Guatemalan peace accords set out to reshape social behaviour in line with the rising neoliberal order. Under the Socio-Economic Accord, writes Short (2007, 99),

> the rural population is explicitly reorganized for production, and the solution to land reform is the market, which "promises" growth out of the historical injustices acknowledged in the accords. This order homogenizes the diversity of economic relationships to the land into one governed by the rational actor and the market, with the sanctioned marginalization of groups that "irresponsibly" do not participate in full ... The Socio-Economic Accord exploits the need to address the social bases of conflict as an opportunity to reconstruct the integral state as a reflection of the market. The raison d'état becomes neoliberal, while citizenship is constructed around the rationality and subjectivity of *homo economicus*.

The intent to establish a neoliberal agrarian regime was laid out in the Socio-Economic Accord, and the selective implementation of the agreement made certain that the neoliberal approach would dominate actual state policy in the years that followed. Where there were elements in the accord that would dampen the market's total domination of agrarian affairs, they were shed either in the negotiation of the legal framework required by the accord or in the actual functioning of the institutions created. Land sold to campesinos through the World Bank–sponsored *Fondo de Tierras*, for example, was supposed to be drawn from a number of sources, including land given illegally to military officers during the conflict, unused state-owned land, land purchased by the government through peace-based funds or international loans, and a limited number of expropriated properties as allowed under the existing constitution (Jonas 2000, 78–9). Instead, FONTIERRAS has functioned solely as a broker between large landowners looking to sell plantations and groups of campesinos who are forced to agree to the prices and terms set by the landowners (see chapter 3). The *Fondo de Tierras* has also coordinated the land registry and land title regularization mandated by the Socio-Economic Accord, again through funds provided by the World Bank. Where the measures were introduced as means to protect small farmers and redistribute improperly registered land, however, the exclusive function of the cadastral project has been to measure, rather than to mitigate, land. Both the land registry and title regularization have also generated a wave of land re-concentration, with large landowners purchasing campesino land to create new plantations, sometimes even before titling is complete (Gould 2014; Hurtado Paz y Paz 2008; Milan and Grandia 2013).

While those close to the creation of the post-conflict institutional framework for rural and agrarian policy insist that the *Fondo de Tierras* was supposed to play just one part among a number of institutions aimed at supporting small farmers, the institution has instead become its central entity (interviews, Funes 2010; Peña de León 2009; Tiney 2010, 2015). The Guatemalan state has been involved in agrarian issues since the end of the armed conflict, primarily through a triad of institutions: the *Fondo de Tierras*, the Ministry for Agriculture, Cattle, and Food (*Ministerio de Agricultura, Ganadería, y Alimentación*, MAGA), and the Secretariat of Agrarian Affairs (*Secretaría de Asuntos Agrarios*, SAA). While the *Fondo de Tierras* takes care of programs aimed at small farmers and Indigenous peoples, MAGA's efforts are aimed mostly at the promotion of large-scale export agriculture. The SAA, for its part, has a mandate based in the peace accords to resolve agrarian conflicts, but it also participates in the violent state repression of campesino demands for agrarian reform outside the market model. Through the language of the peace accords, their selective implementation, and the operation of the institutions created under those agreements, state involvement in rural affairs has thus been dominated entirely by a neoliberal approach to agriculture, helping to consolidate one important element of the post-conflict neoliberal state.

After the establishment of the neoliberal agrarian regime through the peace process, Guatemalan campesino and Indigenous social movement organizations have found themselves organizing within a uniquely difficult environment. When neoliberal restructuring is imposed entirely from outside the sphere of grassroots organizing, as across much of Latin America, the impulse to resist neoliberal policies and institutions is strong. In Guatemala, however, the creation of the *Fondo de Tierras* and its programs, as well as the centralization of agrarian policy under the mandate of FONTIERRAS, was facilitated through participation of multiple grassroots sectors. Regardless of the manipulation and domination of the peace process by elite factions and international donors, the negotiation process nevertheless involved the input of many progressive sectors through the Civil Society Assembly and the direct participation of the organized left as represented by the Guatemalan National Revolutionary Unity (*Unidad Revolucionaria Nacional Guatemalteca*, URNG) guerrillas at the negotiation table. Grassroots civil society organizations in Guatemala – and in particular campesino and Indigenous organizations that focus on land – thus face a situation in which the products of the peace accords represent the result of decades of armed struggle and years of negotiation, the best chance at minimal reform, given the commitment of the government and the elite to support FONTIERRAS, as well as an important vehicle to consolidate agrarian neoliberalism and the renewed power of elites. Escape from participation in the neoliberal project thus becomes nearly impossible under a scenario where most avenues for change have been at once agreed upon by grassroots actors and steeped in neoliberalism.

Challenging Guatemala's Neoliberal Peace

The messy interaction between the organized campesino movement and neoliberal agrarian institutions such as FONTIERRAS and the SAA presents us with the central concern of this book, which is explored from a number of vantage points across the following chapters: how should we understand the relationship between an anti-neoliberal social movement and the neoliberal institutions that they helped to create and have come to rely upon? This question, while tailored to the particular post-conflict neoliberal state in Guatemala, is applicable under many more scenarios. Specifically, when a radical social movement accepts concessions granted by neoliberal institutions, how does this affect the movement's overall ability to affect structural change? Does a social movement lose that potential automatically by engaging directly with, or even supporting, neoliberalism? And if not, how can we make sense of a movement's continued relevance within a neoliberal environment that openly seeks to create a world that is very different from the ones envisioned by social movements?

We can begin to dissect the Guatemalan experience by recognizing that, although the circumstances of the peace process have generated a distinct scenario, collective land titles are actually a frequent concession of neoliberal institutions across Latin America. Most importantly, experiments with territorially based Indigenous governance are often funded by World Bank projects similar to the *Fondo de Tierras*. For more than ten years the anthropologist Charles R. Hale has explored these projects extensively, looking into the conundrum of neoliberal participation in the realization of the territorial goals of Indigenous and

Afro-Latino peoples (Hale 2002, 2004, 2011; Hale and Millamán 2006). Much of Hale's work grapples with the fact that the World Bank has funded the projects through which Indigenous and Black ethnic groups in Central America have gained access to land for territorial autonomy, including through the *Fondo de Tierras* in Guatemala. In Nicaragua, Honduras, and Guatemala, Hale observed varying World Bank projects, all counting with the enthusiastic backing of local elites and neoliberal states, which supported the legal recognition of collective land rights and the establishment of political autonomy. Hale concludes (2011) that the motivation for such neoliberal support lies in two key factors. First, recognition of collective land titles incorporates traditional territories into the land market through their official registration and thus paves the way for economic development projects. But Hale also observes a "spatial differentiation of governance" facilitated by territorial recognition. Under this scenario, areas subject to collective rights are redefined as "empty spaces" and cut off from state support, and their self-governance and political pacification are assumed to be secured by the geographically defined nature of their limited rights (189–96).

Hale thus sees land struggles as facing a particular dilemma under neoliberalism. According to his analysis, movements can choose to accept the concessions of neoliberalism, satisfying their immediate goal for territory but abandoning their broader transformative agenda, since they will "[meet] with success according to circumscribed patterns, in keeping with rules set in advance" (Hale 2011, 202). Or they can ignore their material needs, take a pass on neoliberal territorial projects, and insist on an untainted adherence to their ideals. But the two cannot exist together, for Hale; that is, acceptance of neoliberal concessions necessarily entails a dampening of transformative potential. "The predicament, in sum," writes Hale (202), "rests on the premise that these two modes of struggle – one immediate and pragmatic, the other expansive with sights set on the horizon – are incompatible." The question of struggles corrupted by neoliberal concessions also runs through the earlier products of Hale's studies. When theorizing "neoliberal multiculturalism," or the conditional granting of Indigenous cultural rights by neoliberal states (Hale 2002, 2004; Hale and Millamán 2006), Hale observed "the built-in limits to these spaces of Indigenous empowerment" (2004, 18). In particular Hale warned of the power of neoliberal multiculturalism to incorporate formally radical Indigenous movements into the neoliberal project through practices of governmentality, turning former opponents into the *indio permitido*, or "authorized Indian," whose expression of cultural identity poses no substantial threat to economic power (Hale 2004). Citing Rose's work on Foucault, Hale (496) warns, "The key to resolving this apparent paradox [of neoliberal multiculturalism] is that the state does not merely 'recognize' community, civil society, Indigenous culture and the like, but actively re-constitutes them in its own image, sheering them of radical excesses, inciting them to do the work of subject-formation that otherwise would fall to the state itself."

As we have seen, the attempt to restructure subjectivity is key to international and domestic plans for neoliberal reform. Proponents of neoliberalism, beginning with early theorists such as Hayek, hold that one long-term goal of restructuring is to "change the soul," in the words of Margaret Thatcher (Harvey 2005, 23), to reorient individual behaviour and the relationship between citizens and states to be based exclusively in the rational economic decisions of *Homo economicus*. If this is a stated goal of neoliberalism, however, it is not an *automatic* effect of restructuring. Under Hale's assessment of neoliberalism and land struggles, participation of grassroots actors in World Bank–funded land programs involves an unquestioned metamorphosis into self-governing neoliberal subjects. Such a rigid interpretation leaves out the possibility for the strategic engagement of individual and collective actors with neoliberalism. While some movements may occupy the dichotomous positions of resistance and co-optation in their pure forms, a more ambiguous middle ground appears much more frequently in accounts of social movements: Wolford (2003) shows that the Brazilian MST relies on state agrarian institutions in order to retain members who have gained access to land; Fraser (2009) argues that critiques of traditional power structures levelled by second-wave feminists helped neoliberalism gain footholds in Northern societies; and Zibechi (2012) and others have debated the seemingly contradictory continuation of neoliberal policies by social movement activists elected to power. In these and many other cases, anti-neoliberal movements with sights set on structural change have found themselves participating in and supporting aspects of neoliberalism in order to advance their ultimate goals.

The role of the World Bank in providing collective title to Indigenous land, and the question of land struggles married to Guatemala's neoliberal peace process, provide us with an opportunity to examine strategic engagements with neoliberalism up close. Rather than assuming that the potential of radical movements to effect structural change is defused through participation in neoliberal land institutions, or that the beneficiaries of World Bank–funded market-led agrarian reform projects such as the *Fondo de Tierras* shed their anti-neoliberal activism for neoliberal conformity, we should look to how these grassroots actors behave during and after their dealings with neoliberalism. That the form of agrarian politics presented in the Guatemalan peace accords aids in the establishment of a neoliberal agrarian regime is clear, as is the role of that regime in consolidation of the post-conflict neoliberal state and the affirmation of the power of elites. What we should not take for granted, however, is that campesino and Indigenous activism has been tarnished by this process, or that the results of that activism only feed into neoliberalism without generating additional transformative and anti-neoliberal results.

2 The Guatemalan Campesino Movement: Organizing through War and Peace

Shaded from the scorching coastal sun by a makeshift structure of aluminium siding and wooden poles, I listen to my research project being presented in the Maya Mam language. Juventina López Vásquez, an organizer with the National Indigenous and Campesino Coordinator (*Coordinadora Nacional Indígena y Campesina*, CONIC) in the department of Retalhuleu, had gathered fifty families in the community of Victorias III to consider my request to visit regularly, conduct interviews, and attempt to understand the role that this community plays within CONIC and the broader campesino movement. Dialogue with the approving community followed, and the meeting then carried on to other items of discussion between Victorias III and their CONIC intermediary. Over the course of more visits to Victorias III I sat in on many meetings between the community and CONIC as they coordinated projects ranging from fish tanks to mango groves, established a local health program based on traditional Indigenous knowledge, selected community-based candidates for upcoming municipal elections, and strategized their political decision to refuse payment to the *Fondo de Tierras* agrarian institution.

Victorias III's situation can be taken as a snapshot of much of the social movement of which it forms a vital part. The Guatemalan campesino movement consists not only of a growing number of local or nationally focused grassroots organizations but also of hundreds of aligned communities engaged in daily struggles to access land, to survive with scant resources, and to have their rights and needs respected by their government. In the brief introduction to Victorias III presented here we see evidence of core activities of contemporary Guatemalan campesino organizations: support for communal struggles to access land; accompaniment of communities through agrarian conflict resolution; support for productive projects, infrastructure, and social organization in the absence of state institutions; and grassroots political activism ranging from state-focused pressure tactics to electoral campaigns. But considering Victorias III also points us to the more conflictive and difficult elements of the movement, namely the looming presence of Guatemala's state agrarian institutions and the constraints and opportunities afforded under neoliberalism.

From the Ashes of Revolution and Genocide, 1944–1985

While campesinos and Indigenous peoples in Guatemala have organized collectively for centuries, we can mark the emergence of the distinct Guatemalan campesino social movement with the establishment of the Committee for Campesino Unity (*Comité de Unidad Campesina*, CUC) in 1978. I understand the "campesino movement" in relation to Tarrow's (2011) definition of social movements, to refer to the organizations, people, and activities that engage in sustained collective action to challenge established power in support of the material and cultural interests of campesinos. The Guatemalan campesino social movement draws its membership and political position from the small-scale or landless rural farmers known as "campesinos." Given the ethnic composition of Guatemala – where twenty-two distinct Maya and Xinka Indigenous groups account for around 60 per cent of the population and over 90 per cent in many rural areas – the campesino movement is by default also an Indigenous movement. The 1980s saw the emergence of a separate Maya social movement in Guatemala, with a primary focus on cultural rights. Nevertheless, a strict division between Maya and campesino organizations, and between cultural and material concerns, is difficult given the Indigenous base of the campesino movement, the cultural significance of material demands such as land access, and the ethnic component of class in Guatemala (Bastos 2010; Hale 2004, 2006b; Konefal 2010; Mazariegos 2007; C.A. Smith 1990a; Velásquez Nimatuj 2008). Campesino organizations and communities in Guatemala are described best as belonging to a "campesino-Indigenous movement," and this phrasing is often employed in Guatemala (*el movimiento campesino-indígena*). In the interest of using a neater and more widely referenced term, I refer here simply to the "campesino movement," but the reader should keep in mind the nuanced significance of the word *campesino*.

When the CUC formed in 1978, it became the first Guatemalan social movement organization focused on campesino demands to be founded by campesinos themselves, rather than by well-intentioned outsiders such as labour unions or the Catholic Church. With this the CUC initiated the era of campesino-initiated and campesino-led organizing that we now understand as the campesino movement. The landmark organization did not form in a vacuum, however, as the CUC surfaced at the culmination of a decade of intensive rural organizing and owed much to a political process that began more than twenty years earlier. Jacobo Arbenz's agrarian reform of the 1950s played an important role in the emergence of a campesino movement, as did subsequent cooperative agricultural projects, the new activist role of the Catholic Church, and the response of grassroots movements to a major earthquake in 1976.

A vast body of historical research shows that ever since the Spanish conquest in the early 1500s, Guatemalan Indigenous communities have not ceased fighting to protect or reclaim their land (Cambranes 1992a; Grandin 2011; Lovell 1992; Martínez Peláez 2009; McCreery 1994; C.A. Smith 1990b). Such actions intensified with reforms enacted under the Liberal Revolution of the late nineteenth century, which sought to strip communities of land suitable for coffee crops. However, it wasn't until the radically reformist "democratic spring" of 1944–54 that campesinos began to organize politically on a national scale. Under the government of Juan José Arévalo (1944–50), unionist campaigns to organize plantation workers led the charge towards rapid and widespread organizing in rural communities. By 1952 the National Peasant Confederation of Guatemala (*Confederación Nacional Campesina de Guatemala*, CNCG) and the Confederation of Guatemalan Workers (*Confederación de Trabajadores Guatemaltecos*, CTG) had organized hundreds of thousands of rural workers, and by 1954 autonomous peasant unions had formed in most rural communities across the country (Handy 1994b, 70–5, 117–18; Grandin 2011).

Under the Agrarian Reform Law (Decree 900) introduced by President Jacobo Árbenz in 1952, over 100,000 families gained access to land through a bottom-up procedure that required organized campesinos to identify land eligible for expropriation in their local areas (Handy 1994b, 90–2). This approach helped facilitate the transfer of nearly 800 expropriated farms, totalling 364,587 hectares, between 1952 and 1954.[1] As Handy has shown, however, it also "opened a Pandora's box of conflict in rural Guatemala" (135). Tensions within and between rural communities erupted, labour unions competed for members and influence, and landowners – fearing the rise of Indigenous workers as much as a loss of resources – resorted to violence and counter-revolution in order to halt social change and agrarian restructuring (Handy 1994b).

After re-establishing control through a CIA-backed coup in 1954, the Guatemalan landowning elite attempted to eradicate rural organizing. Land distributed under Decree 900 was reversed, hundreds of campesino leaders were killed and many thousands were jailed or fled into exile, and unions were restructured forcibly to the government's liking (Handy 1994b, 194–8; May 2001, 81–4). Over the following twenty-five years, most campesino organizing took place through a growing number of agricultural cooperatives. The cooperative movement spread through support from the unlikely combination of the liberation theology–inspired work of Catholic Action and other church groups on the one hand, and, on the other, Guatemalan government programs that sought to populate and develop remote northern regions. Added to this was significant funding from the United States Agency for International Development (USAID), which encouraged a transition to Green Revolution technology and saw in the cooperatives an opportunity to redirect campesino energy away from the demand for agrarian reform (Davis 1983; Fledderjohn 1976; May 2001, 95–102; Sinclair 1995).

Much of the land used for cooperatives, as well as many individual family plots, was given out by the government in a series of land distribution programs beginning in 1954. In an attempt to address the pressing demand for land while simultaneously upholding the agrarian status quo, over two million hectares were distributed to campesinos under three programs (Sandoval Villeda 1992; Schneider, Maul, and Membreño 1989; Schwartz 1987). The most prominent of these, operated from 1962 to 1999 by the Institute for Agrarian Transformation (*Instituto de Transformación Agraria*, INTA), provided over 600,000 hectares of land to campesinos, taken primarily from state-owned properties in Guatemala's sparsely populated northern regions. The INTA program was closely coordinated with the U.S.-led Alliance for Progress, which sought to quell political tensions through the correction of rural inequality and was aligned with plans for the expansion of large-scale economic development into remote areas of the country. However, most INTA beneficiaries did not end up owning the land they were given. Paternalistic ownership regulations required INTA beneficiaries to work their land under state tutelage for ten years before gaining legal title, and a military scorched-earth campaign targeted cooperatives and other rural communities, including those based on INTA land. Since 2000 a wave of land sales spurred by a title regularization program has also taken land title away from INTA beneficiaries (Hurtado Paz y Paz 2008, 155–60; Gauster and Isakson 2007, 1530–1; Grandia 2012).

Despite the drawbacks of state agrarian projects from 1954 on, land distributed by INTA and other state programs formed the base of many campesino cooperatives. These grew to 145 in 1967, with a membership of over 27,000 campesinos, and reached 510 cooperatives and 132,000 members in 1976.[2] During the late 1960s and early 1970s cooperatives began to radicalize in outlook, especially through the involvement of Catholic Action, and their focus shifted towards the long-term political goal of agrarian reform and other structural change. When the armed conflict intensified from 1976 on, however, the cooperatives fell out of government favour and became targets of the early phases of military scorched-earth campaigns (Davis 1983; May 2001, 95–102, 120–2; Ponciano 2009, 96–113).

The work of the Catholic Church, and Catholic Action in particular, was instrumental in the eventual emergence of campesino organizations as their own social movement (García-Ruiz 1998; Sinclair 1995). In addition to establishing agricultural cooperatives, activist priests filled a role in rural Guatemala that was quite similar to the work of campesino organizations today, focusing on community development and social organization, producing and disseminating research on the rural situation, and accompanying communities through political processes. Above all, however, the church laid the groundwork for the campesino movement through its emphasis on consciousness-raising (*concientización*), educating campesinos to understand their exploited position in Guatemalan society and to take action towards substantial change (Ponciano 2009).[3]

Rural Guatemala in the 1970s, then, was characterized by heightened organizing through agricultural cooperatives, a transformation in class consciousness as facilitated by activist priests, and a lingering sense of injustice from the reversal of agrarian reform. The first truly campesino social movement organization, the Committee for Campesino Unity (*Comité de Unidad Campesina*, CUC), formed gradually within this national context. Based in a handful of church-organized communities in the municipality of Santa Cruz del Quiché, early CUC leaders first moved from local organizing to collaborate with the newly formed radical National Committee on Labour Union Unity (*Comité Nacional de Unidad Sindical*, CNUS) and then branched out nationally to provide disaster relief following an earthquake in April 1976. In the absence of a coordinated government response to the disaster, Guatemalan communities and associations reached out across the country to assist with reconstruction. Given the overlap of reconstruction with a wave of rural organizing, the efforts proved to be a turning point in the development of Guatemalan social movements (Davis 1983, 164; May 2001, 131–2; Ponciano 2009, 108–11). This was certainly the case with the CUC. The year 1976 became the moment that gave the final push in the development of a national campesino movement, and the CUC publicly announced its creation on 1 May 1978.

Between 1978 and 1980 the CUC carried out a wave of protest and labour actions in an attempt to improve rural working conditions, demand rights for the Indigenous population, and draw attention to escalating state repression. The organization made campesino and Indigenous voices heard, but their demands were met with a campaign of violence so severe that the CUC was driven underground by the end of 1980. The decision to eradicate the CUC was made excruciatingly clear on 31 January 1980 when the military ended a CUC occupation of the Spanish embassy in Guatemala City by setting fire to the building and allowing twenty-eight of the twenty-nine activists inside to die in the blaze; the lone survivor was subsequently assassinated in hospital. Following the Spanish embassy massacre, the CUC organized a strike on sugar and cotton plantations in February and March 1980 which grew to 80,000 participants and forced an increase in the minimum wage for agricultural work from $1.12 to $3.20 per day. More repression followed the strikes, however, culminating in the kidnapping and disappearance of around one hundred CUC activists from a labour march on 1 May 1980 (Davis 1983, 165; May 2001, 131–41; Velásquez Nimatuj 2008, 101–10).

Surviving campesino leaders recounted in interviews that, following the death of much of the CUC leadership during the May Day march and the Spanish embassy massacre, a perception sank in that could no longer be achieved through peaceful measures. CUC members slipped underground or left the country to exile, and for the following five years nearly all campesino organizing took place in conjunction with guerrilla campaigns (Velásquez Nimatuj 2008, 106–7). Mass campesino and Indigenous organizing would not be seen again until 1986,[4] and Guatemala lived the darkest days of its armed conflict in the interim. Unthinkable atrocities were carried out against the civilian population during the early 1980s. Counter-insurgent tactics turned to the genocidal targeting of Indigenous villages, and in an attempt to deny the guerrilla possible support bases, over 660 communities were eradicated, more than 200,000 civilians were killed, and 1.5 million Guatemalans were displaced or exiled (CEH 1999; Huet 2008; ODHA 1998; Schirmer 1998). Campesino and Indigenous groups began to organize again after a transition to civilian rule in 1986, but targeted repression of leaders, organizations, and communities has remained a constant factor of the campesino movement, and the looming violence weighs heavily during nearly every stage of decision-making within contemporary campesino organizations.

The Perils of Peace, 1986–2010

The 1986 transfer of executive power to civilian leadership under President Vinicio Cerezo and the Christian Democratic party marked a turning point for the Guatemalan left, as organizations from many sectors re-emerged or formed anew in a flourishing of social movement activity. The campesino movement re-established itself at the forefront of protest and negotiation during this period, and political activity by new organizations over the following ten years shaped the structure of the movement as it is today and set many of the parameters for political opportunities and constraints faced by contemporary organizations and communities.

The return of campesino organizing was marked with an enormous march led by the Catholic priest Padre Andrés Girón, who brought 15,000 campesinos to Guatemala City between 27 April and 2 May 1986. The march aimed to re-assert the political importance of agrarian reform and rural issues to the transition government, and President Cerezo responded immediately by creating a National Land Commission (*Comisión Nacional de Tierras*, CONATIERRA) to define the new government's agrarian policy (*Central America Report* 1986b; Pedroni 1992; Sandoval Villeda 1992).

Padre Girón's efforts through the National Campesino Association (*Asociación Nacional Campesina*, ANC) – which continued to apply pressure until the priest's election to Congress in 1990 – amounted to political action on behalf of campesinos rather than a return of the campesino social movement, as the campaign was not led by campesinos themselves. Nevertheless, new campesino organizations soon formed to join the revived struggle. Between 1986 and 1988 rural pressure gained momentum as grassroots groups emerged, land occupations were staged across the country, and the Catholic Church backed campesino demands in a 1987 letter, "The Clamour for Land" (*El clamor por la tierra*). Fearing the possibility of agrarian reform, however, the organized land-owning sector, under the right-wing agricultural lobby group National Farmers Union (*Unión Nacional de Agricultores*, UNAGRO), managed to turn the Cerezo government away from any potentially progressive measures through a series of public, legal, and political campaigns in 1988 (Carr 1991; *Central America Report* 1986a, 1987a, 1988; CEUR 1990; Handy 1994a; R. Morán 2002, 65; Pedroni 1992; Sandoval Villeda 1992).

Organized campesino activity between 1986 and 1988 had its most obvious impact in the land distribution program created within CONA-TIERRA. For two decades the National Institute for Agrarian Transformation (INTA) had encouraged the colonization of northern Guatemala by distributing land to campesino families willing to relocate to remote regions. The creation of CONATIERRA marked a change in government land programs, however, as the emphasis shifted away from colonization and towards more politicized instances of land distribution. Fewer cases were attended to and much less land was distributed after 1986, as the official approach became to resolve individual land occupations and conflicts by purchasing alternative farms for the groups, and especially for those connected to Padre Girón's ANC group (*Central America Report* 1986b, 1987b; Handy 1994a, 43–4; Pedroni 1992, 84–9; Sandoval Villeda 1992, 233–4; Schneider, Maul, and Membreño 1989, 22–3).[5] The CONATIERRA model signalled lasting changes in government land programs, both through the reactive approach to distribution and through an early experiment with a market-based model relying on offers from large landowners.[6]

In 1988 the Committee for Campesino Unity (CUC), discussed above, resurfaced within the new context of campesino pressure and government response, bringing with it the ties to guerrilla groups that came to characterize the movement. Across the broad spectrum of left and social movement organizing in Guatemala during the 1980s, integration with the guerrilla struggle was such that a clear distinction between armed organizations and unarmed social movement activity would not always be accurate. Many new social movements, especially those that addressed Indigenous rights and human rights, formed independently of the armed left. But most campesino organizations and many other groups maintained organizational ties to the guerrillas, as the unarmed branches of the revolutionary struggle (Brett 2008, 38–43; Velásquez Nimatuj 2008, 108–17).[7]

CUC leaders had joined the Guerrilla Army of the Poor (*Ejército Guerrillero de los Pobres*, EGP) in 1981 and re-emerged as the CUC in collaboration with that group. Other campesino organizations that formed in the 1980s were likewise connected to one or another guerrilla front. While the connections between the different groups were logical during the revolutionary period, particularly in response to the distribution of territory among the guerrilla armies, these allegiances contributed to many of the divisions within the campesino movement in the years following the end of the war. Campesino organizers who have been active since the war suggest that organizations continue to be split along lines of allegiance to former guerrilla fronts. Another major fracture within the movement distinguishes older groups with guerrilla ties from newer organizations formed in the post-war period (anonymous interviews 2010; van Leeuwen 2010).

As the campesino movement flourished and began to take on its present form in the late 1980s and early 1990s, member organizations united under the first campesino umbrella group. The National Coordinator of Campesino Organizations (*Coordinadora Nacional de Organizaciones Campesinas*, CNOC) formed at the first National Campesino Congress in 1992, bringing together the main groups of the time: CUC, CONIC, CONDEG, and CONAMPRO (CNOC 1999, 2005b, 2011).[8] The founding of CNOC was a milestone for the movement, as it provided a platform for building consensus around campesino demands and proposals and served as the basis of a united campesino movement over the course of the next ten years. However, campesino influence during the final years of peace negotiation was arguably hindered by the ideological and strategic orientation of CNOC organizations towards the guerrilla rather than the emerging autonomous organizations.

Towards the end of peace negotiations, in 1994, a Civil Society Assembly (*Asociación de Sociedad Civil*, ASC) was created with a mandate to bring consensus-based proposals to the discussions, but CNOC declined an invitation to participate in the official discussions (Brett 2008, 49). Sergio Funes, who was active in peace accord negotiation and continues to coordinate their implementation today, notes that the group instead contributed to the internal discussions shaping URNG proposals (interview, Funes 2010). This behind-the-scenes participation was complemented with a campaign of land occupations intended to strengthen the hand of the guerrilla and pressure for agreements favourable to campesinos (anonymous interviews 2010). CNOC did eventually join the Civil Society Assembly in 1995, but by then there was little chance of bringing substantial land reform into what had become a weak accord on socio-economic issues (Brett 2008, 72–3; Short 2007).

As the armed conflict came to an end in 1996, the Guatemalan campesino movement faced a paradoxical turning point. It had become an instrumental and unified actor in Guatemalan politics, and campesino participation in peace negotiation and accord implementation was understood as an important step towards reforming unjust historical patterns of land distribution and discrimination. Nevertheless, the blueprint for reform decided upon in the Socio-Economic Accord also left ample room for the traditional political and economic elite to reaffirm their power, to block even minimal change, and to assist in the neoliberal transformation of agriculture and state agrarian relations. Over the following years, movement organizations would attempt to navigate this terrain to campesino advantage. The task ultimately proved to be too great, however, as the movement split internally at the same time as the neoliberal agrarian model rose to prominence.

Many of the limitations faced by campesino organizations in the post-war period took form through further rounds of negotiation following the peace accords. Although the Socio-Economic Accord called for a less-than-substantial transformation of state agrarian policy, following through on even those diluted compromises required additional discussion to draft the requisite laws and create the institutions called for in the accord. A multiparty consensus-based process similar to accord negotiation followed, and years of discussion produced two key sets of laws and state institutions but little else from the two-hundred-odd reforms that were agreed upon (interview, Funes 2010; Flores Alvarado 2003). Campesino activists and even representatives of state agrarian institutions lament that the more comprehensive blueprint contained within the Socio-Economic Accord was reduced to a near-total reliance on market-led agrarian reform through the World Bank–sponsored *Fondo de Tierras* (interviews, Peña de León 2009; Martín 2010).

The post-war negotiations also shaped the organizational structure of the campesino movement itself. The government formed three "peer commissions" (*comisiones paritarias*) in order to formalize campesino and Indigenous participation in accord implementation. One such commission, the Permanent National Coordinator on Rights Related to Land and Indigenous Peoples (*Coordinación Nacional Permanente sobre Derechos Relativos a la Tierra de los Pueblos Indígenas*, CNP-T), represented campesino and Indigenous groups in the agrarian-related aspects of all accords. The commission absorbed social movement leaders whose focus shifted away from rural activism and into negotiation with the government and the agri-business sector. Their efforts produced the *Fondo de Tierras* Law and the institution with the same name, and, after six years of discussion, the Cadastral Law and its accompanying Cadastral Information Registry project (*Registro de Información Catastral*, RIC) (interview, Funes 2010).

CNP-T participant Sergio Funes believes that the negotiations were necessary to complement traditional campesino activism and social movement involvement ensured that campesinos would benefit from final agreements as much as was possible within the constraints of the market framework (interview 2010). But the process and the reforms facilitated through negotiation have also played an important role in dividing the movement. The issue of campesino and Indigenous social movement representation within the *Fondo de Tierras* divided organizations among those who wished to collaborate and those who would boycott the process, and, among the collaborators, between organizations and leaders who competed for the few representative positions. The post-war negotiations also saw the creation of a rival umbrella group to CNOC, *Plataforma Agraria*, whose distinct political position and leadership structure attracted many new campesino organizations and came to represent another major division within the campesino movement (interviews, Funes 2010; Galicia 2010).

As the movement grew in the post-war years and coalesced around CNOC and *Plataforma Agraria*, CNOC initially held onto its role as the central and most important organizing body of the campesino movement. This was particularly true between 2001 and 2005, when collapsed coffee prices fuelled campesino organizing and radicalism rarely seen in Guatemala.[9] With over 150,000 permanent workers fired and the usual 200,000 temporary jobs not filled in 2001 and 2002 alone, CNOC member organizations mobilized rural communities for a massive wave of street protests and land occupations (Figueroa Ibarra 2003; Velásquez Nimatuj 2008, 37–45). Hundreds of farms were occupied during these years: on the basis of CNOC and CONIC records, Irma Alicia Velásquez Nimatuj shows that over 60 farms were occupied in 2001, around 50 in 2002, and 102 were under occupation as of February 2005 (40–2). These same years also saw the formalization of CNOC's strongest proposals: the Proposal for Comprehensive Agrarian Reform (*Propuesta de reforma agraria integral*, 2005), the Rural Development Proposal (*Propuesta de desarrollo rural*, 2001), and the Proposal for the Alternative Development of Indigenous and Campesino Agriculture

(*Propuesta de desarrollo alternativo de la agricultura indígena y campesina,* 2005), each based on years of consultation with member organizations and rural communities (CNOC 2004, 2005a, 2005b). Together, these proposals provided a vision for political and agrarian transformation to accompany the intensified mobilization of the era.

Following this period, however, conflicts internal to CNOC led a number of groups to withdraw from the umbrella organization. In 2007 and 2008, CONIC, CCDA, and CODECA all pulled out of CNOC, and Kab'awil stopped participating actively. Only CUC, CONDEG, and three regional organizations remained (ACDIP of El Petén, UVOC of Alta and Baja Verapaz, and Xinka of Jutiapa). CNOC was left weakened while the withdrawn organizations acted independently or, in the case of CCDA, formed a new umbrella organization (interviews, Morales 2009, 2010; Pérez Mejía 2010; and Galicia 2010). A CNOC strategic document published in 2008 recognized the need to overhaul the organization, listing among the reasons a "crisis of credibility for CNOC," a lack of unifying vision, lack of sustainable strategy for the organization, and a need to attend to "coherence between our discourse (theory) and our practice" (CNOC 2008, 7–8, 18). As CNOC lost control, the campesino movement grew in the number of organizations, while consolidating around the conflicting umbrella groups of CNOC, *Plataforma Agraria,* and the group formed by the CCDA by the name of the National Indigenous-Campesino and Popular Council (*Consejo Nacional Indígena-Campesina y Popular,* CNAIC-P) (see tables 2.1 and 2.2).

As the campesino movement has fractured, many organizations have also branched out to collaborate with other, non-campesino social organizations. In some cases, campesino organizations teamed up with broad coalitions of the left or with labour umbrella groups. Most prominently, CODECA joined the National Struggle Front (*Frente Nacional de Lucha,* FNL) and CCDA is now a member of the radical Guatemalan Labour, Indigenous and Campesino Movement (*Movimiento Sindical, Indígena y Campesina Guatemalteco,* MSICG). *Plataforma Agraria* represents another kind of multi-sector collaboration, as the ostensibly campesino umbrella group also involves many non-campesino organizations as members, including prominent participation by the AVANCSO social science research institution and the progressive Catholic organization the Interdiocesan Land Pastoral (*Pastoral de la Tierra Interdiocesana,* PTI).

In the midst of this re-alignment of the campesino movement, the Alliance for Comprehensive Rural Development (*Alianza de Desarrollo Rural Integral,* ADRI) has featured as a central convergence space for

Table 2.1. Campesino Umbrella Groups, 2010

	Member organizations	Description
CNOC	ACDIP, CONDEG, CUC, UVOC, and Xinka; Kab'awil a member but not active	The first umbrella group to form, and formerly the central body of the movement. CNOC is made up of campesino organizations that formed during the armed conflict, mostly in association with guerrilla groups. CNOC has lost much of its importance within the campesino movement recently, with some campesino organizations leaving the group and many more forming outside its ranks.
CNAIC-P	CCDA, Defensoría Indígena y Campesina, FESOC, Frente Nacional del Oriente, UCS, UNICAN	A campesino umbrella group formed by the CCDA after that organization left the CNOC umbrella group. CNAIC-P and CNOC still have good relations and even coordinate some actions together.
Plataforma Agraria	ACOMNAT, ADICH, ADIQK, ASUDI, CPR-Sierra, Coordinadora Chortí, Coordinadora de Los Altos, MTC, Red Mujer, REDASCAM, UMCAGEF, Xinka (plus other non-campesino social organizations)	This umbrella group formed after the end of the armed conflict and sees itself as an alternative to CNOC and the campesino organizations that follow the wartime model of social movement organizing. *Plataforma Agraria* does not collaborate with other campesino groups for the most part. The group has taken a firm stance against the *Fondo de Tierras* neoliberal agrarian institution, refusing to participate in any way since 2003.
ADRI	AGER, AEMADIHIQ, AMR, ASOREMA, CCDA, CM-T, CNAIC, CNOC, CNP-T, CONGCOOP, Facultad de Agronomía USAC, FEDECOCAGUA, FLACSO, Fundación Guillermo Toriello, INCIDE, Movimiento para el Desarrollo Rural, Pastoral de la Tierra Nacional, Plataforma Agraria	ADRI is not a campesino umbrella group, but the collaborative effort of campesino organizations, other grassroots organizations, and research groups to have a national rural development law passed in Guatemala. The Guatemalan government drafted such a law in collaboration with ADRI in 2008 and committed to passing it, but the draft law has since remained stalled in Congress. ADRI remains active, and – since it includes every major campesino organization other than CONIC – represents the most thorough cooperation within the movement since the decline of CNOC.

Table 2.2. Campesino Organizations Discussed in the Text

	Full name	Umbrella affiliation	Description
CCDA	Campesino Committee of the Highlands	CNAIC-P	An expanding campesino organization with national impact, the CCDA combines protest and lobbying for political reform with a direct trade coffee export project and an array of alternative agricultural programs in rural communities. One of the first campesino organizations to form in Guatemala, in 1982, the CCDA founded the CNAIC-P umbrella group after leaving CNOC in 2008. The CCDA maintains ties with the *Fondo de Tierras* and has made extensive use of its programs. Chapters 5 and 6 discuss the CCDA as a case study.
CONIC	National Indigenous and Campesino Coordinator	None	Once the largest campesino organization in Guatemala, CONIC focuses on accessing land for rural Indigenous communities, especially through resolution of agrarian conflicts. The group formed from a split in the CUC in 1992 and has remained a controversial outsider to the movement ever since. CONIC made extensive use of *Fondo de Tierras* resources for land access in the early years of the institution. Chapters 4 and 6 discuss CONIC as a case study.
CUC	Committee for Campesino Unity	CNOC	The first campesino social movement organization to form in Guatemala, CUC remains among the most active and radical today.
UVOC	Verapaz Union of Campesino Organizations	CNOC	An organization representing campesino communities in the departments of Alta Verapaz and Baja Verapaz, UVOC focuses on direct action and land occupations, and organizes with over 200 communities engaging in agrarian struggle. UVOC has strong ties to CNOC, and the group has never used *Fondo de Tierras* resources for land access.
Kab'awil	Kab'awil	CNOC (inactive)	A campesino organization based in the Western Highlands. Kab'awil is discussed as a participant in the Salvador Xolhuitz community conflict explored in chapter 5.

most organizations since 2008. ADRI formed with the goal of propos-
ing a Comprehensive Rural Development Law, which would provide
the state with a new mandate for rural and agrarian affairs similar to
that envisioned in the CNOC Proposal for Comprehensive Agrarian
Reform.[10] However, while ADRI brings nearly all campesino organizations together for discussion and negotiation,[11] its focus on one particular element of state reform means that the alliance likely will be
short-lived (interview, Galicia 2010). Despite these attempts to forge an
alliance, the Guatemalan campesino movement today finds itself in a
position of internal division and reduced political impact as compared
to its pinnacle years of unity, proposal, and action during the coffee
crisis of 1999–2004.

The Guatemalan Campesino Movement Today

Despite internal division, the organizations comprising the Guatemalan campesino movement share a set of objectives and primary tasks.
First, the overall goal of the campesino movement can be described as
the structural transformation of Guatemala's political-economic order
for the benefit of the campesino and Indigenous populations, especially
concerning agrarian matters. Second, communal campesino access to
land and land title – along with the protection of the communal use of
traditionally used areas and resources, also referred to as the defence of
territory – serve as an immediate approach to the transformative objective while also satisfying some of the material demands of campesinos
on a case-by-case basis. A third objective, also geared to overarching
structural change, is the political representation of campesinos and
Indigenous Guatemalans at the municipal and congressional levels.
Finally, campesino organizations operate with the short-term goal of
poverty alleviation and rural development, both nationally through
state programs and within individual communities aligned with a
given organization.[12]

These efforts are carried out in three main organizational spaces –
umbrella groups, individual organizations, and rural communities –
but most campesino activists recognize that there is a divide between
organizations and their "base" communities. The political work of
strategy, proposal, and protest are coordinated and largely carried out
at the levels of campesino organizations and umbrella groups, and
communities are usually brought into an action only if numbers are
required or are targeted with assistance if funds are available. While

there is significant interaction among the three levels of the movement, then, it is fluid only between organizations and umbrella groups, and it remains mainly top-down between organizations and communities. Umbrella groups such as CNOC, CNAIC-P, and *Plataforma Agraria* turn input from member organizations into proposals aimed both at government bodies and rural communities, and campesino organizations strive to implement these proposals at the community level. But there is seldom participation by communities within organizations, and the best intentions contained within proposals are often lost in practice as communities make more intuitive or strategic choices.

If campesino organizations are absent from many of the communities considered to form their popular base, this is not so among groups of campesinos actively seeking to access land. A common first step in the quest for land is to find a campesino organization with which to associate, as the organizations have the necessary experience – and sometimes influence – to help a group of campesinos navigate the formal and legal processes involved. In the case of land purchased through *Fondo de Tierras*, 164 of 242 farms distributed by 2009, or 68 per cent of successful cases, were transferred to communities through the assistance of an organization (Fondo de Tierras 2009a).[13]

Campesino organizations play a similar but even more vital role accompanying communities involved in agrarian conflicts. The conflicts range from labour disputes to land occupations and the recognition of historical land rights, to community-based opposition to mining or other mega-projects, and they often end in the formal recognition of community title to disputed land. During the process, which can last years and involve a delicate balance between negotiation and repression, campesino organizations act as intermediaries between communities and government institutions or large landowners, providing experienced representation and legal assistance free of charge (CALDH and CONIC 2009; Santa Cruz 2006; Universidad Rafael Landívar 2009).

Alongside accompaniment for land access and conflict resolution, campesino organizations are active in community assistance and political activism. Community assistance most often comes in the form of advice for the solicitation and execution of funding for community agriculture or infrastructure projects. Campesino organizations themselves rarely have resources for such projects, but their representatives will help a community to find state-based or NGO development projects, submit applications, and act as advisors for project implementation. Occasionally, however, international donors that fund campesino organizations will provide financing for specific projects. These are then delivered to communities under the banner of both the donor and the campesino group, creating an expectation for funds, which can alter the relationship between organizations and communities. As discussed below, campesino activists struggle to be seen in communities as representatives of a political social movement rather than as NGO workers with potential funding.

Finally, campesino organizations dedicate much of their energy to political activism in the municipal, national, and international arenas. To take as an example the CCDA, their regular activities include the formation of political, economic, and legal proposals; negotiation with state agencies through the broad-based ADRI group; denunciation of political and economic abuses through the CNAIC-P umbrella group and the MSICG labour organization; street-level political demonstrations denouncing abuses or supporting proposals; communication with international solidarity organizations about the situation in Guatemala; engagement with local political forums in their home municipality of San Lucas Tolimán, Sololá; and participation in municipal and national elections through the left-wing political parties Alternative for a New Nation (*Alternativa Nueva Nación*, ANN)[14] and the Convergence for the Democratic Revolution (*Convergencia para la Revolución Democrática*, CRD). The CCDA is exceptionally active, but contemporary campesino organizations generally engage to some degree with this full spectrum of political activism, which is referred to in its entirety as *incidencia política* (loosely, to generate political impact).

Of the four main areas of activity for campesino organizations discussed here (support for land access, conflict resolution, community assistance, and political activism), participation in electoral politics may represent the avenue of greatest frustration. Success at the ballot box for candidates based in or supported by campesino organizations is exceedingly rare, matching an overall pattern of left party defeat in post-conflict Guatemala. The country makes for an exception to the regional trend of Indigenous movements forming progressive and ultimately successful political parties, as observed by Yashar (2005). Progressive Indigenous candidates have performed moderately in municipal elections, but national left political parties – including the former guerrilla URNG, and its offshoot ANN, Winaq, and Convergencia parties – together received no more than 3 per cent of the national vote in the 2007 and 2011 (Allison 2016; Pallister 2013). Copeland (2011) suggests that a "radical pessimism" pervades rural and Indigenous

Guatemala, one in which a disbelief in the potential for left parties to win elections or change the country leads progressive voters to instead support right-wing parties that promise minimal local "development" benefits. Observers have also found that the effects of genocidal violence continue to affect elections, through ongoing violent intimidation and in the fallout of a disarticulation of rural social cohesion (Copeland 2011; Remijnse 2001; Vogt 2015). Campesino efforts to bring the movement's work into the halls of power have routinely failed within this hostile political climate.

The difficult situation faced by campesino organizations today is evident when considering together their key objectives (structural transformation, land access, political representation, and rural development) and main activities (support for land access, conflict resolution, community assistance, and political activism). Campesino organizations are caught between the overlapping priorities of the long-term political focus preferred by their leaders and the immediate material concerns of rural communities. To complicate matters more, these priorities are acted upon within an overwhelmingly oppositional climate, consisting of an elite sector and a state apparatus that are both stubborn and coercive; a prohibitive electoral climate; a neoliberal political-economic approach to government and agrarian affairs that is enshrined within the only national progressive political tool available to campesinos, the peace accords; and a social movement so divided as to count itself among its own enemies.

The many divisions within the campesino movement are enormously crippling. These feuds appear along positions of older versus newer campesino organizations, struggles for leadership and representation, and, most importantly, bitter disputes about how to interact with the *Fondo de Tierras* (FONTIERRAS) land market institution. At their core, these internal conflicts are reducible to a combination of competition between organizations and a clash between different strategic approaches to the struggle against neoliberalism.

The most visible division within the campesino movement falls along the lines of CNOC – and former CNOC members such as CONIC and CCDA – versus *Plataforma Agraria*. The division is often described as one of "historical" campesino organizations versus a set of newer groups formed in opposition to the movement's traditional organizational structure. Each of the large campesino organizations associated with CNOC formed during the armed conflict, and each was initially connected to one or another guerrilla front. *Plataforma Agraria* activists argue that the leadership style within CNOC, CNAIC-P, and their member organizations mirrors the command hierarchy of the URNG former guerrilla alliance, in that a small handful of visible leaders control decision-making and argue among themselves for prominent positions. Activists with *Plataforma Agraria* explain that their organization formed as an intentional break from that hierarchy in the post-conflict period and that *Plataforma Agraria* operates according to horizontal decision-making among small regional associations and a rotating system of representatives (interviews with Gómez, Macario, Galicia 2010; conversation with Incer 2010). The result of this perceived difference is a split campesino movement with parallel proposals and duplicated political actions usually undertaken without cooperation, with the exception of ADRI discussions.

The accusations are not without warrant, however, and many leaders outside *Plataforma Agraria* acknowledge that debilitating divisions within CNOC itself fall along lines of guerrilla allegiance (five anonymous interviews 2010). Affiliation with the EGP, FAR, or ORPA guerrilla armies may have laid the foundation for opposing positions within CNOC, but today the conflicts are acted out in competition for political leadership. Most sources interviewed about CNOC – including CNOC General Coordinator Carlos Morales – suggested that changes in internal leadership and competition for key positions among member organizations are responsible for the recent CNOC rupture and the waning influence of the umbrella group over the movement (five anonymous interviews 2009, 2010). These spats further affect the movement at the community level, where opposing organizations may refuse to cooperate on a common issue or even enflame local conflict when two organizations are represented within a single community (four anonymous interviews 2009 and 2010).[15]

The fracturing of the movement between CNOC and *Plataforma Agraria*, and again within CNOC, comes to a head in the relationship that the different factions hold with the *Fondo de Tierras*. On the one hand some note that disputes between CNOC member organizations are most bitter when addressing who will represent the campesino sector before the *Fondo de Tierras* (interview, Galicia 2010).[16] Perhaps of more consequence, however, is the separation between organizations that advocate engagement with FONTIERRAS and those that call for the institution to be closed, a distinction that falls again along the CNOC / *Plataforma Agraria* chasm. Campesino leaders from organizations outside *Plataforma Agraria* tend to be critical of the land market system itself and of the incomplete implementation of FONTIERRAS measures such as technical assistance for beneficiaries. But they also share an underlying support for the institution as a product of the peace accords and the best option currently available to campesinos (interviews, Juracán 2009, 2015; Tiney 2010, 2015; Sánchez Trieles 2010; Martín 2010; Funes 2010).[17] Juan Tiney, a member of CONIC's National Directive Council, presents this position: "First off, the creation of the *Fondo de Tierras* is part of the peace accords. It's not there because of us, it was a product of the peace accords. And many of the people who criticize it now participated in the negotiations; they participated directly as officials or in designing the institution. Today national agrarian policy rests in the hands of the *Fondo de Tierras*. No other institution exists to direct agrarian policy" (interview 2010).

On the other side of the debate *Plataforma Agraria* and its member organizations have renounced the institution entirely. Between 2000 and 2003 *Plataforma Agraria* accompanied at least nine communities through successful FONTIERRAS land purchase, but the organization has since called for disengagement from and the dissolution of the *Fondo de Tierras* (Fondo de Tierras 2009a; Plataforma Agraria 2004, 2010). The same criticism of the land market and the weak functioning of the institution are cited, but *Plataforma Agraria* leaders abandon the argument that peace accord origins or a lack of alternatives justify the continued functioning of the institution. In fact, *Plataforma Agraria* activists tend to take the argument further and accuse leaders who support the *Fondo de Tierras* of legitimizing the institution and benefiting from corruption (interviews, Galicia 2010; Gómez Hernández 2010; and Macario 2010). "Having a representative on the governing council of the *Fondo de Tierras* implies that – and this has actually happened – they give priority to the communities allied with their own organizations ... And they approve land that isn't adequate [for campesino communities]. These are enormously corrupt processes. They negotiate with a landowner and then pressure for the farm to be bought at an overvalued price. The landowner wins because he earns a lot more. The organizations and their leaders win because they are facilitating land for their communities. And the poor people are the ones who lose" (interview, Galicia 2010).

In addition to the political and organizational difficulties troubling the movement at the national level, campesino organizations often have strained relations with the same rural communities that make up their membership. This is partly for lack of resources in all campesino organizations. There is never enough funding, personnel, or time to satisfy the demands of political activism in the national arena while remaining dedicated to each of the hundreds of rural communities linked to an organization. Another factor is the shift in the role of campesino organizations since the end of the armed conflict. Whereas the campesino movement since 1978 has pushed for campesino rights and land access, the recent and somewhat widespread granting of communal title to rural communities has put the organizations in the new position of advising and representing those newly landed groups.

Some campesino organizations were able to adapt to their new role, as exemplified by CONIC's organizational network and CCDA's alternative production model (see chapters 4 and 5). But CONIC, CCDA, and many other campesino organizations have not planned how to interact with communities after they have gained access to land. Rural communities expected that the same campesino organization that helped them through the land access process would continue to support agricultural projects and infrastructure development. In fact, continued community support for an organization often depends on the perception that assistance is being provided. More often than not, however, organizations either lose contact with communities after they move onto their new land, or their plans for the community prove to be unsuited to the particular social group or piece of land.

The high expectations of campesino organizations are elevated even further by the political context of decentralization and competition in neoliberal Guatemala. A series of laws passed in 2002 and based in peace accord recommendations shifted state funds for infrastructure and rural development to the municipal level. Community Development Councils (*Consejos de Desarrollo Comunitarios*, COCODES) based in individual communities now apply in competition to fund basic improvements such as potable water, electricity, and school construction.[18] Campesino organizations regularly assist communities with funding applications, but their involvement has also meant an association with NGO-style development projects. Insistence by communities that campesino organizations provide aid – what I came to think of as *proyectismo*, or "project-ism" – has created a climate where political organization and participation in the broader campesino movement are often relegated to afterthought. Campesino leaders recognized this in interviews and spoke of how they work the situation of *proyectismo* back to a focus on political struggle. Marta Cecilia Ventura, who oversees CONIC's organizational structure, discussed development projects as both hurdles and opportunities: "I've been clear in discussions with communities that [development] projects often end up disarticulating community organization. But the people want them, so we fight for projects ... So the problem as I see it is how our teams of [CONIC] promoters generate discussion with the people. For example, we gain a project from the government – fine. But before the people get the project we need to speak clearly with them about how the project isn't a gift: this project has been a struggle, it involved protests, it took effort, and more" (interview, Ventura 2010).

The style of political organization within rural communities points to another way in which local dynamics have been affected by neoliberal reforms. Mirroring the vision of community councils suggested by the pinnacle CNOC Proposal for Comprehensive Agrarian Reform, communities that have accessed land are almost always governed by an internal *junta directiva*, elected every three years to coordinate community decision-making, manage development projects, and represent the group outside the community. At first glance this organizational structure appears to demonstrate a high degree of political autonomy. But having an elected governing council is actually a stipulation of Guatemalan law. Collective owners of property are required to register themselves legally as associations with the municipal government and with the commercial registry (*Registro Mercantil*). The Ministry of the Interior's regulations for associations then stipulate that groups must elect community leadership, including a legal representative and an accountant, who in turn are responsible for filing monthly reports on the association's financial activities (Congreso de la República de Guatemala n.d., art. 334; Ministerio de Gobernación 1998, art. 3; interviews, Ventura 2010; and Chub Icó 2010).

The system also extends beyond taxes, and having a legally formed community association is a prerequisite of forming a COCODE development council, applying for funding from any government entity, or participating in government discussions including those negotiating the resolution of agrarian conflicts. While the function of the community association and its *junta directiva* do lend themselves to autonomy in political organization and decision-making within the community, the same structures also tie the groups to state regulation and are the direct product of peace accord–based neoliberal decentralization. "In the end," says Marta Cecilia Ventura of CONIC, "we have associations constituted in the communities because the people have seen that they are a medium for accessing resources" (interview 2010).

Conclusion

The Guatemalan campesino movement has made enormous advances over the last three decades. Growing out of waves of rural organizing from the 1950s onward, the movement came into its own when campaigns by the Committee for Campesino Unity (CUC) in 1978–80 forced grassroots campesino demands onto the national political scene for the first time.[19] Since then, and despite a tide of repression that reached unfathomable heights in the 1980s and continues in more selective form today, the movement has grown to include dozens of campesino organizations, multiple umbrella groups, hundreds of organized communities, and tens of thousands of participating campesinos. Rural communities have gained access to hundreds of communal properties through the help of campesino organizations, and movement leaders continue to dedicate their work to assisting campesino communities and advocating on their behalf, often at a high price within Guatemala's ever-present climate of political violence.

But this is also a very difficult time in the history of the Guatemalan campesino movement. As it has grown, internal dynamics have torn apart much of its unity, and campesino organizations now find themselves divided along multiple fronts, even while they continue to share objectives and face the same opposing forces. Guatemala's powerful sectors have also been adept at undermining the success of the movement. As right-wing political and economic factions settled comfortably into their traditional control of resources and power in the years since the end of the armed conflict, they have offered a continuum of negotiations, dialogue, and representative positions, presenting the occasional concession but never allowing consequential transformation of agrarian affairs.

Throughout the post-war period the twin forces of peace and neoliberalism have loomed large within the campesino movement. Participation in the peace process was organic for the Guatemalan left in the 1980s and was itself the result of organized struggle, but a dialogue weighted heavily in favour of elites produced a blueprint for political and economic reform that included little room for structural change. The limited focus of the peace accords – in particular, the prominence of a neoliberal approach to agriculture in the Socio-Economic Accord, which used market-led agrarian reform in an attempt to reconstitute the agrarian economy and relations between the state and organized campesinos – laid the boundaries of political action within which campesino organizations could operate. These boundaries are in part self-patrolled, as many campesino activists accept the peace accord framework and have worked to harvest as many benefits as possible within the neoliberal approach. The *Fondo de Tierras* provides the best example, with campesino organizations participating in the creation and continued functioning of the institution. Nearly all campesino organizations also have assisted communities with land purchase through FONTIERRAS, even while denouncing the conditions those same communities will face after purchase. And while *Plataforma Agraria* and its member organizations boycott FONTIERRAS entirely and accusations are exchanged across a movement that cannot agree on whether or how to interact with the institution, the positions amount to competing strategic approaches to an agrarian climate dominated by peace accord–sanctioned neoliberalism. The question of how much has been accomplished within these constraints is the subject of the following chapters, as we explore strategies deployed first in struggles to access land, and then in the lived experience of two campesino organizations and four rural communities.

3 Between the Bullet and the Bank: Campesino Access to Land

The most significant accomplishment of the campesino movement since the end of the Guatemalan armed conflict has been a tide of community-based struggles to access, reclaim, or hold onto land. Backed by campesino organizations, community-led processes including reclamation struggles and occupations have forged new possibilities for communal access to substantial tracts of land and the formal recognition of traditionally used areas. A World Bank–sponsored market-led agrarian reform (MLAR) has been documented thoroughly (Garoz, Alonso, and Gauster 2005; Gauster and Isakson 2007; World Bank 2010), but alternative forms of rural struggle resulting in access to land have not been catalogued to the same extent, despite significant mention in studies of contemporary rural and agrarian dynamics (Grandia 2012; Hurtado Paz y Paz 2008; van Leeuwen 2010; Velásquez Nimatuj 2008). This chapter presents data collected on forms of land access, offering a system of categorizing cases as either fitting with the market model or as the result of agrarian conflict. I argue that three forms of agrarian conflict – referred to here as historical land claims, rural labour disputes, and land occupations – together account for the majority of instances of land access outside the MLAR system and that these instances together rival the amount of land transferred through the World Bank project. At the same time, however, I conclude that the distinction between these two categories is not as clear as it may seem, as even land accessed through rural struggle comes through cooperation between neoliberal agrarian institutions and the campesino movement.

The Market Model: *Fondo de Tierras*

As peace negotiations progressed during the mid-1990s, guerrilla demands for agrarian reform slowly lost out to a blueprint for post-war agrarian policy based on legal and institutional reform. At the heart of the resulting Socio-Economic Accord lay a World Bank–sponsored project that aimed to redefine the role of the state in agrarian affairs as the facilitator of an efficient private property regime. The bank funded two projects between 2000 and 2007 that together addressed the primary land-related commitments of the Socio-Economic Accord: a Land Administration Project that covered cadastre and land title regularization, and a Land Fund Project to initiate market-based land distribution (World Bank 1998, 2010). Since 1998 government involvement in campesino land access has been limited to the parameters of this market model, and all state-sponsored land distribution has been conducted through the *Fondo de Tierras* (FONTIERRAS), or Land Fund (Garoz, Alonso, and Gauster 2005). As has been observed in similar World Bank projects in other settings, including Brazil, India, and Sierra Leone, the land administration approach to agrarian reform is thoroughly neoliberal (Lahiff, Borras Jr, and Kay 2007; Peters and Richards 2011; Pimple and Sethi 2005; Wolford 2010a). Land administration addresses both the material and subjective aspirations of neoliberalism. The bank's model aims to turn demands for land redistribution into a system of plantation sales benefitting dominant elites, while strengthening the legal framework for property transactions required by the neoliberal state. At the same time the approach demonstrates elements of governmentality, encouraging the creation of a market-oriented, rather than collectively organized, campesino sector.

Fondo de Tierras programs represent the triumph among Guatemalan state institutions of the market-based approach to land access and distribution, but they also draw from a longer history of state-based programs and earlier attempts to mediate agrarian affairs through market transactions. These programs began in the wake of the overthrow of President Jacobo Arbenz in 1954 and the return to large landowners of hundreds of thousands of hectares distributed under the short-lived agrarian reform of 1952–4 (Handy 1994b, 192–207). Recognizing the importance that agrarian reform held for much of the population, successive governments sought to establish programs that would hand out land to campesinos without challenging the agrarian status quo or the power of large landowners. Between 1954 and the creation of the *Fondo de Tierras* in 1999, four main state programs or laws oversaw these minimal distributive efforts: the Agrarian Statute (*Estatuto Agrario*, 1954–62), the Petén Promotion and Development Agency (*Empresa de Fomento y Desarrollo del Petén*, FDYEP, 1959–78), the National Institute for Agrarian Transformation (*Instituto de Transformación Agraria*, INTA, 1962–99), and the National Land Commission (*Comisión Nacional de Tierra*,

Table 3.1. World Bank Support for State Agrarian Projects, 2000–2007 (US$ millions)

Project	Project component	Cost (est.)	Cost (actual)	IBRD loan
Land Administration Project (2000–7)		38.5	33.7	31.0
	Cadastre and Land Regularization	27.2	21.7	
	Land Registry	2.2	1.2	
	Project Management Unit	5.2	10.9	
Land Fund Project (2000–5)		77.2	80.1	23.0
	Access to Land	52.2	56.2	
	Institutional Strengthening	2.0	2.0	
	Community Strengthening	13.3	5.4	
	Community Sub-Projects	9.7	1.5	

Source: World Bank (2010)

Table 3.2. Government Land Distribution, 1954–1989

Program	Years	Cases	Families	Hectares
Estatuto Agrario	1954–62	–	34,426	209,225
FDYEP	1959–78	–	39,000	1,980,000
INTA	1962–89	591	86,813	656,168
CONATIERRA	1986–9	13	1,600	3,420

Source: Schneider, Maul, and Membreño (1989, 18); Sandoval Villeda (1992, 233, 241–2, 256–7)
Note: INTA figures unavailable for 1990–9

CONATIERRA, 1986–9). Nearly a million hectares of land were distributed to around 120,000 campesino families under these four programs (see table 3.2), but the impact of distribution was minimal. In order to avoid the redistribution of private property, plots given out during this period most often came from previously unused or state-owned land in regions deemed ripe for colonization; corruption consumed many hundreds of hectares of available land, especially under the Petén program; and recipients turned out to have little security in long-term ownership for lack of formal title under state regulations and the violence of the escalating armed conflict (Grandia 2009; Pedroni 1992; Sandoval Villeda 1992; Schneider, Maul, and Membreño 1989; Schwartz 1987, 1990).

The shift from land distribution to market-based land sales was noticeable within these programs from around 1987. The transition to formal democracy in 1986 took place alongside a flourishing of organized campesino and other social movement campaigns, including marches and land occupations pressuring the government for agrarian reform. As a result, agrarian policy began to move away from large numbers of colonization-based distributions and towards individual cases of land awarded in order to placate the organizations and communities demanding reform. A national land commission was established in 1987 to develop agrarian policy and, together with the INTA, began delivering land to resolve specific occupations and other agrarian conflicts (*Central America Report* 1986b, 1987b; Pedroni 1992, 84–6; Sandoval Villeda 1992, 233–4; Schneider, Maul, and Membreño 1989). The shift towards case-based distribution melded easily with the market-based approach, which USAID had been promoting within Guatemala since at least 1982 through support for an existing pilot program, the *Fundación del Centavo* (Fledderjohn 1976; Pedroni 1992; USAID 1982). By the late 1980s, both the INTA land distribution program and the CONATIERRA commission facilitated land access according to the "willing seller, willing buyer" principle, giving weight to similar proposals during peace negotiations and paving the way for the creation of the World Bank–sponsored *Fondo de Tierras* in 1999 (*Central America Report* 1986a, 1987b; Stewart, Fairhurst, and Pedroni 1987).

Since replacing other institutions as the primary agency in state agrarian programs, the *Fondo de Tierras* has overseen three programs related to campesino land use: the cornerstone Land Access Program, which conducts a "willing seller, willing buyer" land distribution scheme by providing loans to campesino communities; a land rental program providing grants and loans to individual campesinos since 2004; and a land title regularization program to formalize campesino ownership of properties distributed by INTA. By all accounts, however, the FONTIERRAS institution has lost political and financial momentum, and the future of its initiatives – especially the Land Access Program – is uncertain: World Bank financing was not extended beyond the original ten-year period ending 2008, no more than seven farms have been sold through FONTIERRAS in any year since 2006, and the institution has not reached its goal of financial sustainability through loan repayment (Comisión de Tierras 2008; Fondo de Tierras 2009a; Garoz, Alonso, and Gauster 2005; World Bank 2010).

Even during the height of *Fondo de Tierras* activity, the amount of land sold to campesinos was unimpressive. Between 1998 and 2009, FONTIERRAS transferred 91,811 hectares to 242 campesino communities, benefiting 19,236 families (see figure 3.3). These numbers may appear significant, but as of July 2005, completed cases represented just 18 per cent of the 1,137 applications received by FONTIERRAS (Gauster and Isakson 2007, 1524). Furthermore, Garoz, Alonso, and Gauster (2005, 39–40) estimate that just 1 per cent of the total demand for land in Guatemala had been satisfied by the *Fondo de Tierras*. The area of land distributed is also pitiful when compared to previous government programs (see figure 3.1). Whereas INTA handed out 656,168 hectares over twenty-eight years – 23,434 hectares a year, or 19,239 if we discount a windfall in 1972 – just 8,346 hectares a year

Table 3.3. Farms Purchased through *Fondo de Tierras* Land Access Program[1]

Year	Cases	Hectares
1998	13	4,205.25
1999	17	7,975.35
2000	45	17,276.11
2001	59	26,793.26
2002	21	8,586.14
2003	29	8,991.85
2004	25	6,156.84
2005	15	5,451.87
2006	3	655.17
2007	5	2,169.00
2008	7	3,507.63
2009	3	42.73
Total	242	91,811.20

Source: Fondo de Tierras (2009a)

were transferred via *Fondo de Tierras* (Fondo de Tierras 2009a; Sandoval Villeda 1992, 256–7). This is largely due to the fact that INTA primarily distributed unused state-owned land, whereas FONTIERRAS oversaw market transactions, but the numbers nevertheless point to the ineffectiveness of the market model.

To make matters worse, the relatively few farms purchased through the *Fondo de Tierras* are concentrated in undesirable areas, suggesting that the program has served as a site for landowners to rid themselves of unwanted land. Using the five agrarian regions suggested by the Guatemalan Association for the Advancement of Social Science (*Asociación para el Avance de Ciencias Sociales en Guatemala*, AVANCSO),[2] we see that the majority of *fincas* purchased through FONTIERRAS are found in two areas: 35 per cent on the South Coast and 31 per cent in the Northern Lowlands (see figure 3.2). It may seem positive that land has become available on the South Coast, the traditional stronghold of export agriculture, but, for the most part, campesinos have been presented with either former cotton land that has lost the fertility to produce after decades of chemically intensive farming, or coffee plantations that suffered neglect during the 1999–2004 crash in coffee prices.

Figure 3.1. Hectares of land distributed by INTA and FONTIERRAS, 1962–2008

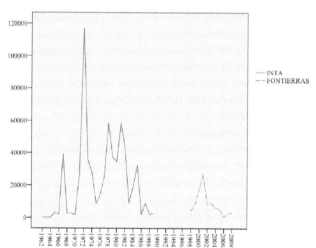

Source: Sandoval Villeda (1992), Fondo de Tierras (2009a).
Note: Figures unavailable for INTA distribution between 1990 and 1999

Figure 3.2. Farms purchased through *Fondo de Tierras*, by agrarian region

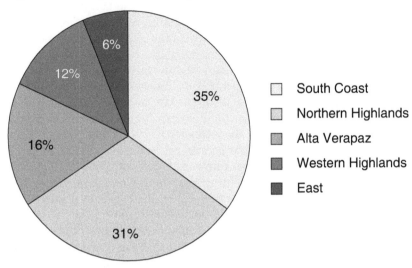

Source: Fondo de Tierras (2009a)

In the Northern Lowlands, comprising the Petén and parts of Alta Verapaz, Izabal, Huehuetenango, and El Quiché, land has come up for sale in extremely remote areas, both geographically and culturally distant from the homes of purchasing communities. By contrast, the current hotspots where soil conditions, topography, and infrastructure make agriculture viable – the ethanol-driven sugar cane valleys of Izabal and Alta Verapaz, eastern cattle lands, and those areas of the South Coast where soil has not been exhausted – have seen very little land made available for purchase.[3]

The FONTIERRAS Land Access Program can be criticized even more severely on the conditions faced by communities after purchase. Poor quality land, lack of technical and financial assistance, and internal group problems often hold communities back from improving their living and working conditions, even years after purchasing land through the *Fondo de Tierras*.[4] Extreme poverty is rampant in FONTIERRAS communities, calculated at 79 per cent of all homes in a review of conditions commissioned by the World Bank in 2003, with a further 17 per cent living in non-extreme poverty. The same study, conducted by German agricultural economist Thomas Miethbauer, showed that subsistence crop production had increased on average, leading to greater food security, but that only 44 per cent of families had seen an increase in financial income since moving to their new land (Miethbauer 2005, 4–7, 21–2). FONTIERRAS beneficiaries commonly live without basic infrastructure such as adequate housing, potable water, and electricity, since the groups are left to their own devices to build a community on what usually had been large commercial farms.

Faced with poor living conditions and unproductive land, many FONTIERRAS communities have trouble paying off their loans. Annual payments are made collectively by the community association, but the common practice is for beneficiary families to contribute their share of the payment through their own individual work. Many families are able to make payments only by finding work outside of the farm or through remittances sent by family members who are working in the United States. Others fall behind on their commitments or abandon the farm, selling their membership in the group to newcomers. No extensive study of FONTIERRAS abandonment has been conducted, but campesino organizers and members of the *Fondo de Tierras* board of directors estimate that 30–50 per cent of all original beneficiaries no longer live on their purchased farms or have sold their membership to someone else (Comisión de Tierras 2008, 9–10; Gauster and Isakson 2007, 1528). Overall, debt non-repayment is severe: 37 per cent of all communities had payment problems by the end of 2008, to say nothing of individuals within each group. This figure rises to 53 per cent if we exclude those farms that were in the grace period or had paid their entire loan with their initial government subsidy (Fondo de Tierras 2009b).[5]

Table 3.4. Debt Payment Status of FONTIERRAS Farms, through 2008

Debt payment status	Cases	%
Behind on payments or no payments made	89	37
Payment completed using FONTIERRAS subsidy	49	21
Payments completed by community	38	16
Payments continuing	38	16
In grace period	24	10

Source: Fondo de Tierras (2009b)

Beneficiary communities also bear the burden of corruption within the *Fondo de Tierras*. Journalistic and academic investigations within Guatemala have uncovered numerous farms sold at overvalued prices, others sold without the knowledge of the registered owner, and, in some cases, titles sold to farms that turned out not to exist. Corrupt land transactions also allegedly benefit campesino and Indigenous leaders who sit on the FONTIERRAS board of directors, an allegation that has gained strength given that the board's membership has not rotated since its creation (de León 2006; Gauster and Isakson 2007, 1529–30; Inforpress centroamericana 2006; Plataforma Agraria 2010; World Bank 2010, 18, 99).

The *Fondo de Tierras* land title regularization program has also fared badly. Financed by the World Bank as part of its land administration project, the program aimed to bring campesinos into the formal private property regime by providing registered titles to land distributed by the INTA state program since the 1960s. If measured in sheer numbers, regularization could be deemed a success, as 15,519 titles were provided to 681,531 hectares of land between 2000 and 2009 (Fondo de Tierras 2010). However, the irony of this program that aimed to provide legal security to small farmers is that it actually contributed to a loss of campesino land. Issuing land titles also means providing the right to sell that land, and an agricultural trend has been established whereby large landowners create commercial farms by buying many plots from newly titled campesinos, especially in areas where agro-fuel crops are expanding. In one such region, the municipality of Chisec, Alta Verapaz, Guatemalan sociologist Laura Hurtado Paz y Paz found that 40 per cent of campesinos from ten INTA-distributed communities had sold their land titles. Between 22 and 63 per cent of members from seven communities sold land following FONTIERRAS regularization; in the three towns still lacking formal title, 0, 8, and 96 per cent of campesinos had done so, with the latter case being explained by a dramatic community history, including forced resettlement (Hurtado Paz y Paz 2008, 160–5). Milian and Grandia (2013, 16–18) similarly found that 31–46 per cent of campesinos in the Petén, whose land had been either regularized or surveyed under *Fondo de Tierras* projects, had since sold their land. One by one, campesinos are convinced or coerced into selling their plots to representatives of agro-industries or drug cartels, who have amassed them to create new plantations in a region previously characterized by peasant subsistence farming (Gould 2014; Hernández 2016; Hurtado Paz y Paz 2008; Solano 2016).

Hurtado Paz y Paz (2008, 194–7) concludes that, even though campesinos look to title regularization as a form of resistance and reclamation in the face of historical displacement, the program has strengthened the property rights regime and fuelled land speculation and land concentration in Alta Verapaz. The same can be said of the *Fondo de Tierras* as an institution, as both the Land Access Program and regularization have attempted to channel the demand for agrarian reform into a land market based on the sanctity of private property. Despite the birth of the institution in peace negotiations on agrarian reform, its primary function has been to strengthen the land market in Guatemala through programs aimed ostensibly at campesino beneficiaries. This should come as no surprise, as both programs were designed within the neoliberal land administration framework, and one of two stated objectives of World Bank support for the *Fondo de Tierras* was "to improve the legal and institutional framework for land markets to work more efficiently" (World Bank 1998, 2).

Nevertheless, it is worth reminding ourselves of this objective, since criticism of the *Fondo de Tierras* often presents the position that the project did not function as intended. For example, the general manager of *Fondo de Tierras*, Luis Fernando Peña de León, told me in an interview,

Table 3.5. FONTIERRAS Land Title Regularization, 2000–2009

Year	Titles issued	Hectares of land covered
2000	10	54,724.0
2001	1,172	119,226.3
2002	47	52,513.7
2003	2,794	127,226.3
2004	2,563	58,371.3
2005	1,534	70,905.4
2006	1,229	31,556.8
2007	3,059	86,306.4
2008	1,642	59,081.7
2009	1,469	21,619.8
Total	**15,519**	**681,531.7**

Source: Fondo de Tierras (2010)

"The creation of the *Fondo de Tierras* as such, according to its law, was a social conquest … In reality, the model … was the best that could have been produced in that moment, and if it could be improved, let's say, it has many strong points. The problem was how … [the model] was applied in practice, there were many weakening factors along the way … There was a series of problems in the application of the model [and] that is what is generating all these problems today" (interview 2009).

Similarly, a report by the World Bank's Independent Evaluation Group found that the Land Administration Project and the Land Fund Project had failed to increase land productivity, tenure security, or the efficiency of the land market. In both cases, the report praised "highly relevant" project objectives and blamed shortcomings on "several flaws in project design" (World Bank 2010, 1–22).

If assessed within its political context, however, the *Fondo de Tierras* has been quite successful. Land access and poverty reduction were secondary objectives, to come about as the result of an efficient land market. If too few campesinos have purchased land, if conditions on FONTIER-RAS farms are deplorable, or if formerly campesino land has been lost after regularization, the World Bank would see these as evidence that land administration and the land market have not been implemented thoroughly enough. But the *Fondo de Tierras* and the World Bank land administration projects were designed as part of the peace process, the political project which allowed for the reassertion of elite power and the reaffirmation of elite control over Guatemalan resources. Thanks to *Fondo de Tierras* programs, large landowners have been able to sell off unproductive land while securing titles in newly desirable areas, and the involvement of campesino and Indigenous organizations in FON-TIERRAS projects has helped to define debt-ridden land purchase as the only acceptable method of agrarian reform.

The land market and its constituent programs, it would seem, have been functional for Guatemala's traditional elite. This sentiment is echoed by campesino leaders, such as Abisaias Gómez Hernández of *Plataforma Agraria*. When asked in an interview if he thinks that large landowners have felt threatened by campesino organizing since the end of the armed conflict, Gómez responded, "These days, large landowners feel even stronger [*el terrateniente ha sentido más fortalecido*]. And they are showing it. Look at the *Franja Transversal del Norte* [a northern highway mega-project], mining, African palm, the mass firings of banana workers in Izabal. And it is the *Fondo de Tierras* that is strengthening them. The *Fondo de Tierras* has strengthened them and they have shown that they are very strong now" (interview 2010).

Agrarian Conflict and Rural Struggle

The *Fondo de Tierras* neoliberal land administration approach has not resolved Guatemala's underlying unequal distribution of land or the weak legal protection for communal land use, a reality that continues to feed agrarian conflict in the country. Conflicts over land ownership and use arise from a wide range of situations, but they very often involve Indigenous campesino communities that have lost land to companies or powerful individuals in the recent past. So many campesino communities have gained communal title to land as a result of agrarian conflicts that their struggles can be considered together as a form of land access alternative to the FONTIERRAS market-led scheme. In this section, I first discuss the particularities of agrarian conflict in contemporary Guatemala and then present what I understand to be the three main forms of land access via agrarian conflict: historical land claims, rural labour disputes, and land occupations.[6]

We can begin to make sense of these conflicts through the concept of *conflictividad*, or conflictivity, used in the Guatemalan literature. Guatemalan researchers use the term *agrarian conflict* to refer to a case that has flared into conflict, over 7,700 of which have been documented since 1997 (SAA 2016), but many also argue that these conflicts arise from an underlying set of factors collectively referred to as "conflictivity." While *conflictividad* is itself a contested term, the concept can be used to refer to the unequal economic, social, and political conditions and a sense of injustice among rural Guatemalans that together give rise to specific conflicts (CALDH and CONIC 2009, 13–19; Santa Cruz 2006, 13–30; Universidad Rafael Landívar 2009, 25–31). Mathijs van Leeuwen (2010, 97–8), for example, describes conflictivity as follows: "This generic but also highly politicized term refers to the historical and structural character of land conflicts in Guatemala. Conflictividad agraria encapsulates a discontent with the extremely unequal distribution of agricultural land, past usurpation of territories of the largely Indigenous rural population and a system of exploitative labour relationships."

The Interdiocesan Land Pastoral of San Marcos (*Pastoral de la Tierra Interdiocesana de San Marcos*, PTSM) – a Guatemalan Catholic Church–based organization that advocates on behalf of campesinos, and with whom van Leeuwen previously worked – understands conflictivity to be composed of eight main factors. PTSM legal advisor Ingrid Urízar explained to me that her group understands the implementation of the agro-export model to be a cause of conflictivity, as is the absence of mechanisms to protect communal Indigenous land, a climate of legal insecurity surrounding agrarian property, a lack of legal definition of state property, agrarian legislation that is positioned against the Indigenous population instead of in protection of it, a labour code that does not function in the countryside, the recent implementation of a new agricultural model including resource extraction and African palm crops for agro-fuels, and the presence of drug-runners in rural Guatemala (interview 2010).[7]

Any agrarian conflict in Guatemala will have resulted from a large number of overlapping historical and recent factors. Given this complex situation, the official government system used to record agrarian conflicts appears excessively simplistic. The Secretariat of Agrarian Affairs (*Secretaría de Asuntos Agrarios*, SAA), the government agency responsible for monitoring and resolving agrarian conflicts, divides them into four categories: a dispute over rights, "when two or more people simultaneously dispute ownership or possession of the same piece of land"; occupation, when "people or communities are in possession of land that is registered as property of another"; land title regularization, when a lack of title sparks conflict; and territorial limits, or conflicts derived from unclear communal, municipal, or departmental boundaries (SAA 2016, 2010b). However, most cases are listed as either a dispute over rights, occupation, or legalization, with just 159 instances of territorial limits listed between 1997 and 2015 (see figure 3.3).

Because there is a limited number of categories for so many conflicts, and since most cases are contained within just three of these categories, the SAA system also tends to lump unrelated scenarios under common headings. The SAA definition of conflicts over the regularization of land titles, for example, refers to land accessed under previous state land distribution programs but not properly documented, to claims made on state-owned or unregistered land, and to any number of situations where no legal title can be shown. The term *dispute over rights* covers everything from historical community claims to land, through properties that have been registered separately by multiple parties, to land erroneously delivered by the state. *Occupation*, finally, is perhaps the broadest of these terms, referring to the intentional occupation of private land, but also to disputed presence on natural reserves, and to the refusal to vacate land that has been used historically but over

Figure 3.3. Agrarian conflicts by SAA category, 1997–2015

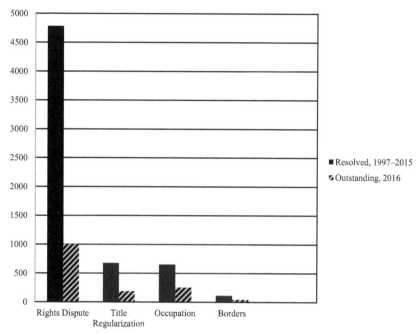

■ Resolved, 1997–2015

▨ Outstanding, 2016

Source: SAA (2016)

which another party claims ownership (Santa Cruz 2006, 29). This small number of comprehensive terms makes difficult any attempt to track instances or trends. An upward spike in "occupations," for example, could be shown from SAA numbers, but one could not determine from available data whether or not this applies to any of the distinct situations contained within that category.

Also missing from the limited categorization used by the Secretariat of Agrarian Affairs are the complicated immediate contexts that give rise to conflicts. Not all conflicts have a struggle for land at their core – violent disputes within and between communities, for example, can take the shape of agrarian conflicts while addressing more fundamentally other social or economic issues. But even when they are fought over land ownership and use, as in the subcategories proposed below, agrarian conflicts involve much more than the acquisition of productive resources by landless campesinos. The term *land access* more accurately describes land purchase via the *Fondo de Tierras*, with needy campesinos coming to own a new piece of land through market transaction. In the case of agrarian conflicts, there is usually deep historical and cultural meaning associated with a particular piece of land, leading to conflict over its ownership and use. Celso Caal, a CONIC organizer in Alta Verapaz, answered an interview question about why communities would choose to fight for their land, given the serious risks they would face: "Let's talk about the S——— community. They have lived their whole lives there, but other supposed owners came along. Why would they put themselves at risk? Why not abandon the area? They never wanted to leave, because where would they go? First, they have no money to buy other land. Second, they don't have anything. Third, they were born there, they have their crops there, and what's more, as Maya Q'eqchi' what hurts us is that they have their sacred altars there. And to defend Mother Earth. Sometimes people show up just to cut down the trees. The community puts itself at risk to defend their land and territory" (interview 2010).

When a community takes on these risks by refusing to leave their property or by attempting to take land, they often face heavy repression. Two cases discussed in the following section – those of Canlún and Xya'al K'obe' (pronounced "Yalcobay") – appeared, when I visited them in January and February 2010, to be examples of successful struggle for recognition of historical land use. Both, however, took tragic turns in early 2011. On 7 March Guatemalan soldiers and police, reportedly numbering over two thousand, forcefully evicted the community of Xya'al K'obe' from contested land, destroying their homes with chainsaws (CONIC 2011a). Further south, in the Polochic Valley spanning Alta Verapaz and Izabal, ongoing negotiations between campesino communities, state agencies, and the Chabil Utzaj sugar cane company fell apart as at least fourteen violent evictions were carried out between January and March 2011 on land claimed by the company. Community cornfields were destroyed in Canlún during the blitz, and private security guards returned to attack campesinos from the group on 21 May, killing Oscar Reyes with twelve gunshots and wounding at least three others (Batres 2011; CONIC 2011b; *Prensa* Libre 2011a).[8]

Xya'al K'obe' and Canlún take us inside implementation of land control in Guatemala (Peluso and Lund 2011). Indigenous communities have been displaced first through armed conflict and then post-war violence, and land and territory have been returned either to governance through conservation (Xya'al K'obe') or to capitalist production in the form of new crops (Canlún). The communities also provide two examples among hundreds of violent evictions, or *desalojos*, since the end of the Guatemalan armed conflict (Amnesty International 2006). As rural communities struggle to hold onto their traditionally used areas or gain access to new land, the Guatemalan government has responded consistently with force. The Public Prosecutor's Office (*Ministerio Público*) responsible for overseeing *desalojos* does not release precise figures, but a study by Camilo Salvadó of the AVANCSO research institution suggests that the government of President Álvaro Colom carried out ninety-nine violent evictions between 2008 and 2010 (Andrés 2011). Similarly, Amnesty International pointed to thirty-six evictions during the first eleven months of President Óscar Berger's administration (2004–7), noting that some campesinos were wounded or killed in most cases (Amnesty International 2006, 6; Santa Cruz 2006, 86–7).

Community activists are also arrested routinely outside the context of evictions, pointing to a marked criminalization of social movement organizing. The frequency of these arrests was made clear to me when I was told stories of jailed leaders in three communities I visited: the president of the San José La Pasión community association was arrested and died in custody during the group's occupation of Finca Chitocán in Cobán, Alta Verapaz; Mario Y was still in jail in early 2010 after being arrested at the occupation of a *finca* in Senahú, Alta Verapaz; and while visiting the community of Xya'al K'obe' I spoke on the phone with Mario Tulio Caal Choc from his jail cell, where he is serving a sentence for living illegally on protected state land.[9]

The ongoing campaign of persecution and state violence, coupled with impunity for attacks by private security guards, leaves all campesinos involved in agrarian conflict and rural struggle vulnerable to repression and subject to a pervasive sense of insecurity. Violence against land struggles demonstrates a continuity with past displacement (May 2001; Grandin 2011; Grandia 2012), just as it reinforces the pivotal role that violence plays generally in agrarian change and land control (Cramer and Richards 2011; Grajales 2011; Kay 2001; Peluso and Lund 2011; Veltmeyer 2005). Despite the ever-present threat of violence, however, thousands of communities have fought for land in recent years, and many have been successful. A review of the database maintained by the Secretariat of Agrarian Affairs suggests that the amount of land retained or acquired by campesino communities as a result of agrarian conflicts surpasses that accessed through the *Fondo de Tierras* system of market-led agrarian reform.

The SAA registered 7,717 agrarian conflicts between 1997 and 2015, with 1,502 of them outstanding as of January 2016. Of the remaining 6,215 closed cases, 4,250 were labelled "resolved," a category defined by the SAA as pertaining to conflicts for which "all parties ... come to agreements based on negotiation, mediation, and conciliation, which satisfy their interests" (SAA 2010b). These 2,326 instances of "resolved" cases represent those most likely to have resulted in campesino land access, and together they cover more than 900,000 hectares of land (see table 3.6).[10]

A thorough case-by-case review of conflicts would be necessary in order to determine conclusively the amount of land accessed or retained through resolved cases or other scenarios.[11] Nevertheless, the large amount of land disputed in cases that ended to the satisfaction of all parties, including campesino communities, suggests quite strongly that a significant amount of campesino land has been accessed through rural struggle identified as agrarian conflicts. In fact, if just one third of "resolved" agrarian conflicts ended with a rural community becoming the recognized owners of a piece of land, the total amount of land accessed or retained through conflicts would have surpassed that sold through the *Fondo de Tierras*.

In the remainder of this section, I present the three most common forms of agrarian conflict to result in land access, as determined by campesino activists working with conflicts: historical land claims, rural labour disputes, and land occupations. My aim is to illustrate

Table 3.6. Land Disputed in Agrarian Conflicts, 1997–2015

SAA category	Resolved	Closed or concluded	Outstanding, 2016
Rights dispute	3,365 cases 636,735 hectares	1,415 cases 149,995 hectares	991 cases 924,681 hectares
Occupation	431 cases 194,499 hectares	220 cases 78,239 hectares	246 cases 417,367 hectares
Regularization	396 cases 68,088 hectares	278 cases 19,054 hectares	189 cases 25,398 hectares
Borders	58 cases 6,869 hectares	51 cases 2,329 hectares	50 cases 26,762 hectares
Total	4,251 cases 908,058 hectares	1,964 cases 249,619 hectares	1,502 cases 1,393,344 hectares

Source: SAA (2016)

the dynamics of rural struggles for land in Guatemala as they occur in the terrain outside of the FONTIERRAS system of market-led agrarian reform. While the examples provided are taken mostly from interviews with CONIC activists, the categories and trends were confirmed by interviews with other campesino groups and analysts.

Historical Land Claims

One of the most common forms of agrarian conflict results from communal struggles to hold on to or reclaim traditionally used lands. These conflicts over historical land claims are concentrated in the northeast of the country – the Petén, Alta Verapaz, Izabal, and northern Quiché – where the primarily Maya Q'eqchi' and K'iche' lifestyles have been threatened for decades by war and large-scale economic projects (Alonso Fradejas, Alonzo, and Dürr 2008; Grandia 2009, 2012; Ybarra 2011). When local communities refuse to leave under threat, or attempt to take back land lost within recent memory, campesino activists refer to the ensuing struggle as one of enforcing *derechos históricos*, or historical rights (interviews, Bol 2010; Caal 2010; and Chub Icó 2010). Canlún and Xya'al K'obe', the evicted communities mentioned above, serve as examples.

   In the late 1960s, 600 hectares of forest surrounded the community of Canlún in the Polochic Valley of Panzós, Alta Verapaz. The protected woods formed part of an agricultural cooperative run by members of Canlún, legally registered under the name Cooperativa Samilhá R.L. When a large landowner cut down the trees in 1970 and claimed the land as his own, community challenges were unsuccessful and the cooperative fell to commercial agriculture. With the sugar cane company Chabil Utzaj holding title to the property as of 2006, a new generation of campesinos from Canlún decided to take control of their land again, symbolically planting a communal cornfield over 157 of the 630 contested hectares. The forty families involved in the reclamation struggle joined forces with the CONIC campesino organization, which managed to bring Chabil Utzaj into legal negotiations with the community and state authorities.[12] Negotiations appeared to be moving ahead during the first year after Canlún planted their corn, but, as detailed above, the cane company and state forces moved violently against Canlún and thirteen other communities within the contested area in early 2011, effectively ending at least the current stage of Canlún's struggle for recognition of *derechos históricos*.

The community of Xya'al K'obe' formed as an extension of the INTA state land distribution program aimed at colonizing Guatemala's northern agricultural frontier in the 1960s and 1970s.[13] The group received land in the early 1960s and established the community of Salacuín in the northern lowlands of Alta Verapaz, near the Río Chixoy (also known as the Río Negro) along the Mexican border. They then branched out to clear surrounding jungle land and claim a new area for themselves, as was encouraged by agrarian legislation at the time. The group was in the process of registering their new land legally in the early 1980s when an attack by the Guatemalan military forced them to retreat back to Salacuín. With the armed conflict over, the children of the original Xya'al K'obe' members began planting their parents' land again in 2000 and moved back to it in 2007. However, the Laguna Lachuá National Park had been established over an area including Xya'al K'obe's land and that of two other communities in 2006, a move that used the creation of conservation areas to enclose community land in a pattern that has been repeated within Guatemala and around the world (Kelly 2011; Ybarra 2011). After the three communities in the Lachuá area returned to the land, park officials charged that they had invaded the protected area illegally.

A long struggle between Xya'al K'obe' and the Lachuá park ensued. At one point the community reacted to military and police presence on their land by surrounding and disarming a group of soldiers, releasing them only when local authorities had signed an agreement to allow the community to remain on the land during negotiations. The case presented by Xya'al K'obe' and CONIC was solid, with evidence of buildings and orchards from the 1960s and even an SAA study of government satellite imagery showing a clearing in the jungle in the exact location of Xya'al K'obe' in 1962. As is so often the case, however, violence won out over official procedure, and Xya'al K'obe' and at least one other community within the Laguna Lachuá park were evicted in March 2011.[14]

The Secretariat of Agrarian Affairs recognizes Canlún's conflict as a "dispute over rights" and that of Xya'al K'obe' as an "occupation," due to claims that the latter are illegal park invaders (SAA 2009b). Neither of the two SAA categories is composed entirely of situations of historical land claims, but trends in both should nevertheless give us an idea of the frequency of such conflicts: despite many cases being resolved or closed annually, hundreds more continue to be registered. Each year since 2000 has seen over 200 – and as many as 500 – new cases of

Figure 3.4. New agrarian conflicts registered annually by the SAA, 1997–2015

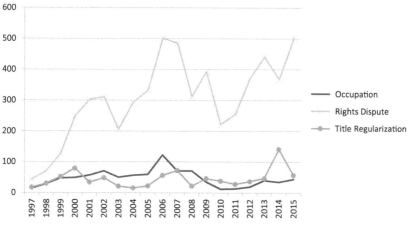

Source: SAA (2016)

disputes over rights and around 20 to 70 new cases of occupations (see figure 3.4). Regional dynamics also make such conflicts more common in the departments of Alta Verapaz, El Quiché, and El Petén: disputes over rights largely took place in El Petén (34 per cent of cases since 1997) and El Quiché (16 per cent), and occupations were carried out in Alta Verapaz (38 per cent) and El Petén (24 per cent).

As in the cases of Canlún and Xya'al K'obe', negotiation is generally initiated once a conflict has begun, involving representatives from the community, an accompanying campesino organization, other parties claiming title to the land, and government institutions. In some cases the community members are found to be the rightful owners of the land and allowed to stay. When it is decided that a community does not have the right to be on the land, and when that decision does not lead to eviction, the situation can occasionally still end in land access. Some cases that are understood to be at risk of violence are resolved through the direct purchase, by the SAA or other government institutions, of alternative land for the community. These cases are celebrated as significant victories by campesino organizers, not only for resolving the conflict at hand but also for pushing the government to deliver land outside of the market-access *Fondo de Tierras* model (interviews, Gómez Hernández 2010; Macario 2010; Monteros 2009; and Urízar 2010). The SAA has provided very little land, however, and a declining budget

Table 3.7. Land Provided through MAGA and SAA Conflict Resolution, 2006–2010

Year	Institution	Cases	Hectares	Departments
2006	MAGA	24	11,565	Alta Verapaz, Baja Verapaz, El Progreso, Izabal, Jalapa, Petén, Quetzaltenango, Quiché, Santa Rosa, Zacapa
2007	SAA	7	966*	Alta Verapaz, Chimaltenango, Escuintla, Huehuetenango, Quiché, Retalhuleu
2008	SAA	6	1,336	Alta Verapaz, Chimaltenango, Retalhuleu, Suchitepéquez
2009	SAA	3	508	Alta Verapaz, Baja Verapaz, Izabal
2010	SAA	5	474	Alta Verapaz, Izabal, Santa Rosa

Source: MAGA (2006), SAA (2010b; 2011)
* Hectare amount available only for 6 of 7 cases in 2007, and inconsistent measurement units in 2006 mean that only 20 of 24 cases are counted here.

for the conflict resolution program suggests that the approach will not be institutionalized to any significant degree (see table 3.7) (interview, Cardona 2009).

Rural Labour Disputes

Communities of *mozos colonos*, or permanent live-in farm workers, have recently begun to demand remuneration after dismissal, an action categorized here as rural labour disputes. The institution of *colonato* was established largely through debt servitude during the Liberal coffee boom of the nineteenth century, and it commonly involves conditions of poverty and restricted freedoms that many *mozos colonos* consider to be a form of slavery (Hurtado Paz y Paz 2008, 202–9; McCreery 1983, 1994).[15] Since the 1950s, however, Guatemalan agriculture has undergone major transformations including the decline of the *colonato* as a system of rural social relations. The number of farms housing *mozos colonos* fell from nearly 30,000 in 1950 to around 10,000 in 1979 and just over 5,000 in 2008. As global coffee prices plummeted between 1999 and 2003 – largely in response to changes in the global market stemming from the dissolution of the regulatory International Coffee Agreement by major coffee companies in 1989 (Fridell 2007a, 89) – the *colonato* was dealt what is understood to be its fatal blow, and close to 200,000 workers were fired from their permanent positions on coffee *fincas* (Álvarez

2009; Hurtado Paz y Paz 2008, 208–14; Segovia 2004). Alongside the last gasp of the *colonato*, however, came an unintended consequence: the collaboration of affected communities with campesino organizations in a campaign to seek compensation in cash or land for their time worked and sudden termination.

With the massive influx of disenfranchised *mozos colonos*, campesino organizations began providing strategic and legal assistance to communities that wanted to follow through on provisions owed them under Guatemalan legislation. Many demanded back pay for years or decades of wages falling short of the legal minimum, or for pay not delivered after coffee prices fell, and most *mozos colonos* who had been let go insisted on the payment of their *prestaciones laborales*, or the constitutionally mandated payment of one month's salary for every year of continuous work rendered if a worker is fired without cause. Standard practice for decades has been to first deny employees their *prestaciones* and then, if brought to labour tribunals and ordered to pay, to offer a drastically reduced amount, which violates the worker's rights but is preferable, in the eyes of campesinos, to non-payment (Serrano López 2008, 69–98).

The strategy employed in recent years by campesino organizations, however, has been to organize entire communities collectively and to bring employers to court in order to ensure full payment. Facing large groups of workers backed by experienced organizations and with legal support, landowners have frequently capitulated and agreed to pay in full, often before legal proceedings even begin. In many cases *finca* owners offer or agree to provide land in place of the payment owed to communities (interviews, Monteros 2009; Urízar 2010). This is how rural labour disputes become instances of land access, when former *mozos colonos* accept property deeds instead of cash in resolution of amounts owing, and thus become the new collective owners of land they may have worked their entire lives.

It is particularly difficult to track land accessed through the pursuit of *prestaciones laborales* and other labour rights due to the number of scenarios and institutions potentially involved. In some cases all that is needed for a dispute to be settled is discussion between a campesino organization and the landowner. If the community moves on to legal measures, the case is mediated by the Ministry of Labour and heard by the Labour Tribunals, but once a ruling has been delivered in favour of a community, negotiations for payment in the form of land are conducted directly with the landowner and outside of any government institution. In addition, not all cases are listed as conflicts with the Secretariat of Agrarian Affairs and thus do not exist even in the flawed data set of potential land access. Since the cases are primarily instances of labour, rather than agrarian, disputes, they are dealt with (but not centrally registered by) the Ministry of Labour. Only when community actions affect land use – usually through a community's refusal to leave the living area provided to them as *mozos colonos* – are they labelled occupations and taken on by the SAA as agrarian conflicts.

Despite a lack of numbers, however, it is clear that this type of dispute has been widespread over the last decade, as have cases resulting in access to land. CONIC alone negotiated land transfer in forty-five instances of labour disputes, making this the most common form of

Illustration 3.1. *In La Tinta, Alta Verapaz, a community begins to build their new village on land purchased by the Secretariat of Agrarian Affairs. The group fought for four years to have labour rights respected as* mozos colonos *from Finca La Mocca.*

land access among CONIC communities. The PTSM has assisted with a number of instances as well, and Ingrid Urízar, the PTSM legal advisor interviewed in March 2010, estimates that upwards of 60 per cent of all cases were resolved by giving land to the communities, even if this was only land for living and not enough for agricultural production.

In one astonishing case, nearly the entire municipality of San Miguel Tucurú in Alta Verapaz turned from *fincas*, or large farms, to collectively owned communities run by former *mozos colonos* during the 1990s and 2000s. CONIC activists who had been involved in the campaign cite a supportive local mayor and well-organized communities working with campesino organizations as helping to transform Tucurú. Between approximately 1995 and 2005, the municipality was transformed from a *finca*-dominated area of over seventy farms and very few communities, to one made up of seventy-four campesino-owned communities and just three remaining farms (interviews, Beb Tut 2009; Monteros 2009; and Tiney 2010, 2015; Hale 2011; Velásquez Nimatuj 2010).[16]

As with all political struggles in Guatemala, the fight for *mozo colono* labour rights has been long and often bloody. Emilio Tzib Quej, the coordinator of CONIC campaigns in the department of Baja Verapaz, told me the story of T———, a community of workers who had recently gained title to their land at the time of our interview in November 2009.

> It was a long struggle. When the community began to organize, the authorities threatened them, they treated them like criminals. The *compañeros* had to hide, and later they came back and occupied another part of the *finca*, way off in a corner; it is a very large property. Some of them spent three months in jail. They had the support of the priest from the La Tinta parish [a nearby municipality in Alta Verapaz]. The police came to evict them, but they couldn't get in because they were the *mozos colonos* from that farm, they couldn't do it ... Then later one of the community leaders was kidnapped, they kidnapped him in La Tinta. So [the community] occupied the central park [in Guatemala City] in 1993 to demand answers about the kidnapping. But nothing came of it so the people went back to the *finca*. They set themselves up on the farm, started planting coffee and cardamom crops and building proper houses. Then the property owner sold the farm to someone else, and the new owner was ready to sell and to resolve [the conflict]. He sold five *caballerías* [225 hectares] through the Secretariat of Agrarian Affairs ... Now the *compañeros* feel very motivated and organized, and now they're managing their own projects. (Interview, Tzib Quej 2009)

Most campesino communities will learn, after achieving land title through rural labour disputes or any of the other methods discussed here, that the next stage of attempting agricultural production and infrastructure development is often as difficult as the preceding struggle for land. Groups may be "motivated and energetic" and "managing their own projects," as Tzib Quej claims, but the result is rarely as transformative as a community might hope. The community cases presented in chapters 4 and 5 – as well as studies with recently landed groups in Guatemala (Hale 2011; Velásquez Nimatuj 2008) and Brazil (Wolford 2010b) – demonstrate a continuity of living conditions more than a road out of poverty. Nevertheless, the very fact of land ownership is enormously important at the end of lengthy struggles for the recognition of labour rights or traditional claims.

Land Occupations

The Secretariat of Agrarian Affairs understands any disputed presence on land registered by others to be an "occupation." In keeping with the definition used by campesino organizations, however, I use the term to refer to the intentional invasion of land known to be owned privately or by the state, and over which the occupiers do not hold historical claim. Used both as an immediate form of land access and as a longer-term tactic to pressure for more campesino land, occupations have a long history in Guatemala and have been conducted over a number of recent waves. Occupations were common during 1953 and 1954 among campesinos seeking land under Jacobo Arbenz's short-lived agrarian reform, but the confrontational tactic was rarely used in the following three decades of state terror and repression (Handy 1994b, 104–6; May 2001).

With the return to civilian rule in 1986 and an accompanying flourishing of social movements, campesino organizations encouraged invasions, and large farms were occupied in at least ten of Guatemala's twenty-two departments between 1986 and 1989 (Cambranes 1992b; CEUR 1990, 102–3). Two main waves of occupations followed this. First, dozens of plantations were occupied across the country during peace negotiations in the early 1990s, partly in response to encouragement from guerrilla and campesino organizations attempting to influence the content of the treaties. News sources noted high-profile occupations in Escuintla, Sololá, Quetzaltenango, Izabal, and Guatemala between 1991 and 1994 – many of which were repressed violently, including multiple

Table 3.8. Land Access Strategies Employed by Campesino Organizations in 2010

Organization	Number of community farms accessed	Via FONTIERRAS purchase	Via agrarian conflicts	Via labour rights	Currently support occupations
CCDA	21	13 farms	Yes	Yes	No
CODECA	3	3 farms	No	No	No
CONDEG	approx. 45	14 farms	Yes: 30	No	No
CONIC	130	36 farms	Yes	Yes: 45	Yes
CUC	approx. 25	Yes	Yes	Yes	Yes
Kab'awil	6	6 farms	No	No	No
Plataforma Agraria	undetermined	11 farms	Yes	unclear	unclear
UVOC	16	No	Yes: all	Yes	Yes
Xinka	0 (protecting existing land)	N/A	N/A	N/A	N/A

Source: Interviews with Sabuc (2009, 2015); Sanchez Trieles (2010); Velásquez (2010) and Pérez Mendoza (2010); Monteros (2009); González (2010); Pérez Mejía (2010); Gómez Hernández (2010); Macario (2010); Carlos Morales (2009, 2010); and Guzmán Grijalva (2010).
Note: Conversations and interviews with Leocadio Juracán of CCDA, Hélmer Velásquez of CONGCOOP, and Eugenio Incer of AVANCSO helped determine the campesino organizations most active in community land access.

instances of campesino deaths – and the government reported in 1995 that eighty-four farms were under occupation or experiencing unrest (*Central America Report* 1991a, 1991b, 1992a, 1992b, 1994a, 1994b; Loeb 1995). Land occupations next regained prominence in the early 2000s, during the years of increased mobilization that accompanied the 1999–2004 coffee crisis (Velásquez Nimatuj 2008, 38–45; interviews, González 2010; and Morales 2010).

Since the easing of the coffee crisis, however, instances of occupation have fallen off, and land invasion is no longer a standard tactic across the campesino movement. Interviews with leaders from nine campesino organizations revealed a hesitancy towards occupations in most cases, and very few examples of current occupations among even supportive organizations (see table 3.8). In large part this is the result of the violent repression of land occupations discussed above. Campesino organizers, understandably, are divided about whether to encourage radical action in the face of repression, and land occupations have continued predominantly in communities associated with three more radical campesino organizations: CONIC, CUC, and UVOC. Marcelo Sabuc, the legal representative for the CCDA, described his organization's apprehension about land occupations:

> In 1992 the CCDA ... occupied unused land [*tierra baldía*] ... Landowners from two farms sent in the army and the police, there was an eviction, people were wounded, people lost their possessions, and community leaders were arrested and jailed. After that we began to reflect on the situation ... In the end [the occupations] were a strain on the community, because what we are doing is motivating, teaching the community so that they will organize. But if in the end when they try to organize this happens – an eviction or violence, for example – then instead of strengthening their organization it is weakened ... So from then on we said, "No more." (Interview 2009)

On the other hand, Hermelindo Chub Icó, a CONIC organizer who works with many occupations in Alta Verapaz and Izabal, explained why groups choose to occupy land: "Some groups have just taken land [*no más que han tomado tierras*], like the two communities evicted [in Chahal, Alta Verapaz]. Those were on a farm that was just taken, but it was their necessity that made them do it. Why do they do that? Because they see a *finca* that is abandoned, that hasn't been worked, and they think, 'Well, these empty lands, or these state lands, well, we are going in there.' That is the reason when a group organizes to enter a *finca*" (interview, 2010).

Some campesino organizations send groups to occupy strategic locations, but Chub Icó and other CONIC activists insist that the communities they work with always make their own decision to occupy land. "When a community wants to occupy a *finca* they always organize it themselves ... We in CONIC don't organize groups and say, 'Go occupy that farm,' because we don't know where there is empty state land. They are the ones who know where the farms are and they organize themselves. The only thing we do is help them to organize better, to organize negotiating commissions, propaganda commissions, a security commission [*comisión de vigilancia*] so that nothing happens to them while they are occupying the farm" (interview, Chub Icó 2010).

Protection of occupied land is usually creative and non-violent, as in the example of Xya'al K'obe' described above, when community members surrounded and disarmed soldiers, holding them until they were assured that their conflict negotiation would be respected. Another activist told me the story of his community's resistance to eviction in the 1990s: traps and lighting tricks were set so that police vehicles approaching at night drove into a ravine instead of entering the village (field notes 2009).

After entering the *finca*, a group will set up makeshift housing, either from materials brought from away such as tin sheets and plastic tarps, or from wood and leaves for thatching found on the property. Corn and other subsistence crops are always planted immediately, as the community seeks to stake their claim over the land and to make the most of their new resource. The occupation then generally follows one of two paths. The group may be evicted forcefully from the land by the landowner's private security or by Guatemalan forces, often within days after arrival. If not, the occupation will be listed with the SAA as an agrarian conflict and negotiation begins and follows the same trajectory of events described above for historical land claims.

As with historical land claims and rural labour disputes, there are no precise records to give an idea of how many occupations have resulted in permanent access to land. The cases are obscured within the broad SAA definition, and campesino organizations count them only haphazardly and without coordination between groups. Nevertheless, each occupation should be thought of as at least short-term land access, as the community works the occupied land and enjoys its harvest if they are able to stay through a growing season, as well as benefiting from a temporary home.

If they are able to stay permanently or are given other land, which occasionally results from SAA negotiation, the group will have accomplished its goal. If forced to leave, however, campesino organizers still tend to chalk up the occupation in the ongoing effort to pressure landowners and politicians. Occupations, it is argued, move landowners away from the practice of claiming large tracts of unworked land, which is illegal under the Guatemalan Constitution (interviews, Monteros 2009; Caal 2010; and Chub Icó 2010). Rigoberto Monteros, the CONIC legal representative who works with every one of the organization's cases of agrarian conflict and land access, describes this strategic thinking,

> The objective is that through an occupation we will demonstrate that there is a lot of land that large landowners have usurped and that isn't

being used rationally, it isn't being used for the benefit of society ... One way of breaking that system is for people to organize and occupy. So the landowners see that their farm is occupied and they start to run around with lawyers and everything, they need to figure out how to have the land labelled as private property, and they start to think that they need to work the land ... rent it out or work it themselves ... But at least they come to realize that land shouldn't be abandoned, it's to be used. That's one way, and in some cases occupying farms has had an impact. (Interview 2009)

Conclusion

Campesino organizing in rural Guatemala has adapted to a recent flurry of agrarian change. Spurred by neoliberal restructuring, acted out through new waves of enclosure, territorialization, and legalization (Peluso and Lund 2011), and underlined by historical inequality, these changes have altered the options for land access available to campesino communities. The campesino social movement and its allied rural communities engage in direct action in search of land and in response to factors ranging from wartime or post-war displacement, to the creation of conservation areas, and the violation of labour rights. Campesinos are confronted with violence that can accompany land control in any scenario, and the threat of repression is a reality for all rural communities in resistance or occupation. Nevertheless, hundreds of communities have carried these efforts forward, and a recent tide of successful direct action has led campesino communities to become communal owners of agricultural land.

Highlighting these scenarios helps to challenge the central role that the World Bank–funded *Fondo de Tierras* claims in agrarian politics. Nevertheless, we must be careful not to elevate the campesino movement to heights of unrealistic expectation. Specifically, the cases discussed here shed light on two substantial difficulties: the amount of land accessed through rural struggle remains insignificant on the national agrarian scene, and even this most successful alternative to market-led agrarian reform has not been able to escape participation in the neoliberal agrarian model.

As discussed above, data provided by the SAA suggest that the amount of land acquired or retained by campesino communities as a result of agrarian conflicts surpasses that transferred by the *Fondo de Tierras* for market-led agrarian reform (see table 3.6). Despite this encouraging assessment, however, the overall pattern of land ownership and use has not been affected by campesino efforts. Agrarian censuses conducted by the Guatemalan government in 1979 and 2004, and agrarian surveys carried out each year between 2005 and 2008, demonstrate convincingly that Guatemala's unequal land tenure remains unchallenged, regardless of a few hundred thousand hectares won through rural struggle. Land ownership in Guatemala is divided into various legal categories (*condiciones jurídicas*), including individually owned, cooperative, and communal properties. The division of land is weighted heavily towards the individual and has changed very little since 1979: individually farmed land remains consistently around 90 per cent, suggesting that the communally owned properties resulting from all of the aforementioned forms of land access have not made a dent in Guatemala's overarching agrarian structure (INE 1979, 2004, 2008).[17]

We must also consider the role that neoliberal institutions play within conflict-related land access, a sobering reality that further dampens the hope that substantial agrarian reform might result from these forms of grassroots organizing. Campesino organizers speak proudly of land accessed through processes other than *Fondo de Tierras* purchase, considering them to be examples of "alternative" land access that help to push the government away from the market model (interviews, Gómez Hernández 2010; Macario 2010; González 2010; Monteros 2009; Carlos Morales 2009, 2010; Tiney 2010, 2015). These alternatives, however, still rely on direct or indirect participation in the neoliberal agrarian system in at least three ways.

First, *Fondo de Tierras* land transactions are necessary in many instances of conflict resolution, even when the beneficiary community does not incur the cost of the purchase. In cases where the Secretariat of Agrarian Affairs has provided land to communities in order to end a conflict (see table 3.7), for example, the SAA uses its own funds to purchase land from large landowner "willing sellers," with FONTIERRAS facilitating the transaction. Beneficiary communities are spared the debt, and the cases are not counted among the instances of FONTIERRAS land purchase, but they nevertheless should not be thought of as having circumvented the market model.[18]

Second, agrarian conflict resolution is an element of the World Bank land administration model, and the SAA itself was founded within this approach. The literature on neoliberal land administration refers to agrarian conflicts as obstacles to property rights and land tenure security, since these goals rely on clearly defined and formally titled ownership

(Dale and McLaughlin 1999, 33–5; Deininger and Binswanger 1999; Deininger and Feder 2009; World Bank 1998). As such, the Presidential Office for Land Conflict Legal Assistance and Resolution (*Dependencia Presidencial de Asistencia Legal y Resolución de Conflictos sobre la Tierra*, CONTIERRA), the institution created under the peace accords and later became the SAA, was selected by the World Bank to be among the six coordinating bodies to carry out its Land Administration Project (Garoz, Alonso, and Gauster 2005, 34–9; World Bank 2010, 63, 71–2). CONTIERRA and the SAA did not receive World Bank funding under the project, however, and the SAA's official budget has been minimal, leaving conflict resolution as a neglected element of the land administration project (Garoz, Alonso, and Gauster 2005, 66–71). Nevertheless, the SAA remains a tactical component of the neoliberal approach to land in Guatemala.

Finally, agrarian conflicts help to define the boundaries of acceptable *campesino* struggle under the neoliberal governance model. In his seminal essay "Rethinking Indigenous Politics in the Era of the 'Indio Permitido,'" Hale (2004) discusses the "neoliberal cultural project" as one that appears inclusive and willing to engage in dialogue, but it uses this engagement to justify a hard line against any attempts to redress economic inequality. By embracing some but shutting out more radical actors, Hale argues (17), neoliberalism seeks "the creation of subjects who govern themselves in accordance with the logic of globalized capitalism." While campesino subjectivity may not be affected automatically, as discussed in the final chapter of this book, such *intent* is clearly present in the agrarian system enforced by the *Fondo de Tierras*, the Secretariat of Agrarian Affairs, and Guatemalan state forces. Debt-ridden land purchases are defined as the only acceptable form of agrarian change. Access to land through negotiated conflict resolution is tolerated for the larger goal of updating the private property regime, but agrarian struggles that rub too closely against specific economic interests are shut down through violent eviction.

The neoliberal agrarian approach seeks to enforce a self-discipline in organizations and communities whereby repression is avoided by limiting campesino organizing to petitions for land purchase. In some ways this scenario has in fact played out, and campesino organizations have unwittingly played a role in defining the parameters of the neoliberal model despite engaging in anti-neoliberal campaigns. On the one hand, the *Fondo de Tierras* land market has been legitimized through the participation of campesino organizations in land purchases and as representatives on the FONTIERRAS governing council (interviews, Galicia 2010; Gómez Hernández 2010; and Macario 2010). And on the other, the hard fact of violent repression has led campesino organizations to scale down their activity in many cases from demanding agrarian reform to negotiating the resolution of specific conflicts.

This critical assessment of agrarian conflicts and land access should lead us to cautious conclusions about the role of the Secretariat of Agrarian Affairs. While no one would hope for the SAA to be the source of structural agrarian change in Guatemala, there is a tendency to view the institution in a more positive light than is usually afforded Guatemalan state actors. Campesino activists and members of communities in conflict usually hold out hope for resolution and land access through SAA negotiations, and research often overlooks the role of the SAA or accepts its mediatory function at face value (Amnesty International 2006; CALDH and CONIC 2009).[19] While the SAA does play an immensely positive role in negotiating the resolution of individual cases, however, there should be no doubt that the institution also holds an important position in the neoliberal restructuring of rural Guatemala. In fact the secretariat is as emblematic of neoliberalism as is the *Fondo de Tierras*: under both institutions, the demands and tactics of the rural poor have been co-opted to further the agenda of wealthy Guatemalan and transnational actors. On the one hand FONTIERRAS has turned demands for agrarian reform into a system that helps large landowners rid themselves of unwanted land while acquiring new property, and, on the other, the work of the SAA with community struggles has limited broader demands and legitimized violent repression.

Rural communities and campesino organizations, under the neoliberal economic and governance regime, have been trapped between the bullet and the bank. Drawing attention to efforts to escape the model, such as the community-based struggles for land discussed here, can highlight alternative and creative grassroots forms of organizing, but the constraints and repression associated with neoliberal restructuring and an unjust agrarian system endure as pivotal factors in rural Guatemala today.

4 CONIC: A Campesino Organization Apart

The National Indigenous and Campesino Coordinator (*Coordinadora Nacional Indígena y Campesina*, CONIC) formed out of a split within the CUC in 1992, when a group of Indigenous activists attempted to prioritize land access and the resolution of agrarian conflicts within campesino organizing. The tension behind that division never faded entirely, and CONIC has often been isolated for its perspective and tactics. Despite a somewhat ostracized position within the movement, however, CONIC grew to be the largest campesino organization in Guatemala during the first decade of the 2000s, and its focus on communal land issues has positioned it as the most accomplished facilitator of community land access in the country.

In this chapter we examine CONIC as an example of campesino organizing in Guatemala, at both the organizational and community levels. The community case studies introduced here present us with detailed accounts of land access, agrarian conflict, and rural development. Considered together with an account of CONIC's history and organizational structure, those community cases allow for the exploration of our central line of inquiry, namely the relationship between organized campesinos and the neoliberal agrarian regime that dominates the rural sector in Guatemala today. While CONIC's unique approach to campesino organizing has led to considerable accomplishments, however, the group has also suffered major setbacks in recent years due to its growing closeness to successive government administrations. This chapter focuses on the history and core operations of CONIC, leaving the questions surrounding its more recent and controversial changes for the final chapter, which considers the two case study organizations in comparison with one another.

CONIC and Territorial Collectives

CONIC was founded amid turmoil in 1992, the result of a split within the Committee for Campesino Unity (*Comité de Unidad Campesina,* CUC), and it continues to be a controversial group within the movement. But during the main period of research for this book in 2009–10, CONIC stood as the largest and in some ways the most successful of Guatemalan campesino organizations, and the sources of tension that led to the group's formation – Indigenous identity, autonomy from guerrilla groups, and a focus on community land rights – have proven to be the basis of CONIC's strength.

The details of CONIC's split from the CUC have been largely the stuff of rumour for nearly two decades. Nevertheless, the few materials published on the division agree that a need to ground political demands in Indigenous identity created a rift within the leadership of the CUC and brought the future founders of CONIC into disaccord with the Guerrilla Army of the Poor (*Ejército Guerrillero de los Pobres,* EGP) (Bastos and Camus 2003; Brett 2008; CONIC 2010; Velásquez Nimatuj 2008).[1] Following eight years of clandestine organizing, the CUC re-emerged publicly as a campesino organization in 1988 with the support of the EGP. Interviews with key actors from the time, conducted by Velásquez Nimatuj (2008, chap. 3), show that in 1992 the guerrillas continued to exert control over the CUC's political decisions. Despite the EGP having appointed the first two Maya men to leadership positions within the guerrilla army, many activists maintain that there was no room within the CUC and EGP to approach rural issues from a standpoint other than one of class-based agrarian reform. When four Indigenous members of the CUC leadership bypassed EGP orders and negotiated directly with the Guatemalan government in an attempt to resolve land-rights agrarian conflicts in Indigenous communities, they faced retaliation from within both the CUC and the EGP.

Juan Tiney, Pedro Esquina, Juana Vásquez, and Federico Castillo were forced out of their appointed CUC positions at a meeting in May 1992. A campesino march that month had pressured President Jorge Serrano into a meeting with CUC, and Tiney and Esquina used the opportunity to focus discussion on Indigenous rights and land conflicts. Direct negotiation itself was taken to be out of line: the URNG guerrilla command had entered into peace negotiations, and all grassroots demands to the government were supposed to be channelled through the formal command structure. That the content of the negotiations was framed in explicitly Indigenous-based terms also touched a nerve within a revolutionary movement that, according to Tiney and others, already discriminated against Indigenous activists and their priorities (Velásquez Nimatuj 2008, 123–4).

The 1992 negotiations and the resulting rift within the CUC can be interpreted as the culmination of the rising importance of Indigenous issues within some elements of Guatemala's organized left. Velásquez Nimatuj (2008, chap. 3) argues that Tiney, Esquina, Vásquez, and Castillo represented an Indigenous current within the CUC that had begun with a consultation with base communities in 1985 and grew until the 1992 rupture, and matched a broader emergence of Indigenous activism across Guatemala during the same years. Similarly, Brett (2008, 119) argues that the international Indigenous rights current in the early 1990s allowed the CUC leaders who would later found CONIC to express an "Indigenous perspective of social struggle … [that] was not compatible with a Marxist conceptualization of identity."[2]

The 1992 CUC negotiation with the Serrano government thus represented both an open opposition to the guerrilla command's rigid control over grassroots campesino organizing and a reframing of rural demands in Indigenous terms based in the resolution of community land conflicts. For this mutiny, the four leaders were expelled from the CUC, accused of selling out to the government (Velásquez Nimatuj 2008, 117–21). On 16 July 1992, less than two months after being expelled, Tiney, Esquina, Vásquez, and Castillo – along with eighteen other campesino organizers from within and outside of the CUC – founded CONIC.[3] The new campesino organization would grow tremendously over a few years and eventually surpass the CUC in the number of communities allied with the group. Furthermore, the issues that led to the CUC split would continue to define CONIC. To this day CONIC exercises a rare level of autonomy within the campesino movement as well as a willingness to negotiate with state institutions, and the group is still criticized harshly for this. CONIC's approach to campesino issues is also based more directly in Indigenous perspectives than is the case with other campesino organizations. Finally, the defence of community and Indigenous land rights and the resolution of agrarian conflicts have proven to be the most effective areas of CONIC action.

Over nearly twenty years of organizing, CONIC's strategy has been to combine direct action, political pressure, and negotiation in the struggle to access or recover land for Indigenous and campesino communities. The organization has been flexible in adjusting the relative weight of the three aspects of this approach, fluctuating between an emphasis on land occupations or negotiation with the government. This has allowed CONIC to respond to changing circumstances, but autonomous shifts in tactics have also earned the group the scorn of the broader campesino movement.

CONIC took a defiant stance during its first few years, coordinating massive grassroots political action while engaging tepidly with the official peace process. Two large-scale CONIC mobilizations in 1995, running from February through May and then again in September and October, used an array of direct action tactics to force concessions on campesino access to land. Demonstrations, roadblocks, and pressure on local landowners and politicians were combined with around 100 land occupations and ultimately led to the formation of two government commissions and negotiations resulting in land access for a number of communities (Bastos and Camus 2003, 67–71; Brett 2008, 133–8). These actions were carried out during the final stretch of peace negotiation, however, and CONIC was criticized by the left and right alike for bypassing the official process and risking a derailment of peace negotiations. But CONIC had already distanced itself from the peace process, declining to participate in the Civil Society Assembly (*Asociación de Sociedad Civil*, ASC) and criticizing the heavily compromised accords on Indigenous rights and socio-economic issues for their lack of movement on land issues. In his assessment of CONIC's engagement with the peace process, Brett (2008, 141) argues that CONIC made an intentional choice in favour of grassroots activism over formal negotiation, and that the organization "[judged] its relative gains in land ownership and campesino mobilization as sufficient trade-offs for the institutional constraints of civil inclusion."

Despite its hesitancy to participate in the peace process, CONIC quickly shifted its policies to fit in with the new political context following the end of the war. The organization announced in 1996 that it would no longer support land occupations and would focus on resolving land conflicts and other Indigenous-campesino issues through formal channels, including the new agrarian institutions established under the peace accords (Brett 2008, 142). In addition to participating in the *Fondo de Tierras* council and facilitating around thirty instances of community land purchase through FONTIERRAS, CONIC also continued to negotiate the resolution of Indigenous and campesino issues with government officials. Through three successive presidential administrations since 2000, CONIC managed to extract accords benefiting campesinos, including debt reduction for communities that have purchased land through INTA and FONTIERRAS, land purchases in order to resolve agrarian conflicts, and delivery of agricultural benefits for small farmers, including free fertilizer and subsidized land rentals (interviews, Bol 2010; and Tiney 2010).

These negotiations have been backed at times by grassroots mobilization – as in a return to land occupations in 2002–3 and a "Maya and popular uprising" in 2006 – but at other times the CONIC talks have been characterized by the absence of the group from ground-level political pressure, as has been the case ever since the 2006 actions. Both the tactic of direct negotiation as well as the willingness to withhold from mobilization in order to advance government talks have helped to keep CONIC in the position of outsider to the campesino movement. This uneasy relationship with other organizations also has been maintained by CONIC's withdrawal or abstention from umbrella organizing. Despite having helped to found CNOC, Guatemala's first campesino umbrella group, CONIC withdrew in 2006 following internal turmoil. Similarly CONIC has refused to join the multi-sectorial Alliance for Comprehensive Rural Development (*Alianza de Desarrollo Rural Integral*, ADRI) in negotiating a rural development law, preferring to attend government discussions as a separate representative of the campesino sector (interviews, Galicia 2010; and Tiney 2010). CONIC's staunch insistence on autonomy in political organizing and negotiation has its roots in the organization's founding conflict in 1992, a divide that has never quite healed. During interview discussions in 2009–10, leaders of other campesino organizations warned me that CONIC had sold out to the Colóm government. CONIC continued to strengthen its rural base and to support land occupations and other agrarian conflicts during the Colóm period, however, leading to my assessment at the time that CONIC remained true to its values. Events since 2015 have given this assessment a more complicated balance, as discussed in chapter 6, but the strategies employed by CONIC, controversial as they may be, have generated immense benefits for its campesino members.

If measured through successful instances of community land access, CONIC's tactics have been overwhelmingly successful. Between 1992 and 2014, CONIC helped 144 groups gain legal title to communal land, which represents many more cases than those of any other Guatemalan campesino organization (see table 4.1). The cases have been spread out evenly, with around ten communities gaining land with CONIC each

Table 4.1. CONIC Communities, by Method of Land Access

Form of land access	Cases
Fondo de Tierras	55
Rural labour disputes	41
Secretariat of Agrarian Affairs	27
Other state institution	14
Community purchase	4
None listed	3

Source: CONIC (2015)
Note: Category *"Fondo de Tierras"* includes 6 cases of land title regularization through FONTIERRAS 4 purchases through INTA, which FONTIERRAS replaced. "Secretariat of Agrarian Affairs" includes joint purchases between the SAA and FONAPAZ (13 cases), SAA-MAGA (2 cases), and SAA-FONTIERRAS (1 case). The other state institutions listed are CONAP, CONTIERRA, FONAPAZ, FORELAP, and FUNDAECO.

year until 2008 and around five per year since then. The land accessed has been located in fourteen of Guatemala's twenty-two departments,[4] although it has been concentrated heavily in Alta Verapaz, which counts with 50 of 144 instances, or 34 per cent (CONIC 2015).

The concentration of cases in Alta Verapaz, and also within a small number of municipalities, reveals some of the reasons for CONIC success in land access. Just five municipalities account for seventy-five instances of land access: San Miguel Tucurú and Senahú in Alta Verapaz (thirty-six and seven cases); Purulhá, Baja Verapaz (fourteen cases); Champerico, Retalhuleu (ten); and Livingston, Izabal (ten). In San Miguel Tucurú, Senahú, and Purulhá, most land accessed by CONIC communities resulted from the legal battles over labour rights discussed in chapter 3. In Champerico, campesinos from the highlands purchased large farms in areas where they had previously migrated for seasonal work (interview, Monteros 2009). These areas of large-scale land access point to the importance of basing community struggles in local conditions rather than only following top-down strategy. According to Rigoberto Monteros – who as the CONIC legal representative works directly with each of the community land struggles supported by the organization – the regions that have seen many farms turned over to campesinos have high levels of internal community organization. Similarly CONIC cofounder Juan Tiney told me that for a community to gain access to land, its members need to be well organized and to have secured the support of a dedicated local CONIC activist (interview, 2010).

CONIC's strong record of helping campesino groups gain title to communal land is thus the result of successful organizing at the community level, dedicated support from CONIC activists, and local conditions that help cases move forward. Dealing with land access on a case-by-case basis through support for community organization has meant that many finalized cases of land access have been based in the resolution of agrarian conflicts and the three categories of alternative land access discussed in chapter 3: historical land rights, rural labour disputes, and land occupations. Of the 144 instances of CONIC land access recorded by 2014, 55 were community land purchases through the *Fondo de Tierras*.[5] Of the remaining 89 cases, at least 68 were carried out under our categories of alternative land access: 41 instances of labour rights and 27 purchases by the Secretariat of Agrarian Affairs (see table 4.1). Furthermore, in 2009 CONIC was managing another 71 cases of ongoing agrarian conflicts aimed at community land access (CONIC 2009e).

Any group of campesinos in Guatemala can join together in order to purchase land through the *Fondo de Tierras*, and most campesino organizations are willing to help them through the required administrative process. But supporting agrarian conflicts aimed at gaining or reclaiming communal land implies much greater involvement and familiarity. CONIC manages this through an effective organizational system with fluid communication between communities and leadership.[6] The cornerstone of the system lies in CONIC's eleven *Colectivos Territoriales*, or Territorial Collectives, consisting of local volunteers who regularly visit each CONIC community in their region. The volunteers, called *promotores* (promoters), are leaders from communities organized with CONIC who speak the predominant Indigenous language of the area and understand regionally specific socio-economic issues and who provide continuing organizational support through monthly visits to each group. These communities – numbering 619 across fifteen departments – include those that have accessed land, those that are still fighting for land, and those that have not engaged in land struggles, as is the case with many highlands villages.

The role of CONIC promoters in the Territorial Collectives is to facilitate community organizing, guide the group through community development and internal problems, provide or seek out technical and legal support, and help to instil CONIC's political and ideological positions (CONIC 2009a). This is a mutually beneficial relationship, as rural groups enjoy organizational support and counselling in community development, and CONIC maintains the support of an organized rural base numbering nearly 40,000 families (CONIC 2009c).

The flow of information between communities and CONIC's national leadership also runs both ways, through a strategic plan adopted at a national assembly every four years (CONIC 2009d). What makes the plan especially democratic, however, is its implementation through the Territorial Collective system. Each of the seven thematic "strategic lines" that comprise the strategic plan has a coordinator who works with the eleven Territorial Collectives to ensure that those objectives are being carried out within communities. The coordinators of the strategic lines and the eleven Territorial Collective coordinators also meet once a month in Guatemala City, together with CONIC's central leadership, the National Directive Council (*Consejo de Dirección Nacional*, CDN). Finally, a number of regional councils were being organized during my time of research with CONIC, including plans to establish departmental and municipal councils across the country. When researching with the San José La Pasión community, for example, I attended some of the first municipal councils that brought together the eighteen CONIC communities of Chahal, Alta Verapaz. Altogether, this system means that not only are the strategic priorities of the CONIC leadership disseminated within rural communities, but that perspectives and concerns from all CONIC communities are voiced regularly to the national leadership.

Where this model is implemented diligently, as in the cases of Victorias III and San José La Pasión discussed below, the result fully integrates rural communities into CONIC's political decision-making process and helps to form new community, organizational, and political leaders within CONIC. This is evident in the composition of CONIC's national leadership. While many of the organization's original founders still form part of the CDN, many newer leaders from communities organized with CONIC have been voted into important positions. The story of the National Directive Council's sub-coordinator, César Bol, is typical of many CONIC activists who come into the organization through their own community struggles.

> I'm from the community of Tres Cruces in Cobán, Alta Verapaz. We are working on getting our rights to that *finca*. My grandparents and parents were *mozos colonos* there ... When I was ten years old I couldn't speak Spanish. I started studying at the age of ten ... We joined as members of

Illustration 4.1. Hermelindo Chub Icó, Territorial Collective promoter in Alta Verapaz and Izabal, speaks at a municipal council meeting of representatives from 18 CONIC communities in Chahal, Alta Verapaz.

CONIC in 1998. I was a community leader there, and since I was the only one to have had the opportunity to go to university – ninety-five families and I was the only one who could read and write, so [people said], "César will be our leader." I joined the CONIC youth structure later, and from there I went on to be a member of Cobán's Municipal Directive Council. Then I rose really quickly, and in 2004 I joined the National Formation Commission. In 2005 I was elected sub-secretary [of the National Directive Council]. In 2007 I was elected secretary, and in this 2009 assembly, sub-coordinator, just like that [*laughs*]. I feel like it's been a very quick ascension. (Interview 2010)

The model has not always been successful. Although CONIC has been more adept than other organizations at maintaining ties with rural communities and incorporating local organizers into its national structure, the organization still suffers from the disconnect between communities and leadership that is characteristic of the Guatemalan campesino movement (see chapter 2). CONIC organizers lamented in interviews that campesino groups are often much less dedicated to participating in CONIC after successfully completing their struggle for land.

When communities don't have land they are very active. But the problem is when communities win their struggles, recover land, they start to leave CONIC, they start to get disorganized, they even start to think about dividing their land quickly, divide mine here and someone else's over there ... Why? Because they see that there are lots of meetings: protests over here, protests over there, meetings over here, meetings over there, political negotiations here and there, when they feel that it's not necessary for themselves. They think to themselves that their own problem has ended, but CONIC's vision wasn't for it to end like that. (Interview, Caal 2010)

Marta Cecilia Ventura, the sub-secretary of the National Directive Council whose responsibility it is to oversee CONIC's organizational structure, views the problem in terms of three groups of communities. The first are communities that completely share CONIC's vision for political organizing and that remain active; they have usually been with CONIC since its early years. The next are those communities that are currently struggling to access land or resolve agrarian conflicts, and that identify with CONIC as an organization that will help to solve their problems. And the third group comprises communities that do not identify strongly with CONIC's political vision but that see the organization as an asset for acquiring resources, especially community development projects. The challenge, Ventura explains, lies in building relationships with communities once they have accessed land, and in using development projects as a platform for building a community's political-ideological affiliation with CONIC (interview 2010).

This points to a major weakness in CONIC's work with rural communities. While CONIC has been tremendously successful in assisting campesino and Indigenous groups with land conflicts and struggles to access land, and while it has created an organizational structure that ensures continuous direct engagement with all of their associated rural communities, it lacks an overarching strategy for community improvement following land access. As opposed to the CCDA discussed in chapter 5, whose direct trade coffee production in a small number of communities has helped campesinos move forward after purchasing land, agricultural production and sales in CONIC communities depend almost entirely on case-by-case initiatives. In ethnographic research with two CONIC communities, Velásquez Nimatuj came to the same conclusion, finding that while CONIC was effective at accessing land for the communities of Aztlán and Nueva Cajolá in Retalhuleu, "they were not effective in the second stage, when having land is complicated by the need to produce and to pay off debt ... CONIC did not grow enough to be able to convert itself into an institution capable of financing itself or diversifying" (Velásquez Nimatuj 2008, 276).

Plans for rural development, production, and marketing exist within CONIC's strategic planning documents (CONIC 2009d), but even members of the national council admit that the extent to which these are carried out depends on each community and on the work of the local Territorial Collective (interview, Bol 2010). There are successful cases of cooperative production and community infrastructure improvement based in support from CONIC, and the Victorias III case study provides an excellent example, but these are rare and, more importantly, are not coordinated centrally as an element of CONIC's work with communities.

Gender equality in community organization is another aspect that has been slow to catch on. Even at the basic level of having a parallel women's association alongside the community *junta directiva*, or directive council, CONIC has fallen far behind its goal: fewer than half of the 619 communities have organized women's groups where the stated goal is to have one in every community (CONIC 2009c). Where women do participate in community organization and CONIC activities, Marta Cecilia Ventura notes that they are mostly single or widowed. Patriarchy continues to exert a strong influence in even the most politically organized rural communities, and it keeps women tied to household duties and children, or holds them back from becoming active in community decision-making (interview, Ventura 2010; Velásquez Nimatuj 2008). CONIC's national leadership has taken important steps, creating a Women's Secretariat and mandating that a minimum of seven of the thirteen positions on the National Directive Council be held by women. These accomplishments were hard-won by female CONIC activists, however, and women within the national leadership continue to insist that there is gender discrimination within CONIC, from the communities up to the national council (interview, Ventura 2010; field notes, 19 November 2009).

The strength of CONIC's organizational model can also be called into question on the basis of its difficulty in translating the large base of 40,000 affiliated campesino families into local electoral success. Organizers from the Alta Verapaz, Baja Verapaz, and Retalhuleu Territorial Collectives interviewed in 2009 were hopeful that members of their communities would be elected to mayoral positions (interviews, Tzib Qej 2009; López Vásquez 2010; and Chub Icó 2010). CONIC partnered with Nobel laureate Rigoberta Menchú's Indigenous political party, Winaq, and supported local community leaders to run as Winaq candidates for municipal positions in the 2011 national election. The election results, however, were crushing. Not a single Winaq candidate was elected as mayor, not even in the highly organized CONIC municipalities of Champerico, where more than half of the population lives in CONIC communities, and San Miguel Tucurú, where organized former *mozos colonos* own most of the land.

To what extent, then, are rural communities associated with CONIC integrated into the organization's movement for political change? Do base communities mirror CONIC's vision of anti-neoliberal or even post-neoliberal socio-economic organization? Are the difficulties associated with navigating Guatemala's neoliberal agrarian terrain replicated at the community level? We turn now to Victorias III and San José La Pasión, two communities whose histories and internal political and economic organization are windows onto many aspects of CONIC.

Victorias III: "We're Screwed but Happy"[7]

Illustration 4.2. A house under construction in Victorias III

Victorias III is a tight-knit community that has made extraordinary accomplishments. Its members remain cohesive as a group after more than a decade on their new land, they benefit from strong organizational support from CONIC, and the community has benefitted from numerous agrarian and infrastructural development projects. Yet Victorias III faces economic hardship. The soil on its land, located in the former heart of export agriculture on the South Coast, has been depleted through decades of chemical-based cotton farming and intensive livestock grazing. Similar communities have accessed land in the surrounding area, yet the region has almost no state services or infrastructure, since it had, until recently, been the terrain of commercial farming. Victorias III thus faced building a new community from the ground up, on land that barely produces enough harvest for survival, and with a lack of additional work in the area due to changes in the regional economy. The community of Victorias III presents an excellent case for considering what kind of community development is possible in an overall disadvantageous context, but one that nevertheless can count on the strong support of a campesino organization.[8]

The Maya Mam families that made up the first members of Victorias III came from the village of Victoria, municipality of San Juan Ostuncalco in the highlands department of Quetzaltenango, as well as from the neighbouring municipality of Palestina Los Altos, Quetzaltenango. There they participated in the *minifundia-latifundia* system, with household economies based in small subsistence plots and complemented by wage labour and sharecropping on the South Coast coffee and cotton plantations, or *fincas*. When asked why they left their home town, almost everyone said it was for lack of land in their area, with some detailing the difficult conditions on the *fincas*. "Where we used to live we weren't at home much, we lived more on the *fincas*, with the *patrones* [bosses], enslaved, discriminated" (interview, Felipe, 15 January 2010). Alberto told a story about the strict control that landowners exercised, even on rented land: "One man planted a chilli plant, an *ayote* plant, and a cotton plant. They called the owner. 'Who gave you permission to plant that? I gave you this land for you to plant corn – don't you plant any cotton!' And he chopped it all down with a machete in front of everyone" (interview, 12 February 2010).

The war was also a factor in driving people to look for land away from Victoria. One thirty-year-old man followed his politically active father, who told him, "If we don't win the struggle through war, we'll join the struggle for land" (interview, 15 January 2010). But repression during the armed conflict was a greater factor: San Juan Ostuncalco suffered multiple raids, disappearances, and murders at the hands of the military, as documented in the report of the Historical Clarification Commission (*Comisión para el Esclarecimiento Histórico,* CEH) truth commission (CEH 1999, ss. 817, 2024, and 4357). Timoteo recounted, "When we first thought about coming here was during the war, when many of us died in the village of La Victoria where we lived. Many died, around seventy people. The soldiers came and took them out of their houses and killed them who knows where. So we thought, 'Why don't we unite to find *fincas*, because those farms are ours, they belonged to our ancestors'" (interview, 23 October 2009).

A nine-year struggle for land followed. The Mam coordinator of the Municipality of San Juan Ostuncalco (*Coordinadora Mam del Municipio de San Juan Ostuncalco*) land committee was formed in Victoria in 1990 and grew to include around 650 families from across San Juan Ostuncalco and Palestina Los Altos. Weekly meetings were held, and people walked from villages up to eight hours away to participate as steps were taken to request land from the government. The Institute for Agrarian Transformation (*Instituto para la Transformación Agraria,* INTA) was at the time issuing loans for land purchases in an early market-based land distribution scheme, and the Victoria-based committee wanted to participate. Having joined with CUC from the beginning, and then later with CONIC, the group took part in a common pressure tactic of the time and occupied the plaza in front of the national palace in Guatemala City. There they endured the rainy season without shelter and suffered the death of two children during their occupation. In 1994 the group finally accessed Finca La Braña through INTA, but it was too small. One hundred and five families stayed there, and a second farm was purchased through INTA three years later, Finca San Marcos Nisa. One hundred and fifty families stayed on that second farm, and a third location was found in 1999 (interview, Alberto, 12 February 2010; conversation with Timoteo, 15 January 2010; Xunta de Galicia 2007; Velásquez Nimatuj 2008, chap. 5). This final farm, the Finca Guayacán where ninety-four families would form the Victorias III community, was among the earliest *Fondo de Tierras* transfers, sold by Hector Briz Santos through a FONTIERRAS loan of Q4,386,925.81, or around half a million dollars (BANRURAL 1999). Indemnification would later forgive the debt of the first two farms bought through INTA, but Victorias III continued to owe their full amount to the *Fondo de Tierras* until a second debt forgiveness in 2015.

When the ninety-four families of Victorias III first moved to the Finca Guayacán in 1999, they were met by dry, treeless terrain with depleted soil and no infrastructure aside from a dirt road running through the property. Today the community is green and shaded, lush with crops, and a central schoolhouse and football field are ringed by communal buildings, churches, and neat rows of houses. The story of this transformation is based equally in luck and determination. The community first lived in makeshift housing with plastic sheets for roofs, put up alongside a river that runs through the farm's lowest point. Hurricane Stan devastated Guatemala in 1999 and hit Victorias III hard, with the community enduring the wind and rain without proper shelter. Cristina Nieto of the *Xunta de Galicia* – the international cooperation agency run by the Galician state

Table 4.2. Projects Funded in Victorias III, 1999–2010

Project	Funding Agency	Year	Project Status
Training in cattle ranching(7 people)	SARES Foundation, via FONTIERRAS	2000	Complete
Communal drinking wells (3)	MSF	2001	Complete
Composting outhouse toilets (94)	MSF	2002	Complete
Health training	MSF	2002	Complete
Cement houses (74)	ASF & CONIC	2003–6	Complete
Training in construction work (30 people)	INTECAP	2003–6	Complete
Primary school construction	FIS & municipality	2005	Complete
Cattle: 36 cows, with corral	ACSUR & CONIC	2007	Altered, from communal to individual
Small-scale irrigation and vegetable planting	ACSUR & CONIC	n/d	Abandoned
Reforestation	MAGA	n/d	Complete
Mango trees	MAGA	n/d	Complete
Fish tanks (3, for 30 families)	TechnoServe	2009–10	In progress as of 2010

Source: Xunta de Galicia (2007) and field notes, 22 September 2009
Note: The above organizations are the Foundation for Rural, Equitable, and Sustainable Food Security (Fundación SARES); Doctors without Borders (Médecins sans Frontières, MSF); Architects without Borders (Architecture sans Frontières, ASF); the Technical Institute for Training and Productivity (Instituto Técnico de Capacitación y Productividad, INTECAP); the Inter-American Development Bank's Guatemalan Social Investment Fund (Fondo de Inversión Social, FIS); the Association for Cooperation in the South (Asociación para la Cooperación en el Sur, ACSUR–Las Segovias); and the Ministry of Agriculture, Cattle, and Food (Ministerio de Agricultura, Ganadería, y Alimentación, MAGA).

government in Spain – happened to visit the community around this time. Nieto collected information about the group and promised to do her best to find financing to build houses, thus initiating a long relationship between the community and the Galician development agency. Today the *Xunta de Galicia* works with CONIC in Retalhuleu and coordinates infrastructural, agricultural, and organizational projects in Victorias III and seventeen nearby communities. Many major developments in Victorias III came from outside funding, and most of that was secured through the work of the *Xunta de Galicia* (see table 4.2) (interview, López Vásquez 2010).

The *Xunta de Galicia* first partnered with Doctors without Borders to bring three communal drinking wells and a composting outhouse toilet for each housing lot. The seventy-four lots, measuring 20 × 40 metres each, now also have two-bedroom cement houses that were built in stages as funding became available between 2003 and 2006.[9] Thirty members of the community were trained in construction work, and the full group participated in the construction of each house. Other buildings have been built through funds raised by community members: three churches of varying degrees of formality, from a wooden shack through to a cement building; a communal hall consisting of a tin roof over a floor space open to the breeze; and a building to house the *alcaldes auxiliares* (auxiliary mayors), or Indigenous authorities, and their two holding cells (see illustrations 4.3–4.6) (field notes, 22 September 2009; Xunta de Galicia 2007). Community members are extremely proud of these advances, and especially of their new houses, the benefits of which are often explained in connection to weathering storms: "These houses were the most important thing for us, to be living more securely. The roofs we had before were made of palm leaves, not very secure, but this house is a little better. It can stand up to more and we can live calmly inside. When there is strong weather we have a place to live well, to sleep well" (interview, Andrés, 23 October 2009).

Community members also recognize that they have a long way to go before their basic needs are met. At a strategic planning session facilitated by CONIC and the *Xunta de Galicia* in November 2009, community members listed and prioritized their needs, in order to improve long-term planning and coordination between community committees (field notes, 4 November 2009). Projects were listed by the group and listed by priority, with the first four receiving the strongest backing.

Illustration 4.3. *A house in Victorias III. Seventy-three identical homes were built by Architects without Borders, one for each family.*

1. Formal land title[10]
2. Electricity
3. Running potable water
4. Health post
5. Gravel roads
6. Better stoves
7. River bridge
8. Communal hall
9. School
10. High school

Of the 248 hectares that make up the Victorias III property, all but 10 hectares are dedicated to farming. The farmland is divided into three sections, with every family working an individual plot within each section (see illustration 4.8). The area surrounding the housing

Illustration 4.4. *The building used by the Victorias III alcaldes auxiliares (auxiliary mayors), with two holding cells visible on the right side of the building*

Illustration 4.5.
The composting outhouses built for each home by MSF

Illustration 4.6. *One of three communal wells*

Illustration 4.7. *Community leaders from Victorias III show local CONIC promoter Juventina López Vásquez a communal fish tank under construction*

lots and community centre is flat and dry, referred to as the *seco*, or dry ground, and each family has a plot for *milpa* and sesame production measuring one *manzana* (0.7 hectares). This section ends where the elevation drops slightly around the Río La Unión river flowing through the middle of the farm. The land in the river area is dramatically different from the rest: lush and green all year, with trees in abundance and water for bathing and laundry. The area is intended for firewood and grass, since extremely wet soil and frequent flooding make for less ideal growing conditions, but some families plant corn and fruit trees in their plots. Continuing out of the *bajío*, or river lowlands, the farm returns to its regular elevation and dry ground, and each family has another one-*manzana* plot intended for cattle grazing. Since the number of cows kept by a family varies, and some families have no cows, the cattle area is also used by many as additional land for corn and sesame production.

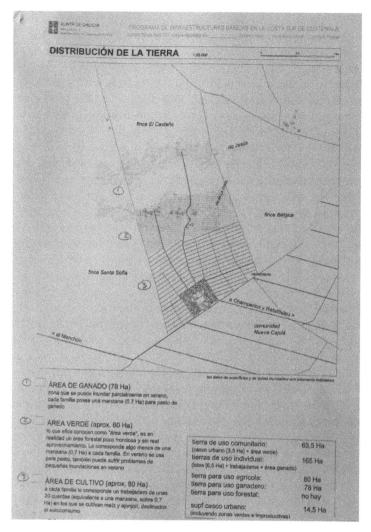

Illustration 4.8. Map of Victorias III, Municipality of Champerico, Department of Retalhuleu

This map of Victorias III farm and surrounding areas was drawn as part of a socio-economic study of the community conducted by the Xunta de Galicia (2007). The Victorias III community and land are located in the middle, between the Río Jesus to the north, and Finca Santa Sofía and Finca Bélgica to the west and east. Four areas of the farm are marked: the cattle land in the northern third of the property, followed by the wet lowlands and then the corn and sesame plots in the south; the busy square surrounded by a grid of farm plots marks the housing and communal area.

While each family has access to close to three *manzanas* across three plots, few consider their land to be adequate for farming. The land at Victorias III is often extremely dry, with little water and no irrigation to ease the drought. Corn and sesame, the two main crops grown in the community, are both affected by the fluctuating weather: not enough rain makes for low corn yields, and rain during picking season can ruin a sesame harvest. As a result, harvests are erratic from year to year, leaving food and income uncertain. Community members also note that the soil is poor, having been depleted through years of chemically intensive cotton and pig farming. In response to an interview question, only three people out of thirty-seven considered their land to be good, with the rest split between those calling it bad land and those referring to it as average. When referring to their land as average, many people qualified their answer to say that the land is bad when it isn't farmed with sufficient water or fertilizer: "The land here doesn't have any nutrients left, it's a little tired and can't produce with strength like virgin land, so this land is only good for producing our own food now" (interview, Gavino, 25 February 2010). "The land here might have been good before, but when the *patrones* came they started to plough the land. The land is washed out now and doesn't have any potency … It's going to take some time to be able to restore this land" (interview, Felipe, 15 January 2010).

Soil conditions leave people in Victorias III with few options for production. *Fondo de Tierras* agronomists encouraged the community to diversify their farm, but crops either failed, as in a women's tomato project, or didn't earn the community any money for their efforts. A papaya project exemplifies the second scenario: the trees gave good fruit, but after hiring pickup trucks to take the papaya to market the farmers were left with no profit and the project was abandoned (interview, Marciana, 14 January 2010). The distance from markets also holds people back from a healthy diet, since the cities of Retalhuleu (forty-three kilometres away) and Champerico (twenty-three kilometres) are too far for regular trips to be affordable, and meat, dairy, and vegetables won't keep in the hot town with no electricity.

Faced with poor soil and a remote location, Victorias III farmers rely on corn, sesame, and cattle. The system adopted by the community is to alternate between corn and sesame on the same land, growing one harvest of each per year. With two plots of one *manzana* each available outside of the *bajío* river area, 58 per cent of households grow corn and sesame in one plot, and 42 per cent use both plots for greater harvests. Corn yields fluctuate with the weather, but the harvest prior to my interviews in 2009 and 2010 was described as an average one, with each *manzana* of land producing between fifteen and forty *quintales*, or 100-pound bags of dried corn kernels. This put the average yield per *manzana* at 27.8 *quintales*, with a household average of 37.9 *quintales* of total production (see table 4.3). In most cases this was enough corn to feed a family for the year and have a varying amount left over for sale, but nine out of thirty-seven people interviewed reported not producing any surplus. Sesame yields varied more wildly, partly as a result of the risk of water damage while drying the seeds. A *manzana* of sesame produced between one and twelve *quintales* of dried seed, with an average of 500 pounds per *manzana* and 720 per household.

Most Victorias III residents raise cattle as well, grazing cows in riverside plots, sometimes in one of their two *seco* plots, and in the communal field in the middle of town. The cows came as a development project from the Spanish development agency Association for Cooperation in the South (*Asociación para la Cooperación en el Sur*, ACSUR–Las Segovias), and the original intention was for the cattle to be raised as a communal venture. It wasn't long before the residents of Victorias III decided to raise the cows individually, however, handing out two cows to each household. Some people have sold all their cows, but most survey respondents still raise cattle, holding onto between one and six cows and selling calves for around Q2,300 once a year. Adult

Table 4.3. Crop Production in Victorias III, 2009–2010 (*Quintales*)

	Corn	Sesame
Per *manzana*		
Low	15	1
High	40	12
Average	27.8	5
Per household		
Low	15	1
High	80	20
Average	37.9	7.2

cows serve as financial security as well and can be sold when money is needed, as was the case with Nolberto, who sold his when his wife fell ill (interview, 15 January 2010).

Paid work is scarce, but it can be found within the community, in the neighbouring community of Cajolá, back home in the town of Victoria, Quetzaltenango, and on the large farms surrounding Victorias III. Men are often paid to help with agricultural tasks within the community or in Cajolá, an adjacent town that also gained land through CONIC. The going rate is Q50 per day – which is the national minimum wage but surpasses what is often paid for plantation work – and labour is in demand during planting. Around half of the community members I interviewed say they or their spouse work on nearby plantations, often staying away from Victorias III for a week or two, but most also noted that very little work can be found. The South Coast region where they live used to be full of cotton farms, but most of these have fallen out of

Illustration 4.9. The transition between harvests: sesame plants grow among drying corn

production, sold to communities of landless campesinos like Victorias III or abandoned after deforestation and chemicals drained the soil of its nutrients.

Instead of working the *fincas*, wage labour is more often found back in *tierra fría* (the "cold land," because of the mountain climate), the San Juan Ostuncalco and Palestina Los Altos highland municipalities from which Victorias III drew its members. Strong family and community ties mean that most members of Victorias III visit their home towns regularly, and campesinos from the resettled community can find wage labour helping in plots back home. The connection to highland communities and their cooler temperature also plays an important role in the Victorias III economic strategy. Corn keeps better in the mountain climate, so most people will bring their harvest to store with family in Quetzaltenango. The home communities thus serve as a bank. When visiting family, campesinos from Victorias III often sell a bag or two of corn to earn cash and also take home the corn that they need for upcoming household consumption. A single harvest of corn, tucked away with family in the highlands, presents cash flow and food over the course of a full year for most people in Victorias III. Conventional wisdom holds that this is the best way to ensure economic stability. "If you have some money in cash and you put it aside to save, the time will come when you need money and say, 'Let's borrow a bit,' but you don't end up putting it back. With corn, on the other hand, you have food to eat and you can put some of it aside" (interview, Alberto, 12 February 2010).

Victorias III has flourished largely as the result of strong relationships with communities and organizations outside of their town. Alongside the economic benefits stemming from family connections in the highlands, the community has drawn strength in social and political organization from CONIC and the *Xunta de Galicia*. The campesino organization and the Galician development agency have melded in Retalhuleu over the years, to the point where it is difficult to draw a distinction between the two. Under CONIC's model of Territorial Collectives, local Maya Mam organizers from recently landed communities in the area regularly visit Victorias III and other nearby communities and support their socio-economic progress. Unique to the Retalhuleu collective, however, is the additional financial and technical support of the *Xunta de Galicia* as a development agency that works exclusively in the Retalhuleu area and only with CONIC communities. Four local CONIC organizers have crossed over to work full-time with the *Xunta*, and one of them, Juventina López Vásquez, continues to serve as the CONIC promoter for Retalhuleu, thus blurring even further the line between CONIC and the *Xunta de Galicia*.

The *Xunta* has financed or secured outside funding for development projects in Retalhuleu for many years, but as of 2008 their activities have supported political organizing as well. Together with CONIC, the *Xunta* initiated an ambitious three-and-a-half year comprehensive development program called *Oxlajuj Tz'ikin* that would carry out projects in housing, basic services, economic production, and risk management, but that also focuses on strengthening community and institutional organization. The program was pitched in 2007 to aid agencies and grassroots organizations as well as to the thirty communities working with CONIC within the department of Retalhuleu. Fourteen organizations agreed to participate, including CONIC, Architects without Borders, Education without Borders, the pharmaceutical organization *Farmacéuticos Mundi*, and local Indigenous and development groups. And of the thirty CONIC communities in the area, eighteen decided to take part in *Oxlajuj Tz'ikin*, including thirteen who had gained land through the *Fondo de Tierras*, INTA, or SAA, two that had held onto land distributed under the Arbenz agrarian reform in the 1950s, and three groups without land (interview, López Vásquez 2010).

An enormous amount of work was carried out by *Oxlajuj Tz'ikin* in 2008 alone: houses and toilets were built; schools were improved and scholarships awarded; cattle, fish, and vegetable projects were started; and health workers and midwives were trained, pharmacies and health posts were established, and medicinal gardens were planted. A more lasting impact may have been generated, however, from the organizational work conducted by the program. Victorias III and the seventeen other CONIC communities involved in *Oxlajuj Tz'ikin* each elect two community representatives, one man and one woman, to sit on a "micro-regional council," the decision-making body that determines spending and distribution priorities for the program. This generated a shift in community involvement with CONIC, from the regular meetings to support organization and development that are the standard fare of CONIC organizers, to the sustained interaction with other local communities focused on regional decision-making. Such an initiative suggests a change in community outlook. Instead of being a community working to improve itself alongside the outside support of CONIC and the *Xunta de Galicia*, conversations in Victorias III made clear that community members now see themselves as part of a larger formation of similar communities working together to improve living conditions for all. The *Oxlajuj Tz'ikin* program in a sense created a parallel municipal government of CONIC communities, with funding provided by aid agencies and with decisions resting on the consensus of representatives from every community (Xunta de Galicia 2008; interview, López Vásquez 2010).

Victorias III is highly organized for community management. In addition to the regional council, elected positions play a strong role in community life, with over half of all participants serving in committees at the time of my interviews. Women in the community have also fought to participate, and female interview participants mentioned that *machista* culture is slowly being eroded. Marciana, director of the Victorias III elementary school and former member of the community

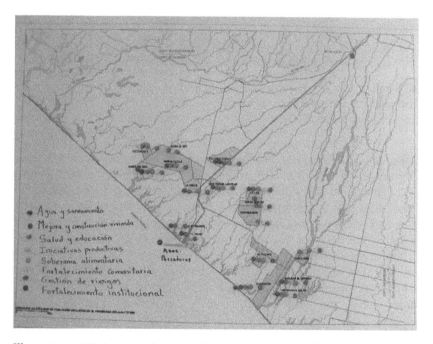

Illustration 4.10. *A map on the wall of the* Xunta de Galicia *office in Retalhuleu shows development projects under way with the* Oxlajuj Tz'ikin *program. Shaded areas indicate the location of the 18 CONIC communities participating in the program, most of which own former plantation land.*

Illustration 4.11. *At a strategy session for infrastructure projects held in Victorias III, community member Marciana explains her group's choices while Mónica González Ferreiro of the* Xunta de Galicia *and Juventina López Vásquez of CONIC look on.*

Women's Commission, told me that women have participated in most commissions as well as in the *junta directiva* leadership council and the auxiliary mayor system. Marciana says that women are often less active than their male counterparts, since many women cannot read or write, but that participation rates have risen nonetheless. "Before there was a lot of that, of men not letting women participate, but not anymore. There are maybe two or three [men] now who say, 'My wife's not going out because she has to cook for me, because we have a lot of children and I don't want her to go out' … But the majority now give their wives time … they give them the opportunity" (interview, 14 January 2010).

The community vision at Victorias III matches overall with CONIC's ideas of agrarian transformation and alternative socio-economic organization. Nevertheless, the community depends heavily on outside support for the realization of that vision. When discussing Victorias III with CONIC's national council, I was cautioned not to hold the community up as an example of how CONIC communities should operate: their reliance on the *Xunta de Galicia* and other funders, I was told, has generated an unsustainable situation (field notes, 24 March 2010). The benefits of that outside support are many. Projects have improved living conditions in the community immensely, reaching a level of development often understood to be unattainable within a climate of total state neglect for rural communities. Constant support from CONIC has also helped keep the group living and working together happily, even as many other *Fondo de Tierras* beneficiaries descended into internal conflict. But *proyectismo*, the emphasis on development funding for agriculture and infrastructure that is common within the movement, is rampant in this community that has always benefitted from a flow of financial assistance.

Despite constant external support, Victorias III also finds itself in a difficult economic situation. The community does have important resources. Corn production sustains families throughout most years, there is water and firewood for all, and the three agricultural plots that each family has access to allow residents to live according to the campesino lifestyle, taking time for family, religion, and non-agricultural chores in the afternoons and evenings. Money for additional expenses is scarce, however, as is wage labour. The lack of cash adds to adverse growing conditions for most crops, meaning that many residents of Victorias III feel their economic hardship daily, in a lack of sufficient or nutritious food. "Our diet is thin [*comemos escasito*]. We eat meat maybe once every two weeks, beans maybe three times in two weeks. And we eat plants [*yerbitas* from the maize plots] ... We're only buying sugar, salt, and oil, and vegetables when they come in on a truck" (interview, Zenovio, 23 October 2009).

Another source of much concern in the community, until 2015, was a lack of formal land title. While Victorias III purchased their farm from the *Fondo de Tierras* in 1999 and was required to pay back the loan by 2011, the group refused for sixteen years to make any payments. The community was supported in this by CONIC, which encouraged its FONTIERRAS communities not to pay their debt (interview, López Vásquez 2010), and its support surely made it easier for Victorias III to remain on its land and fend off FONTIERRAS. In 2015, following the restructuring of FONTIERRAS community debts initiated in response to a campesino protest march, Victorias III had its debt reduced by 75 per cent and was in the process of paying the remaining amount in order to receive formal land title (field notes, 13 and 15 December 2015).

When interviewing community members in 2009–10, many made the case to me that they should not pay for land because they had built significant infrastructural improvements that were in fact the duty of the state to provide, such as a school and drinking water (field notes, 14 January 2010). I imagine they must have also felt that it would be unfair if Victorias III had to pay their debt while the other two groups from their land struggle had their debts forgiven by the FONTIERRAS predecessor, INTA. Nevertheless, not having the land title in hand made the residents of Victorias uneasy, and for a long time there was an ever-present fear that the *Fondo de Tierras* or the bank responsible for the loan – the Rural Development Bank (*Banco de Desarrollo Rural*, BANRURAL) – would evict them from the land they had worked hard to improve and make their own.

Victorias III can be assessed as a successful project of alternative socio-economic organization and an example of reinforced Indigenous autonomy, albeit with severe limitations. The resources made available to the community through land access and external support allow them to reproduce the highland Indigenous lifestyle based in subsistence agriculture while freeing themselves from mandatory participation in *latifundista* production and its associated migratory patterns. To the contrary, a reversed travel pattern from the lowlands to highland villages presents members of the community with the economic advantage of long-term corn storage and savings.

For all their success in subsistence and autonomy, however, campesinos from Victorias III remain heavily dependent on outside funding, and they have been unable to produce enough on their land to feel that even their basic needs have been met. The agricultural cards were stacked against Victorias III from the beginning, with poor soil in a region of inconsistent rainfall and distant markets. In addition, Victorias III demonstrates drastically the total abandonment by the Guatemalan state of many rural areas. Such basic services as roads, electricity, running water, and schools must often be secured by communities and their allies if they are to be installed at all, as government bodies routinely neglect their responsibility to provide them. For these challenges of agricultural misfortune and governmental disregard, Victorias III has been helped immensely by its relationship with CONIC, which has brought community organizational support and has helped to secure long-term financial assistance. The success of Victorias III should be measured in terms of autonomy, organizational strength, and social well-being, rather than either its lack of economic advancement or its wealth of infrastructure development. The *Oxlajuj Tz'ikin* program and the micro-regional council of eighteen CONIC communities promise to strengthen further the pillars of autonomy and organization in Victorias III.

San José La Pasión: "We Have to Work Together, the Community and CONIC"[11]

After a long and painful search for land, including involvement in two land conflicts, the fifty-six families of San José La Pasión gained access in 2007 to enough land to continue their Maya Q'eqchi' subsistence lifestyle. The community settled on land provided by the Secretariat of Agrarian Affairs in the remote region of Chahal, northern Alta

Illustration 4.12. A typical house at San José La Pasión, with the communal forest seen in the closest mountain in the background

Verapaz, where they are cut off from infrastructure and state services.[12] Nevertheless, they have the regular support of CONIC promoter Hermelindo Chub Icó and are surrounded by other CONIC communities. With strong internal cohesion resulting from their participation in land occupations, and with more fertile land than they need for subsistence production, San José La Pasión serves as a beacon for CONIC, an example of ideal conditions for land access and community development.[13]

As night fell on my first day in San José La Pasión, on 22 July 2009, the town authorities gathered in the Catholic church. We had met earlier in the day to discuss my research, together with the full community, and spent the afternoon touring the property on foot, surveying crops, and hiking through the communal forest that covers a mountain on the eastern edge of the farm. After becoming familiar with group leaders during the day, this second meeting was more intimate, and sombre. The group gathered to tell me the story of their struggle for land. Sitting on wooden benches set on the church's dirt floor, lit by candles, the CONIC promoter Hermelindo Chub Icó translated as four men recounted the community history at length. The version of that history told here comes from those four testimonies and subsequent comments made during interviews and conversations, as well as from mention of the Chitocán land conflict in Amnesty International's *Guatemala: Land of Injustice?* (2006, 25–9).

Of the fifty-six families living in San José La Pasión, and 316 residents in 2009, all but five households came to the new community from a land occupation at the Chilté cooperative in Cobán, Alta Verapaz. The core group that occupied the Cooperativa Chilté came from the Finca Chitocán, also in Cobán, where agrarian conflicts had been active since the 1980s. Some of the families that eventually settled San José La Pasión were thus engaged in conflicts on two farms, and they suffered repression in both cases. Three people were murdered at the conflict at Chitocán in 2000 and the group was evicted by police in 2004; the Chilté occupation was evicted three times and was subject to thirty-five arrest warrants and one death.

The conflicts at Finca Chitocán, and CONIC's involvement there, led to the formation of the group that would become San José La Pasión. Chitocán is an enormous farm with thousands of residents, including *mozo colono* resident workers as well as a separate village of wage labourers based on the property. Since the mid-1980s, *mozos* from Chitocán had organized to demand respect for their labour rights.[14] CONIC began supporting the group in 1996, and demands for settlement continued through at least 2004. During 2000–1 another conflict flared up on Chitocán around an access path across the farm from which residents had been cut off. Three people were murdered in those years, including a community leader and a lawyer working with the group. Chitocán workers occupied the hub of the farm in 2002 in order to create pressure upon resolving their case for labour rights, and they were evicted violently by over 500 police officers on 5 May 2004. Houses were burned, there was a confrontation with police, and six campesinos were arrested, including one who was hospitalized for injuries sustained during the eviction.

With residents of Chitocán active in land and labour struggles and connected to CONIC, organizers encouraged a group from the *finca* to branch out and occupy other land. Domingo, a community authority from San José La Pasión, remembers CONIC's work preparing the group for occupation: "I never forgot how they came from Santa Ines and they worked on organizational strengthening for occupying a farm. 'Occupy a farm not just to occupy it,' they said. There will be threats, evictions, arrest warrants, and other threats, the *compañero* told us. But thanks to his experiences, and we put them to work, that's why we won the land where we are now" (San José La Pasión group testimony, 22 July 2009).

The occupation of Cooperativa Chilté lasted from 2000 to 2005.[15] Three days after occupying the land in 2000, the group was evicted by the cooperative members. They reoccupied and were evicted again two more times, with the third being the most violent. The police burned down the homes that the occupying campesinos had built on Chilté and destroyed their possessions, and a number of people from both sides of the conflict were arrested. The president of the occupying group, Don Antonio, suffered injuries during the eviction, including internal bleeding, of which he would die one month later. After Antonio died, CONIC helped bring in another man to head the group, Don Pablo, who remained president of San José La Pasión community association in 2010. Don Pablo, who had lived through another conflict around land claimed by former Guatemalan president General Fernando Romeo Lucas García in Chisec, Alta Verapaz, insisted on calming the situation and finding a solution to the Chilté conflict. Don Pablo helped the group to join forces with members of the cooperative in pressuring state authorities to find land to end the occupation. The occupying group managed to stay on the land, and by the end of 2006 the Secretariat of Agrarian Affairs had purchased the Finca Asunción Cebac farm that would become San José La Pasión, in order to end the occupation and the conflict.[16] "Four years on, Don Pablo took over as president of the association. He managed it all, he oriented us a lot: looking for a solution to the land conflict should always be peaceful, that's the advice that Don Pablo always gave us. But there were some *compañeros* who were angry and wanted to hit the *cooperativistas* because they couldn't stand all the harm they had caused us. That's why they wanted Don Pablo as the representative of the association, and thanks to God we made it and in the end that's why we're here" (Domingo Chub, group testimony, 22 July 2009).

The fifty-six families that formed the community of San José La Pasión settled their new land in late January 2007, moving their possessions in trucks from the Chilté occupation and the Chitocán farm over the course of one week. Fifty of those families came from the Chilté occupation and were originally from Chitocán or other communities from which CONIC drew supporters for the occupation. The remaining six families were brought together by CONIC to fill the SAA's requirement that exactly fifty-six families be settled on the land provided. After arriving, the community lived under plastic sheeting while they all pitched in to the communal work of cutting lumber and thatching palm from their new land in order to build houses. The residents consider these houses to be temporary, inadequate living conditions: one large room, with a wood-burning stove built inside; dirt floors; wooden walls with gaps between boards that let the mosquitos in; thatched roofs and the occasional stretch of aluminium siding.

Three years after moving to the farm, as I conducted my research in San José La Pasión, living conditions were still rough. There was no electricity, although a project to connect to nearby power lines was underway in 2010, and water was drawn from just six outdoor taps distributed throughout the village. As adults mostly in their thirties with young children, the residents of San José La Pasión prioritized building a school on the farm as their first development project. They were successful in that goal, securing Q8 million (US$1 million) in funding from the Guatemalan government-based National Peace Fund (*Fondo Nacional para la Paz*, FONAPAZ) to build a large primary school consisting of two buildings. While FONAPAZ contributed the money for building materials, the community provided the labour, and all men from San José La Pasión put in equal hours of unpaid work over a six-month period in order to complete the school.[17]

The egalitarian spirit at San José La Pasión, seen in the community's pitching in to build the school and houses, extends to land distribution as well. On their 299-hectare farm (6.65 *caballerías*), each family has a total of six *manzanas* of land for farming, and plots were allocated through a lottery system. The farming land is divided into two sections:

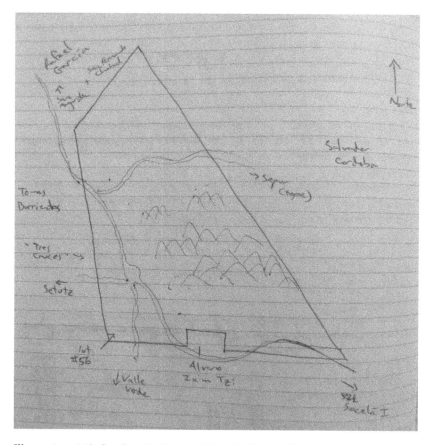

Illustration 4.13. San José La Pasión, Municipality of Chahal, Department of Alta Verapaz

Property borders for this map were traced from a land registration document in the possession of the community. Roads and mountains were then added by a community member, who also told me where to label the neighbouring communities and farms. Housing in San José La Pasión is clustered along the main road that runs north, on the left-hand side of the map. Each family holds two agricultural plots, one west of the main road, and one to the east of it.

the hilly western side of the farm where families have plots of two *man-zanas* each, and the eastern side with plots of four *manzanas* in size (see illustration 4.13). While the plots in each section are of equal size, their shape varies as the community tried to keep any one plot from holding too much rocky or hilly ground. Still, the uneven terrain keeps the plots from being equal in quality, so the lottery system at least prevented any favouritism in determining the initial distribution.

As in Victorias III, the campesino economy of San José La Pasión is based primarily in corn production. In contrast to Victorias III, however, San José receives a reliable yield from their harvests, two harvests per year instead of one, and fertile land that can produce a variety of additional cash crops. Families in San José La Pasión also have more land than most will use at any one point, with interview participants reporting an average of 2.5 *manzanas* in use out of 6 available. Since they usually use less than half of the land available, farmers at San José La Pasión rotate between areas within their large plots in order to allow the soil to replenish. About one-third of interview participants also say they intentionally farm less of their own land and rent an additional plot of 1–3 *manzanas* from nearby *fincas*, in order to maintain the quality of their own land. Paolo recounted the strategy: "The neighbouring *fincas* will rent land to us. So we go there first, to work there while our land is being saved. When they won't give us anything anymore in other *fincas*, then that's when we can put our own land to work" (interview, 18 November 2009).

The six *manzanas* that each family has are divided into two plots: one to four *manzanas* are used for *milpa* production of corn, beans, squash, and other plants, and another of two are *manzanas* used for other crops. At an average of 26.8 *quintales* per *manzana*, corn production is similar to the yield reported at Victorias III. The average household is producing much more corn than in Victorias, however, since two harvests a year, in April and October, mean that each family produces an average of 95.5 *quintales* of dried corn a year (see table 4.4). With one *quintal* of corn usually feeding four people for a month, the high level of production in San José La Pasión allows for a lot of surplus for sale. Most families will store this extra corn at home and sell it by the *quintal* over the months between harvests, with the town's president buying corn at Q10 ($1.25) per *quintal* below the market rate and transporting it to sell in nearby markets.

In addition to producing enough corn for subsistence and market sales, many people in San José La Pasión experiment with other cash crops, especially beans, chilli peppers, peanuts, and cardamom. Black beans are the most commonly grown crop after corn, but the amount of land used and beans produced varies significantly within the community. Eighteen of twenty-eight interview participants grow beans, and they use between one *cuerda* (one-sixteenth of a *manzana*) and 1.5 *manzanas* of land to produce between one and forty-five *quintales* of beans. A household will usually eat around 100 pounds of beans over the course of a full year, leaving an average of about five *quintales* of beans for sale at Q300 ($37) per *quintal*.

In addition to beans, some families grow chilli peppers or peanuts, and some have experimented with cardamom. Growing chillies can be

Table 4.4. Corn and Black Bean Production in San José La Pasión, 2009–2010

	Corn (*quintales*)
Per *manzana*	
(one harvest)	
Low	10.0
High	50.0
Average	26.8
Per household	
(two harvests)	
Low	20.0
High	250.0
Average	95.5
	Beans (*quintales*)
Per *cuerda*	
Low	0.5
High	3.0
Average	1.4
Per household	
Low	1.0
High	45.0
Average	6.3

Note: 8 of 28 surveyed households also rent 1–3 additional manzanas of land for corn production on other farms. The additional corn is not counted here.

lucrative, as the dried peppers sell for around Q1,300 a *quintal*. The crop is labour-intensive, however, and just half of the families interviewed were growing chillies in 2009–10. Those families dedicated between one and eight *cuerdas* each to the crop, and with a *cuerda* of land producing around one *quintal* of dried chillies, the earnings per household from the peppers varied between Q1,300 and Q10,400 ($162–$1,300). Peanuts were a less popular crop, with just two interview participants using two *cuerdas* each to grow peanuts, one at one *quintal* per *cuerda* and one at four. Finally, a number of people in San José La Pasión planted cardamom in their first years on the farm. Residents of San José are familiar with cardamom from working on plantations in the Cobán area, where it is a common crop, but weather conditions in northern Alta Verapaz proved difficult. No one interviewed had seen any earnings from the plant yet and most commented that their efforts weren't paying off.

Across the fifty-six households of San José La Pasión, the amount of land used and the area dedicated to cash crops vary significantly. Unlike Victorias III – where nearly all families use all available land for one harvest of corn and one of sesame, and then hope for adequate weather conditions – the campesinos of San José La Pasión have options. Each family decides how much subsistence and cash crops to grow, and whether to rent land away from the community, and in very few cases will a family work all of their land. This means that each family can guarantee their subsistence corn production while planning for a somewhat dependable income from farming. Two examples illustrate the possibilities of varied production in San José.

José is a thirty-nine-year-old Q'eqchi' man from Carchá, Alta Verapaz, who worked as an agricultural labourer before joining San José La Pasión as a latecomer, just before the SAA purchase of the farm. Using three *manzanas* of land, José and his family plant corn, beans, chillies, peanuts, and cardamom. The family collects around sixty-seven *quintales* of corn during each of two harvests and eat about 15 bagsful over the course of the year, leaving about 119 bags to sell for approximately Q11,900.[18] Adding to that three *quintales* of beans (Q900), one *quintal* of chillies (Q1,300), and two *quintales* of peanuts (Q600), José and his family bring in about Q14,700 ($1,837) a year in agricultural sales. By contrast, Doña Maria and her family earn around Q7,600 ($950) a year. The fifty-two-year-old is San José's midwife, and she joined the occupation of Cooperativa Chilté after being forced to leave a *finca* in Lanquín, Alta Verapaz, where she had lived and worked. She and her family plant two *manzanas* of corn that produce eighty *quintales* and leave sixty-eight for sale at about Q6,800. Doña Maria says her family eats about half of the *quintal* of beans they grow, meaning about Q150 in earnings from the other fifty pounds, and they also sell half of their *quintal* of chillies for about Q650.

Neither family rents land for additional agricultural production outside San José La Pasión, but both see some money come in from work outside of their community. José owns a chainsaw and lends his skill to other communities, but he doesn't have time for the work with so much land planted. Both families have children who work on *fincas* outside San José and contribute money for household expenses, and José's brother-in-law occasionally sends money from the United States. When considering annual income, Doña Maria said about half of her money comes from her children working outside of the community and half from farming, whereas José said his family's money comes almost entirely from working their plots.

Overall, the families of San José La Pasión face a stable and relatively comfortable economic situation. They have more than enough land to consistently produce enough corn and other crops for consumption and sales, a large communal forest of seventy-four *manzanas* provides firewood for the whole community, and the surrounding area presents opportunities for waged agricultural labour for those who want it. In addition, their costs are few: with good soil, most families don't feel the need to buy chemicals or fertilizers, and seeds are saved and planted from one harvest to the next. Having won their land through an occupation, community members also have no agrarian debt to repay. Nevertheless, many families still reported in interviews that they preferred their previous living conditions, where harvests were apparently better.

The success of San José La Pasión as a recently settled village is also due to strong political organization within the community. San José is organized according to the common system of an elected *junta directiva* governing council that answers to a community assembly, and the community has also organized a parallel Women's Committee as encouraged by CONIC. In addition, people in San José elect representatives to a Community Development Council (*Consejo de Desarrollo Comunitario*, COCODE) and other committees, as well as an *alcalde auxiliar*, the auxiliary mayor who serves as a village connection to the nearby municipal government in Chahal. The lines are blurred between the various committees, however, and people in San José La Pasión speak of "the community authorities" rather than considering there to be separate bodies operating within the community. Tasks are distributed according to their corresponding position, but the collected community authorities act as the political leadership of San José. Furthermore, people in the community stress that decision-making rests with the *asamblea*, the gathering of all men and women in town, and that people are elected to committees to carry out priorities determined by the assembly.

Internal organizing at San José La Pasión has been strengthened even further through a solid bond with CONIC. The group of campesinos that would become San José La Pasión had worked with CONIC since 1996, through the land conflicts at Chitocán and Chilté. Although CONIC did not work on a comprehensive development plan with the community after it moved to new land, the local Territorial Collective promoter, Hermelindo Chub Icó, maintains regular contact with the community. Chub Icó makes the rounds through regions of Izabal and Alta Verapaz, visiting San José and many other communities to discuss their progress and work through any difficulties. Chub Icó also keeps the groups connected to CONIC's national programs. Over the course of 2009–10, as I travelled through Alta Verapaz with Hermelindo Chub Icó, I saw him gather representatives from San José La Pasión and seventeen other CONIC-affiliated communities in the municipality of Chahal into a municipal council to formulate political strategy. At those meetings, San José La Pasión serves as an example to other communities, about how to successfully access land and how to form a community on new land. And residents from San José are proud of their role as an exceptionally well-organized community within Chahal. "The communities are frozen here in Chahal, because they can't act, they can't propose, they can't explain, and they can't manage commissions where they should be able to. If the communities were like us when we suffered, I think Chahal would have risen up by now. But sadly the communities are cold and they can't do it, they just wait for things to come … but that's not how things are accomplished … If we had been frozen up, I don't think we'd be here now" (San José La Pasión authorities group testimony, 22 July 2009).

San José La Pasión fits within Marta Cecilia Ventura's category of communities that share CONIC's political vision and maintain strong ties to the organization, despite having gained access to land. With no opportunities for development funding in the area, residents of San José La Pasión don't discuss CONIC as a source of *proyectos*, but as a partner in the political journey from land occupation to land access to community development. Although he was referring to their past struggle for land, Domingo communicates the attitude that continues today. "We can't leave the work of gaining land just to the organization

[CONIC]. We have to do it together: the community as much as the organization. That's how we'll get what we're looking for. If we leave it to just the organization and we leave it in your hands, you won't be able to solve the problem. So we have to search together, the organization and the community. That's how we'll get what we're looking for" (group testimony, 22 July 2009).

Conclusion

Access to communal land and the resolution of agrarian conflicts have been the central concerns of CONIC since the organization formed in 1992. Many CONIC organizers, from the group's founders through to the regional and national leadership today, come from communities engaged in struggles for land, which has helped to sustain a shared concern for land access. The organization has generated significant accomplishments as a result, with fourteen communities gaining land access or land title through CONIC between 1992 and 2014. The communities of Victorias III and San José La Pasión encapsulate the CONIC approach, which prioritizes land access without debt, particularly through the resolution of agrarian conflicts. Victorias III was one of the first communities to purchase land through the *Fondo de Tierras* in 1999, and they subsequently managed for fifteen years to refuse payment for land to which they felt entitled. They are supported by CONIC in their stance, both through a dedicated local activist in Retalhuleu and through CONIC's overall position that loans to FONTIERRAS communities should be forgiven. In the case of San José La Pasión, a group of campesinos fought two land occupations over seven years before settling on new land in northern Alta Verapaz. Their new home was facilitated through years of CONIC support and was purchased under the Secretariat of Agrarian Affairs' Crisis Attention Program, leaving the community with no agrarian debt.

Despite a similar foundation of communal land access without debt repayment, the two communities' experiences with post–land access development have seen significant differences. The community of Victorias III generated a long-standing relationship with the *Xunta de Galicia* development agency and has benefitted from infrastructure and agricultural projects that have entirely reshaped its formerly barren plantation. Growing conditions on Victorias III are difficult, however, and the community has struggled economically, relying on connections to their former highlands homes and still lacking enough to satisfy even basic nutritional needs. In San José La Pasión, no outside development projects other than a state-sponsored elementary school had been built in the first three years, but agriculture fared much better. Corn and cash crops were grown in abundance both on the farm and in rented plots nearby, giving most families in San José food throughout the year and a steady income. These divergent experiences are nevertheless consistent with the CONIC approach to rural community relations. The organization does not work according to blueprints for rural development in communities that have accessed land. Each community instead works out its own approach and is supported by the guidance of local CONIC activists who visit communities on average once a month. The importance of those activists was evident during my time in Victorias III and San José La Pasión. The achievements I witnessed were the result of the ongoing collaboration between the community and CONIC, and of an adaptation to the resources and immediate conditions of each case.

We must remember the role that neoliberal agrarian institutions play in even the most successful and "alternative" instances of land access. The market model of campesino land access, within which both the *Fondo de Tierras* and the Secretariat of Agrarian Affairs play integral roles, absorbs demands for agrarian reform and restricts advances to individual cases of private ownership generated through registered transactions. CONIC may be the Guatemalan campesino organization with the most success in facilitating debt-free campesino land access, but even in exemplary cases such as Victorias III and San José La Pasión those achievements were made possible by collaboration with that same market-based model. However, when examined at the community level, we see that groups of campesinos and local activists are not hostage to the market once their transactions have been carried out. Victorias III dug into their new land and refused to repay the *Fondo de Tierras*, and San José La Pasión used their SAA land to sustain their traditional Q'eqchi' lifestyle. Both communities, while enduring differing conditions of hardship, base their economies in subsistence production and the local sale of surplus or cash crops. Seen from the perspective of everyday existence, these cases show how campesino organizations and communities can navigate the neoliberal agrarian terrain to their advantage and according to alternative visions of socio-economic organization.

5 CCDA: A Revolutionary Enterprise

From their headquarters in the village of Quixayá, nestled in the volcanic foothills of Sololá, the Campesino Committee of the Highlands has organized since 1982 to support a large number of alternative rural development projects while also pushing for national agrarian change. While the CCDA shares the goals and many tactics employed by CONIC, the two organizations represent substantially different approaches to campesino organizing and to navigating the neoliberal terrain. The CCDA was until recently a relatively small organization, but the group has expanded to command a strong national presence in recent years. Having formed as an unarmed revolutionary organization during the height of the armed conflict in 1982, the CCDA later transformed its political work in conjunction with a direct trade coffee project based in the organization's allied communities.[1] Fewer farms have been accessed by campesinos working with the CCDA than with CONIC, and most of those were purchased through the *Fondo de Tierras* rather than won through agrarian conflict. The CCDA's unique strength as an organization, however, lies in its highly successful productive support for the communities and individuals involved in its direct trade coffee project. Whereas CONIC attempts to circumvent the market for land access and community development, the CCDA has stimulated alternative socio-economic organization by engaging and subverting both the Guatemalan land market and the international coffee market. This approach eventually allowed for a strengthening and expansion of the CCDA, and in recent years the group has assumed a leadership role within the national campesino movement.[2]

A second difference between the CCDA and CONIC lies in the two groups' expression of Indigenous identity. While CONIC formed as an

Indigenous organization in opposition to the dominant class analysis of the guerrilla movement, the CCDA continues to hold a class perspective as central to its analysis and tactical approach. The leadership and membership of the CCDA have always been predominantly Indigenous – Maya Kaqchikel for the most part, but with the recent inclusion of many activists and communities from Q'eqchi', K'iche', and other ethnicities. If the group's work has long focused on economic issues, the CCDA's own description of it has always contained a strong component of indigeneity. It could be said that CONIC is a primarily Indigenous organization that focuses on work traditionally carried out by the campesino movement – such as land access – whereas the CCDA is a primarily campesino-focused organization that nevertheless understands itself in terms of Indigenous identity.

This chapter outlines the work of the CCDA and explores the opportunities and challenges presented by its approach through a discussion of two communities, Salvador Xolhuitz in Retalhuleu and Don Pancho in Escuintla.

The CCDA and *Café Justicia*

Until recently, the CCDA was often overlooked by Guatemalans and foreign observers alike, in favour of larger and more visible groups such as CONIC and the Committee for Campesino Unity (*Comité de Unidad Campesina*, CUC). The CCDA has deep roots in rural Kaqchikel communities in the highland departments of Sololá and Chimaltenango, however, where it has long practised an innovative approach to agriculture and community development. Over the last few years the CCDA has expanded its presence across Guatemala, especially in the Quiché and Alta Verapaz, while also becoming one of the more visible organizations dedicated to grassroots activism in Guatemala. If the CCDA has become more recognized since around 2012, its activism is not new, having exerted significant influence behind the scenes over its more than thirty-five years of political organizing. In fact, the CCDA intentionally maintained a low profile over most of its history, because the group was formed during the height of the armed conflict. Forming as a campesino organization in 1982, when nearly all social movement groups had been eradicated or forced into exile, the CCDA has faced repression from its earliest days. It is understandable, then, that the group often chose to minimize its visibility, organizing instead behind the banners of various umbrella groups. Nevertheless, the CCDA has become more vocal in recent years, and the support that the group built for its work in the highlands has grown to include backing from rural communities across the country for its political initiatives.

The CCDA marks its origin as 2 March 1982, when the group announced its formation in the highland municipality of San Martín Jilotepeque, Chimaltenango (CCDA 1982c).[3] At that time, the CCDA was quite likely the only civilian campesino organization in Guatemala, and only the second of the contemporary form of campesino organization to form, following the CUC in 1978.[4] San Martín and the surrounding mountainous area were a stronghold for the Rebel Armed Forces (*Fuerzas Armadas Rebeldes*, FAR), and the CCDA was connected intimately to the guerrillas from its outset (CCDA 2008b, 35; Martínez 2006). During the CCDA's first year, as the Guatemalan genocide reached its peak and civil society organizations had been eliminated, the CCDA played the important role of documenting and publicizing human rights abuses. In its original constitution, the CCDA states as its first objective "to denounce before national and international public opinion, the massacres and destructions that the country's communities are suffering from the repression unleashed by the military" (CCDA 1982c). This objective was acted upon with considerable success, as early CCDA documents contain the details of thousands of acts of murder, massacre, disappearance, torture, rape, theft, and more, with information compiled from across the country and describing in particular detail the events occurring in the CCDA home department of Chimaltenango (CCDA 1982a, 1982b, 1982c; Noticias del Istmo 1982).

By 1983 the CCDA had been driven underground, its leaders assassinated or forced into exile. The group re-emerged publicly on 20 October 1988, but for more than a year earlier the CCDA had been organizing in Chimaltenango communities. The focus was no longer solely denunciation but was expanded in 1987 to include economic and relief programs with victims of the war.[5] In 1987 the CCDA launched at least two such programs: one for "widows, orphans, and campesinos" to produce candles for home use and sale, and another to train twenty young people in sewing and carpentry (CCDA 1987a, 1987b). In 1989 the group began organizing communal stores in rural communities and added a project to provide emergency relief to people affected by the violence (CCDA 1989a, 1989b). By the early 1990s the main programs engaged in by the CCDA included the continuation of the communal stores, youth apprenticeships, and emergency aid, along with poultry production with widows and the production of traditional crafts for export. Some of these projects had expanded beyond Chimaltenango to include work in the highland departments of Totonicapán, San Marcos, and Huehuetenango (CCDA 1990, n.d.; Support Group for the Peasant Committee of the Highlands 1992). These productive projects organized by the CCDA in the late 1980s and early 1990s foreshadow the direct trade coffee program that it would launch in 1999, with a shared emphasis on a search for campesino self-sufficiency and the involvement of international solidarity groups in both trade and project financing.

While the CCDA returned to community work in 1987 and announced itself publicly in 1988, its caution in the face of repression prevented the group from registering legally until 2000. Around that time, the CCDA passed from what it considered to be a first phase, defending highland campesinos during the war, to a second phase of *la lucha reivindicativa*, or the struggle to recover the resources and rights historically denied to Indigenous campesinos (CCDA 2009a, 4). Daniel Martínez (2006, 89–92, 118–24) argues that this transition is best understood through the CCDA's adoption and reinterpretation of coffee farming. Between 1998 and 2000, the CCDA assisted in its first four instances of land access, helping communities move to communal farms in the core CCDA municipalities of San Antonio Palopó, Sololá, and San Pedro Yepocapa, Chimaltenango (see table 5.1). Three of those farms – two in Sololá and one in Chimaltenango – had existing coffee production and presented the CCDA with the opportunity to help the new communities grow their crops and sell them through a network of alternative trade. According to Martínez, who explored the roots of the CCDA coffee project through six months of participant observation, the CCDA's early engagement with direct trade coffee allowed the organization to reimagine and recreate themselves in the post-war era: "The CCDA reinterpreted coffee to transform it into 'something constructive and positive.' What I was witnessing with the CCDA's core-members' reinterpretation of themselves (and thus of the organization) I was also witnessing with coffee; it was skilfully being reinterpreted from a marginalizing product, blessed with a few bouts of prosperity, to a tool for political change, a complement to their *lucha reivindicativa*" (Martínez 2006, 120–1).

From an organization that defended campesino rights, the CCDA took on the role of advocate for political reform based in the peace accords, and of advisors and participants in community development through their nascent coffee program. Hélmer Velásquez – director of the Coordinator of NGOs and Cooperatives (*Coordinación de ONG y Cooperativas*, CONGCOOP), an organization that works with agrarian analysis and

Table 5.1. Community Land Accessed through the CCDA, 1998–2009

Case #	Location	Year accessed	How accessed	Debt status (2009)
1	San Antonio Palopó, Sololá	1998	Church loan	Paid
2	San Antonio Palopó, Sololá	1998	Church loan	Paid
3	San Antonio Palopó, Sololá	1998	Church donation	No debt initially
4	San Pedro Yepocapa, Chimaltenango	1999	FONTIERRAS	Outstanding
5	San Antonio Palopó, Sololá	2000	FONTIERRAS	Paid
6	Patzún, Chimaltenango	2001	FONTIERRAS	Outstanding
7	San Pedro Yepocapa, Chimaltenango	2001	FONTIERRAS	Outstanding
8	Guanagazapa, Escuintla	2001	FONTIERRAS	Outstanding
9	San Juan Bautista, Suchitepéquez	2001	FONTIERRAS	Outstanding
10	Chimaltenango, Chimaltenango	2002	FONTIERRAS	Outstanding
11	Escuintla, Escuintla	2003	FONTIERRAS	Paid
12	Taxisco, Santa Rosa	2003	FONTIERRAS	Outstanding
13	Patulúl, Suchitepéquez	2003	FONTIERRAS	Paid
14	Patzún, Chimaltenango	2004	FONTIERRAS	Paid
15	Nuevo San Carlos, Retalhuleu	2004	FONTIERRAS	Outstanding
16	Cobán, Alta Verapaz	2007	FONTIERRAS – Regularization	No debt
17	Patzún, Chimaltenango	2007	FONTIERRAS	Paid
18	Cobán, Alta Verapaz	2009	Labour rights	No debt
19	Cobán, Alta Verapaz	2009	Labour rights and community purchase	Owing
20	Cobán, Alta Verapaz	2009	FONTIERRAS – Regularization	No debt
21	Cobán, Alta Verapaz	n.d.	FONTIERRAS – Regularization	No debt
22	Patulul, Suchitepéquez	n.d.	Labour rights and community purchase	Paid

Source: Discussion with Marcelo Sabuc, CCDA legal representative, 16 December 2009; and Fondo de Tierras, "Fincas entregadas, 1998–2009" (2009a).

community agricultural projects in Guatemala – holds that the roots of CCDA members allowed them to form a unique organization.

> From what we've seen, in general the [campesino] organizations have a problem, and that is they access land without a plan for managing the land and much less with productive organization for managing land … I would say that the CCDA is the exception … the CCDA since it was born effectively was *reivindicativa*, but it also was very clear the side of production and sales, and they already had experience because they were *finca* workers, they knew the coffee process and all of that. They knew it, albeit from a dominated position, but they knew how to run a farm, from their parents and the like. (Interview, Santiago Atitlán, 2 March 2010)

This reinvention of the CCDA for the post-war context relied heavily on the framework for political reform laid out in the peace accords, and in particular the Accord on Socio-Economic Aspects and the Agrarian Situation. The CCDA draws an explicit connection between the goals of armed revolution and the spirit of the accords: "During the civil war, the *lucha reivindicativa* was carried out in the mountains and in clandestinity; using guns as weapons, words of war and the mountains themselves as revindicative tools. Today, the struggle out in the public light has as its weapons the Peace Accords, the Constitution, international treaties, the Cadastral Law, the Decentralization Law, the political wisdom of leaders, organizational membership [*bases*], and processes in which international solidarity has played an important role" (CCDA 2008b, 19).

The CCDA fits squarely among the "historical" campesino organizations discussed in chapter 2, those that formed during the armed conflict and that, through a primarily class-based analysis, view the peace accords as the best framework for moving towards the political goals of agrarian reform and campesino political representation. For example, the CCDA included among their guiding programs for a number of years that of "Peace Accords and Rural Development," which included CCDA plans for land access, labour rights, and food security and sovereignty (CCDA 2007). Through their membership in the campesino umbrella group CNOC until 2008, and with Leocadio Juracán serving as the CNOC sub-coordinator between 2005 and 2007, the CCDA also promoted the creation of the Cadastral Law, the functioning of the *Fondo de Tierras*, and implementation of other aspects of the Socioeconomic Accord. The CCDA and CNOC shared the perspective that the elements of the accord, if implemented fully, would together act as important steps towards a comprehensive agrarian reform, the *Reforma Agraria Integral* proposed by CNOC in 2003 (CNOC 2005b; CCDA 2005, 2007). Furthermore, since 2008, the CCDA has played a key role in the Alliance for Comprehensive Rural Development (*Alianza de Desarrollo Rural Integral*, ADRI), the multi-sectorial umbrella group that managed to have the Colóm government agree in principle to a Comprehensive Rural Development Law (ADRI et al. 2009; Inforpress centroamericana 2009).

As with other campesino organizations, the CCDA's attitude towards the *Fondo de Tierras* market-led agrarian reform program is telling in its chosen response to the neoliberal agrarian regime. Whereas CONIC makes use of FONTIERRAS as a less preferable method of land access after agrarian conflict, and *Plataforma Agraria* has chosen to boycott the institution altogether (see chapters 2 and 4), the CCDA has relied heavily on the *Fondo de Tierras*. Theirs is a complicated reliance, however, as the CCDA has remained critical of the institution despite using its resources, and the organization has adopted a strategic approach that minimizes the risk taken on by beneficiary communities. Since the *Fondo de Tierras* began to disburse loans in 1999, thirteen of the nineteen communities that the CCDA has helped to access land have been bought through that institution, and another three were accessed through FONTIERRAS land title regularization (see table 5.1). The CCDA has also had involvement in the institution, given that one of the two representatives of the campesino sector to sit on the *Fondo de Tierras* governing council for many years, Gilberto Atz, is a close collaborator with the CCDA and CNOC.[6]

Nevertheless, the CCDA has been critical of FONTIERRAS's shortcomings and deviations, even while continuing to support the spirit of the institution. The CCDA began to describe FONTIERRAS in an overall negative light, especially after about 2006, once funding for the *Fondo de Tierras* had begun to dry up, fewer loans were provided, and corruption within the institution had become apparent (Garoz, Alonso, and Gauster 2005). Mention of the *Fondo de Tierras* in the CCDA annual operating plans since 2007 has reflected this position, with the documents' continuing criticism of the institution for its inability to provide land, lack of support for beneficiary communities, and corruption, including overvalued or even non-existent land (CCDA 2006, 6, 2007, 6–7).[7] CCDA activists were severely critical of the institution during interviews in 2009, with CCDA General Coordinator Leocadio Juracán even claiming "negative intentions on the part of the *Fondo de Tierras* so that [small producers] aren't productive ... because that way they have the argument that campesinos aren't capable of making land productive and being successful" (interview, San Lucas Tolimán, 29 September 2009).

Despite noting the deficiencies of the FONTIERRAS system, the CCDA continues to support state-based initiatives to facilitate campesino land access, whether through a renovated *Fondo de Tierras*, creation of an Agrarian Tribunal as suggested in the Socio-Economic Accord, or measures laid out in the proposed Comprehensive Rural Development Law (interview, Marcelo Sabuc, Aldea Quixayá, Sololá, 14 October 2009). This qualified support for the *Fondo de Tierras* and state-sponsored land distribution, even in its market-led variety, is best explained by the CCDA's highly successful utilization of the resources available through FONTIERRAS. The CCDA has developed an approach to navigating the *Fondo de Tierras* that avoids high debt or poor land wherever possible. First, the organization and its agricultural workers, skilled in assessing land quality from their work in organic agriculture, accompany communities through the land access process and encourage campesinos not to rush into overpriced purchases or bad land. Next, the CCDA encourages communities to use the agricultural subsidies allotted to them by the *Fondo de Tierras* to pay off immediately as much of the loan as possible, avoiding debt and interest in the long run.

This approach to FONTIERRAS loans was evident in some of the newly landed CCDA communities I visited in 2009 and 2010. One community in Chimaltenango already had small housing lots and some agricultural plots, but the group wanted land for agriculturally based income. Together with the CCDA, the group looked at a first potential *finca* but turned it down since the farm had too many outstanding debts. They then found their current farm around 2004, but the asking price was too high, at Q4 million. Three years later, as the group was still searching for land, the owner of the second farm came back and offered the land for around Q500,000 ($62,000). With just over Q1 million in subsidies from the *Fondo de Tierras* (Q34,000 for each of twenty-eight families), the group paid off the farm entirely and had close to half a million *quetzales* with which to start agricultural projects (field notes, 8 July 2009).

A second group, from Sololá, has a similar story. The community has been established on land for a long time, and in 1998 a small group from within the village became the owners of the first CCDA-backed coffee farm. Since not all members of the community were a part of the original coffee project, another group formed in 2001 to find another coffee farm. The group bought a second *finca*, one hour's walk from their homes, in 2004, and were able to pay their Q700,000 debt immediately from the Q1.2 million in subsidies received (field notes, 20 July 2009). Altogether, of the seventeen farms accessed together with the CCDA that were bought through the *Fondo de Tierras* or through other loans, eight have been paid back entirely (see table 5.1).[8]

Land access through the *Fondo de Tierras* has also helped in the success of the CCDA direct trade coffee program, which increasingly forms the backbone of the organization's financial sustainability and political activities. The CCDA coffee program began as a very small project through the support of Canadian volunteers. After the first coffee harvest picked by two communities in 1999, fifteen volunteers from the BC-CASA solidarity group brought 100 pounds of coffee back to Canada in their luggage. This initiated BC-CASA's foray into coffee roasting and sales, as well as the push into the Canadian fair trade and direct trade market. Five years later, in 2004, the CCDA had established new relationships and tripled their annual exports. The group reached out to the Guatemalan Federation of Coffee Cooperatives (*Federación de Cooperativas Cafetaleras de Guatemala*, FEDECOCAGUA) for assistance with exports, and joined up with the Nova Scotia–based Just Us! Coffee Roasters Cooperative while also maintaining sales through BC-CASA's *Café Justicia* label. What began as 100 pounds of coffee exported in 1999 had grown to 1,200 pounds in 2003 and, after a cross-Canada speaking tour promoting the coffee and the CCDA's wider political work, grew to 30,000 pounds in 2004. Sales kept rising, and in 2009 the CCDA exported 67,600 pounds between BC-CASA (which bought 87 per cent of the exports) and Just Us! (13 per cent) (CCDA 2008a, 22, 2009a, 14–15).

Sales are growing tremendously for the CCDA, but only a fraction of coffee production from their associated communities makes it to the international market. The 2008–9 harvest saw over 36,000 100-pound bags (*quintales*) of coffee cherries picked by the thirteen CCDA communities (see table 5.2). Had all of that coffee been processed and dried by the CCDA, it would have amounted to around 6,600 *quintales* of dried beans ready for export – nearly ten times what was actually sent to Canada.[9] This is mainly the result of the limited market offered by the two Canadian importers. Even if BC-CASA and Just Us! could purchase all coffee produced by the CCDA, however, much of it would be ineligible for export since the two importers market exclusively organic CCDA coffee, and fewer than half of the producing communities have been certified as organic. The CCDA thus estimates that, of the coffee produced by the thirteen communities involved in their coffee program, 85 per cent – including a great deal of organically certified coffee – is sold by individual producers to local middlemen at standard rates (CCDA 2009a, 14–15).

Even though the major portion of coffee produced in CCDA communities is not sold through the CCDA, the organization's approach to direct trade ensures that all producing communities benefit from the sales. Prices paid to the organization through its direct trade model exceed the international minimum set for fair trade,[10] but the profit generated is spread across all communities instead of being concentrated among the few producers who are able to access the limited export market. Money earned from CCDA coffee sales are returned to coffee producers and other CCDA-affiliated communities in three ways. First, those communities involved in the *Café Justicia* project – regardless of their progress in organic certification or how much of their coffee is bought for export – receive continual support from the CCDA in the form of technical assistance, credit programs to cover production costs, and access to the CCDA's coffee processing facilities. Included in the technical support is demonstration and instruction in many alternative agricultural techniques aimed at self-sufficiency, such as the traditional *milpa* mixing of corn, beans, and squash; mixed-method farming of fish ponds together with fruits and vegetables, all within coffee plots; and backyard worm composting, gardens, and chicken coops. In addition, producers that form part of the *Café Justicia* network avoid the wild fluctuation in prices typical of the coffee market, with minimum prices set in direct trade agreements.

Second, coffee producers and other communities also benefit from community development projects sponsored by coffee sales and international funds secured by the CCDA, including educational scholarships and the construction of houses, water filters, and chicken coops. Finally, coffee sales help to finance the CCDA's political activism, which involves their member communities both directly and indirectly: directly when this works towards successful land access, and indirectly when CCDA pressure and negotiations result in the adoption of government programs or laws that benefit the campesino and Indigenous populations (CCDA 2008a, 20–7, 2009a, 9; Martínez 2006, 126).

Table 5.2. CCDA Coffee Producers by Municipality, 2008–2009

Community	Land accessed through CCDA	Number of producers	Coffee produced
San Lucas Tolimán, Sololá (I)	No	35	Conventional
San Lucas Tolimán, Sololá (II)	No	30	Conventional
San Lucas Tolimán, Sololá (III)	No	25	Conventional
San Lucas Tolimán, Sololá (IV)	No	2	Organic and conventional
San Lucas Tolimán, Sololá (V)	No	30	Organic and conventional
San Lucas Tolimán, Sololá (VI)	No	11	Organic and conventional
San Lucas Tolimán, Sololá (VII)	No	60	Organic
San Lucas Tolimán, Sololá (VIII)	No	25	Conventional
San Antonio Palopó, Sololá (I)	Yes	33	Organic and conventional
San Antonio Palopó, Sololá (II)	No	15	Conventional
San Antonio Palopó, Sololá (III)	Yes	25	Conventional
Santiago Atitlán, Sololá (I)	No	30	Organic and conventional
Santiago Atitlán, Sololá (II)	No	125	Organic and conventional
Patzún, Chimaltenango	Yes	50	Conventional

Source: CCDA (2009a, 14); discussion with Marcelo Sabuc (2009).

All five of the CCDA's operational programs – Rural Development and Food Sovereignty; New Model of Campesino Organizing; Agricultural Production, Transformation, and Sales; Organizational Empowerment for Campesina Women; and Social Services[11] – are funded by a combination of coffee sales and international donations.

The overview of the CCDA's *Café Justicia* project and the community programs funded by it point to the balance between class and identity in the group's work. We can highlight an emphasis on class analysis and economic change in the CCDA's focus on community-based economic projects and on the acquisition of formal political power towards structural economic change – both of which, in turn, align with the revolutionary roots of the CCDA. However, the CCDA's own description of their economic work has always been based in terms of indigeneity. One of the community-based projects launched following the group's resurfacing in 1988, for example, states as an objective, "To compete in the international and national markets with products made and marketed by the communities. These products are native to the community and their production will enhance traditional Indigenous cultural values" (CCDA n.d.). Similarly, CCDA coffee and other agricultural production today is explained as strengthening the recovery of traditional practices. As mentioned in the introduction to this chapter, the CCDA can be understood as holding an analysis slightly different from that of CONIC: whereas CONIC presents itself as an Indigenous organization engaging in work focused on campesinos, the CCDA works through an analysis of campesinos as an exploited economic class, but without losing sight of the ethnic composition of that class or the importance for cultural identity of any positive economic change.

In regards to its direct trade coffee program, the CCDA considers *Café Justicia* to stand apart from conventional fair trade, referring to the project as one of *"Comercio Justo Plus,"* or Fair Trade Plus (CCDA 2008a). The organization is well aware of the dangers involved in a sales-driven fair trade model that equates social justice with increased financial compensation – an approach to fair trade that has been adopted by corporations in search of "niche markets" and increasingly dominates fair trade sales (Fridell 2007a, 2009; Crowell and Reed 2009; McMurtry 2009). Instead, the organization models its enterprise according to the "solidarity trade" model based in cooperative principles and the promotion of social justice through production in Guatemala and distribution in Canada (Crowell and Reed 2009). As CCDA describes Fair Trade Plus,

> Fair trade is a movement of hope and for the future, but it won't become an alternative if it is integrated into the mercantilist economic system, and, if that happens, it will be reduced to mere rhetoric. Fair Trade Plus, implemented by the CCDA, is based in the sale of agricultural goods produced by small producers for international solidarity groups. It is the communication between peoples [*pueblos*] based in the sale of products ... And it also alternates between commerce and social benefit, since in addition to paying a very good price for the product, it seeks to raise the conscience of the consumer in order to change the life of producers working in Fair Trade Plus. That is, a communication between peoples prevails in

Fair Trade Plus, as a fundamental aspect of human development and not only as a transaction aimed at economic growth. (CCDA 2008a, 15)

The CCDA has been clear on its intention to maintain a solidarity trade model of coffee sales. However, a debate has been carried on within the organization on how to remain true to that vision. The CCDA registered a business in 2008, Highlands Campesino Services, Inc. (*Servicios Campesinos del Altiplano, S.A.*), to manage coffee processing and sales separately from their political work as the *Comité Campesino del Altiplano*. But with the two aspects of the CCDA's work tied intimately together, and with increasing time spent on specific community development projects funded by the coffee or by international groups, some leaders of the CCDA worried that the group's broader goals and political activism were being neglected. At a four-day meeting in January 2010 to compose an annual operating plan for the year ahead, discussion returned to this question a number of times. One core member in particular identified a gradual shift in the CCDA towards community projects and assistance, and worried that "we have begun to lose the overall vision [*se ha empezado a perder la visión grande*]" (field notes, 4–7 January 2010).[12]

These concerns point to some of the most important strengths and weaknesses evident in the CCDA as a campesino organization. On the one hand, the CCDA's work has been effective at the community, national, and international levels. Internationally, the CCDA has been particularly adept at generating long-term support from international solidarity organizations while maintaining autonomy in political and financial decision-making. The CCDA funding model revolves around relationships of solidarity rather than instances of charity. Reaching back to its early guerrilla connections, and thus to international support for the movement in the 1980s and 1990s, the CCDA has relied on a small number of trusted organizations that participate in their movement rather than merely supporting it financially (CCDA 2008a, 22–4). The group manages this by soliciting and accepting funding from international organizations for specific projects outlined by the CCDA. For example, in 2010 the American Jewish World Service funded a series of CCDA regional encounters with campesino communities, and the Irish Catholic development agency *Trócaire* supported the CCDA's disaster-relief program.[13] The CCDA also encourages funding organizations to visit the group's headquarters, coffee processing plant, and allied communities; in January six such group visits were already planned for 2010 (field notes, 4–7 January 2010).

Within Guatemala the CCDA has been a strong national lobbyist for campesino and Indigenous rights and has had a large impact in some rural communities. Until 2010 the CCDA chose not to be very visible, but rather to participate in national politics through umbrella organizations. For example, CCDA Coordinator Leocadio Juracán acted as sub-coordinator with the CNOC campesino umbrella group between 2005 and 2007; the group played a strong role in drafting and negotiating the proposed Rural Development Law with the Alliance for Comprehensive Rural Development (ADRI), with Juracán acting as the ADRI representative who signed the proposed law alongside President Alvaro Colom in 2009; and the CCDA helped to write a report on the repression of the labour movement presented in 2010 by the Guatemalan Labour Union, Indigenous, and Campesino Movement (*Movimiento Sindical Indígena Campesino Guatemalteco*, MSICG). After leaving CNOC in 2008, the CCDA formed another campesino umbrella group, the National Council of Indigenous People and Campesinos (*Consejo Nacional de Indígenas y Campesinos*, CNAIC),[14] and organized national protests and meetings under the CNAIC name rather than as the CCDA. When working in rural communities, however, the group always presents itself as the CCDA. Those communities that have been involved in the *Café Justicia* project have benefitted from their interaction with the CCDA, as outlined above, and other, non-coffee producing communities have sporadically benefitted from infrastructure improvements or technical training provided by the CCDA and funded by a combination of international support and proceeds from the coffee project.

On the other hand, the CCDA has had inconsistent and often poor relations with many other rural communities, those that are supposedly allied with the organization but are not integrated into the coffee project. In 2009 the CCDA counted 122 communities in eleven departments as having organized with them (CCDA 2009b).[15] But the CCDA lacks the practice of constant interaction with rural communities that we saw with CONIC in the previous chapter. While those communities that are active at any stage of the coffee project engage regularly with CCDA activists, others – including groups that had worked with the CCDA to access land as well as others that had joined under other circumstances – see little of the campesino organization or have lost contact with it altogether. For example, in one community that I visited when searching for case study communities, a CCDA organizer had to update the community on the work of the CCDA and remind them of their relationship when introducing me (field notes, June 2009). The

CCDA recognizes this shortcoming, as evidenced by efforts to revitalize community relations and by statements made in interviews, such as one with Leocadio Juracán, who suggested, "We have to recognize that we have had a weakness, let's say, in accompanying communities," and "There are communities that tell us that the CCDA has abandoned them" (interview 2009).[16]

We saw that CONIC's strong and active relationships with allied rural communities led to the constant formation of new local and national activists taking leadership roles within the organization. This is another major CCDA shortcoming: a lack of turnover in leadership, partly stemming from weak ties to the communities. The tireless dedication of these core activists to the CCDA and the campesinos they represent has been overwhelmingly apparent over the fifteen years that I have known the CCDA leadership. But it should also be noted that, over those years, the same group of fewer than ten CCDA leaders have rotated positions, alongside some other people as well, within the elected CCDA National Coordination Council (*Junta Coordinadora Nacional*). This also results in the top-heavy concentration of power among a few CCDA activists, despite their best intentions to distribute decision-making to their base communities through regional gatherings and national assemblies.

The CCDA leadership recognizes these shortcomings, however, and steps have been taken to address them after my fieldwork. Importantly, a plan was implemented to reactivate relationships with rural communities and to integrate them into a political and socio-economic structure labelled the New Model for Campesino Organization (*Nuevo Modelo de Organización Campesina*). Beginning in 2009, the CCDA carried out a series of community visits and regional consultations re-establish direct contact with each of the 122 communities listed as CCDA supporters (interview, Juracán 2009; field notes, 4–7 January 2010). Over the following six years, the attempt to renew relationships with communities was impressive. One indication can be seen in a national march organized by the CCDA and the CUC in March 2012 to bring campesino demands to Guatemala's new far-right president Otto Pérez Molina.[17] The march saw thousands of campesinos – drawing heavily from CCDA communities, according to CCDA President Lesbia Morales and evident in photos of the event – walk the 217 kilometres from Alta Verapaz to the national palace in Guatemala City. Not only did the march avoid state repression, but its leaders gained an audience with the president in negotiation of the campesinos' demands (Batres 2012; Gobierno de

Guatemala 2012; Marcha Indígena Campesina y Popular 2012). The march, in turn, connected the CCDA to many new rural communities, especially in Alta Verapaz, and contributed to a wave of new community leaders, many of them young people, who have recently become active in the CCDA.[18]

The 2012 campesino march is just one example among many in a new wave of CCDA activism. In fact, the changes are so great that I have come to think of the period since 2010 as a third phase in the CCDA's organizational history. The first phase began with the founding of the organization in 1982 and saw the CCDA organizing on behalf of Indigenous and campesino rights while maintaining strong ties to guerrillas. With the CCDA accompanying its first two communities for land access in 1999, a second phase saw redefinition of the group's work around coffee production for direct trade export and implementation of the promises contained in the peace accords. I watched the CCDA survive an onslaught of threats and attacks between 2008 and 2010 – including an attempt on Leocadio Juracán's life in 2008 and paramilitary-backed threats to Juracán and his family in 2010 – only to return to the national political scene more openly and belligerently. The group had begun to agitate more heavily in conjunction with the Comprehensive Rural Development Law in 2008, but when Juracán returned from exile after the 2010 threats, the CCDA ceased to carry out actions behind the banner of umbrella organizations.

By 2015 the CCDA had carried out nationwide protest campaigns, opened regional offices in three more departments, and navigated a wave of popular support to have Leocadio Juracán elected to the Guatemalan Congress. The renewed and open activism of the CCDA since 2012, alongside a coffee project that has grown and become more organized through the Highlands Campesino Services, Inc., all underline the new phase in the organization's history.

The CCDA as a campesino organization is active in a number of spheres, from community agriculture and development projects, through land access and national political activism, to an ever-expanding international direct trade coffee project. Their role in and position on neoliberal agrarian institutions is perhaps more complicated than that of CONIC, since the CCDA has heavily criticized the *Fondo de Tierras* while simultaneously using the institution for community land access and continuing to advocate for the full implementation of the Socioeconomic Accord. Below, we explore two communities that accessed land through the CCDA. Both are instances of purchases through *Fondo de Tierras* loans, but the outcome of the two groups has been dramatically divergent. In exploring these communities and their relationships with the CCDA as well as with state institutions, we consider the same questions that guided our discussion of CONIC communities: How involved are these communities in the CCDA as a movement? Do they mirror the CCDA vision of socio-economic change? And have they experienced the same difficulties of navigating Guatemala's neoliberal agrarian terrain evident in other instances of campesino organizing?

Salvador Xolhuitz: A Divided Community

Illustration 5.1. Eighty-three-year-old Don Bonifacio dries coffee from his trees in Salvador Xolhuitz

The story of Salvador Xolhuitz[19] is a tragic one, an example of what can go wrong following communal land access. It is a story of internal division, violent conflict, and the ineffective support of state institutions and campesino organizations alike. The community showed initial potential: eighty-nine campesino families, including former *mozos colonos*, took out a *Fondo de Tierras* loan to purchase the very coffee plantation that those former *mozo* residents had worked for decades. The farm had already established infrastructure, including roads, houses, and coffee-processing machinery; and the land itself promised to provide, with rich soil, existing coffee and macadamia trees, and abundant water sources and forests. That potential soured early on, however, after extrajudicial negotiation and lack of cohesion among community members. Three years after taking ownership of the land, the community of Salvador Xolhuitz had split in two, and violence and accusations of corruption flew in both directions. As I conducted fieldwork in late 2009, the conflict reached one of its intermittent eruptions and the threat of further violence kept me from completing my research: the two sides of the conflict were arming themselves in response to a shooting and an attempted lynching.

Before deciding to stop visiting Salvador Xolhuitz in January 2010 I had been to the community four times and had interviewed eleven community members about their lives on the farm, as well as recording testimony about the conflict by members of the *junta directiva* of one group. In the months that followed I spoke with leaders from campesino organizations representing both sides of the conflict and with *Fondo de Tierras* staff familiar with the case. I was also given full access by the *Fondo de Tierras* to their documents on the Salvador Xolhuitz sale and subsequent conflict. However, despite wading through well over 100 pages of documents produced by both sides of the conflict, and having spoken with people on both sides,[20] I recognize that I cannot possibly understand this conflict in its entirety from the outside. Instead, what follows is an account of the Salvador Xolhuitz situation that attempts to present both versions of the conflict while focusing on an assessment of what the community and its problems can tell us about the *Fondo de Tierras* market-led agrarian reform program.

The early events of the story are not contested. Between 2000 and 2004 a group of campesinos formed to access land through the *Fondo de Tierras*. The group's internal composition changed, and they eventually bought the coffee plantation that became the community of Salvador Xolhuitz. The group formed in the municipality of Santa Cruz Muluá,

Retalhuleu, to purchase land through the *Fondo de Tierras*, and it called itself the Santa Cruz Land Committee (*Comité Pro-Tierras Santa Cruz*) before changing its name to the Santa Cruz Association for Comprehensive Development (*Asociación de Desarrollo Integral Santa Cruz*, ADISC). After being declined for two *finca* purchases in 2001 and 2002, ADISC came across the Finca Salvador Xolhuitz in Nuevo San Carlos, Retalhuleu, in late 2003. At this point the group had grown from its original twenty-three member families to forty, and had the support of the Kab'awil campesino organization as well as the CCDA's, both through the coordination of the CNOC campesino umbrella group.[21] In order to satisfy FONTIERRAS requirements on land extension per capita, ADISC had to increase its numbers to eighty-nine families before they were allowed to purchase the farm.[22] This was accomplished by first including the twenty-six *mozo colono* resident-worker families living on Salvador Xolhuitz, and then by Kab'awil bringing in a third group of campesinos to round out the numbers. In February 2004 the eighty-nine families that now made up ADISC purchased the Finca Salvador Xolhuitz through a *Fondo de Tierras* loan of just over Q4 million ($500,000) (ACROX 2008; ADISC 2006).

The coffee farm was in bad shape, but improvement was within reach. The 184 hectares (four *caballerías* and four *manzanas*) that make up Salvador Xolhuitz are mostly covered with coffee trees but also have groves of macadamia nut trees, a large patch of forest taking up 30 per cent of the farm, and a small area dedicated to subsistence crops grown by the *mozos colonos* (see illustration 5.2). In addition, the farm had a large plantation house, shacks occupied by the resident workers, a church, a warehouse, an office, and a coffee processing plant, including German-made drying equipment (see illustrations 5.3–5.5). The coffee trees, which require constant care during the year, had been neglected since low international prices had led the plantation owner to abandon the crop. In addition to being poorly maintained, many of the trees were nearing the end of their productive lives. Nevertheless, campesinos from Salvador Xolhuitz report that the soil conditions are good and that the farm could easily become very productive with a few seasons of care (field notes, 24 June 2009; Fondo de Tierras 2004).

Unfortunately, however, the community of Salvador Xolhuitz was not able to get their productive projects going as the result of an internal conflict that began to consume the group's energy. The two sides explain the origins of the conflict differently, but both begin with additional negotiations with the plantation owner outside of the official

Illustration 5.2. Map of Salvador Xolhuitz, municipality of Nuevo San Carlos, department of Retalhuleu.

This map, drawn by Salvador Xolhuitz community member Herlindo, is a survey of the land after the group moved to their new land. Sections of the farm dedicated to macadamia nut trees, coffee trees by variety, bananas, corn, and community housing are indicated by colour-coding in the original. The eastern edge of the property is marked by a river that runs the length of the border.

Fondo de Tierras process. The representative of the farm who negotiated its sale brought two extra items to negotiate with the campesino group: an unregistered piece of land that he considered to form part of the farm, and back payment owed to the *mozos colonos*.[23] In addition to the amount agreed upon through the *Fondo de Tierras*, the representative wanted Q500,000 for the additional fifty-two *manzanas* (12.4 hectares), and he insisted that the group pay the *prestaciones laborales* that were owed to the twenty former resident workers for their years of service. The workers were owed either Q352,178, according to the original ADISC group, or Q500,000 according to the small group that would later break away under the name Rosario Xolhuitz Campesino

Illustration 5.3. Harvesting coffee from an old tree

Association (*Asociación Campesina Rosario Xolhuitz*, ACROX) (ACROX 2008; ADISC 2006).

Marcelo Sabuc of the CCDA, and current representatives of ADISC – which remained the name of the larger of the groups when the community split into two – say that the representative would not sell the farm if those two demands were not satisfied (interview, Marcelo Sabuc, Aldea Quixayá, Sololá, 14 October 2009; ADISC 2006). Herlindo, a former *mozo colono* member of Salvador Xolhuitz, claims that the seller forced the workers to sign a document stating that they had been paid when in fact they had not. The community of resident workers didn't know better back then, Herlindo told me as we walked through the coffee trees one afternoon, and if they were organized and aware of their rights as they are today, they would have stood up to the landowner (field notes, 17 July 2009). Nevertheless, the ADISC *junta directiva* leaders agreed

Illustration 5.4. *The community turned the* casa patronal, *or plantation house, into a day care.*

to the terms, and the group paid the landowner his half-million *quet-zales* out of the initial FONTIERRAS "work funds" subsidy (*capital de trabajo*).

From this initial deal struck outside of *Fondo de Tierras* negotia-tions, differing positions on the use of community funds quickly sped towards conflict. The group of sixteen families that would eventually break away from ADISC – referred to in the documentation as Group 2, and occasionally as ACROX – point out that the ADISC leadership agreed to pay for the extra fifty-two *manzanas* without consulting the group assembly, who found they were in debt for an extra half mil-lion *quetzales* only after the deal had been struck (interview, Pérez Mejía 2010). Starting with that point, members of the small group allege mis-use of communal funds. They point out that the purchase of the extra land was illegal and claim that other funds were mismanaged by the

Illustration 5.5. *Drying coffee beans by hand at the Salvador Xolhuitz* beneficio *(processing plant).*

ADISC leadership. An audit of the community's finances was conducted by the *Fondo de Tierras* at the request of ACROX (FONTIERRAS audit AI-29-2006), and "various thousands of quetzales" were found to be missing, according to an ACROX statement.

People in ADISC, on the other hand, highlight other financial problems during the same period. According to their version, the back payment owed to the *mozos colonos* was supposed to be paid from the proceeds of the first year of coffee and macadamia harvests. Indeed, they say the landowner sped up the sale so that the community would take possession of the farm before the harvests began, in order to use the sales to cover the costs that he insisted on. However, ADISC members claim that two men from the small group took hold of the macadamia nut harvest, sold it, and refused to pay either the debt to the *mozos* or wages to community members for picking the harvest (ADISC 2006; PDH 2007).

With the seeds of conflict sown by way of financial disagreement, the community split in two. Twenty-six families broke away from ADISC and formed the smaller ACROX group in 2006 – although ten would soon return to the big group, leaving 16 in the small one. Members of ADISC claim that two men from one family have been responsible for much of the violence they have faced in the years that followed the split.[24] And there have indeed been many instances. A package prepared by ADISC and delivered to the *Fondo de Tierras* in 2009 collects documentation from state institutions, including the national police, the public ministry, and the human rights ombudsman, detailing 15 counts of aggression between 2006 and 2008. Among these are multiple death threats, attempted kidnapping, and intimidation using guns and machetes (ADISC 2006, 2009; PNC 2007).

At the same time, in the words of Eliseo Pérez Mejía, a campesino leader with the Kab'awil organization representing the small group, "The people in the big group aren't little angels, either" (interview 2010). Since the community split, the big group has been accused of their own share of aggression. Previous to the clashes of late 2009 the most severe accusation – documented in the minutes of a meeting between representatives of the small breakaway group and government agencies – holds that armed members and supporters of the ADISC *junta directiva* accosted a leader of the small group in his coffee plot, stealing his entire harvest while firing their guns. On two other occasions in July 2008, members of ADISC are alleged to have attempted to forcefully evict the members of the small group from their homes (URNG 2008).

Many confrontations since 2006 arise from divergent interpretations of who belongs to the Salvador Xolhuitz community. Members of the big group do not consider those in the small group to be *asociados*, or legal members of the association, while those in the small group still consider themselves partners in the FONTIERRAS-purchased land. To make matters worse, both sides have been backed by different people within the *Fondo de Tierras*. In 2006 the large ADISC group voted in its member assembly to expel the sixteen families of the small group from the association "for their negative, belligerent, and destructive attitude … [and] for being responsible for the crisis in which we currently live and which does not allow us to develop as a campesino movement" (ADISC 2006). ADISC cites their notarized internal statues as allowing for the change in membership: "Article 36. Loss of membership as an associate. Active membership as an associate is lost … b) By expulsion" (ADISC 2009). The *Fondo de Tierras* supported the expulsion and revised their list of Salvador Xolhuitz associates accordingly. The small group doesn't recognize the legal grounds of expulsion, however. They instead request that the farm and its debt be divided proportionally according to the membership of the two groups. This proposal has also found support within FONTIERRAS, and the plan to divide the land has received attention in conflict negotiation meetings. Attempts to resolve the conflict have fallen flat, since both sides feel that theirs is the legitimate position before the law (Fondo de Tierras 2008; PDH 2007).

In the final days of 2009, the Salvador Xolhuitz conflict reached a new extreme. Earlier the large ADISC group had installed a chain across the only access point to the community and farm (see illustration 5.6). When I visited throughout 2009, ADISC members watched the chain in shifts and decided which vehicles could come and go. The barrier was installed, they insisted, to stop the removal of community resources

Illustration 5.6. Entrance to Salvador Xolhuitz. When I visited in 2009, members of the ADISC group controlled access to the community and farm with a metal chain hung between two concrete posts, taking shifts to guard the entrance.

by ACROX. Since 2007, members of the small group had been cutting down trees and selling the wood, which ADISC reported as theft. ACROX responded that the chain amounted to harassment aimed to chase them off the farm (ACROX 2008; INAB 2007). On 29 December 2009 the local justice of the peace for the municipality of Nuevo San Carlos ruled that the chain must be removed. He also indicated in his decision that the sixteen families of the small group must still be considered members of the community and co-owners of the farm.

According to members of ADISC, the small group cut the chain and removed the concrete posts the same day. Disregarding the ruling, ADISC set out to rebuild their checkpoint on 30 December and were stopped violently when an ADISC member, Ananias, was shot in the leg while bringing sand to the site. In response, the large ADISC group gathered firearms and set out to forcefully evict the remaining members of the small group in an action described as an attempted lynching (interview, ADISC Junta Directiva, Salvador Xolhuitz, 13 January 2010; field notes, 4 and 13 January 2010; Creelman 2010).

The conflict was calmed temporarily through the intervention of the campesino organizations representing the two sides of the conflict, as well as by the police, who stationed a patrol truck on the farm around the clock for a few days.[25] If various agencies have been able to calm particular events, however, their efforts have failed to resolve any aspect of the conflict itself. On the contrary, and despite best intentions, the manner in which the *Fondo de Tierras* in particular has intervened in Salvador Xolhuitz has been counterproductive. With both sides of the conflict finding FONTIERRAS support for their position – ADISC had its expulsion of the small group recognized, while FONTIERRAS officials have also backed the ACROX request to divide the farm – these mixed signals have only reinforced the determination of each side to not back down.

But the *Fondo de Tierras* bears more responsibility for the Salvador Xolhuitz conflict than just their negative participation in negotiations: the institution is partially responsible for the two root causes of the conflict. First, the *Fondo de Tierras* should not have allowed additional negotiation to occur outside of the official process. Evidence suggests that, when the purchase of an extra fifty-four hectares of land and the settlement of *mozo colono* wages was tied to the Salvador Xolhuitz sale, the *Fondo de Tierras* technician working with the group was aware of at least the extra land sale (Fondo de Tierras 2008). According to both groups of Salvador Xolhuitz community members, those additional negotiations generated the initial disputes that led to their conflict. And once those differences had been established, a lack of internal cohesion allowed the community to fracture in two more easily. This is the second area of FONTIERRAS responsibility for the conflict, given the institution's prioritization of meeting set numbers of families per hectare of distributed land, instead of considering the internal dynamics of that group. The group that bought Salvador Xolhuitz was patched together from at least three previous communities: the original members of the *Comité Pro Tierras* from Santa Cruz Muluá, the former resident workers living on the plantation, and a selection of campesinos brought in by Kab'awil shortly before the deal was finalized.[26] Despite this heterogeneous blend, a *Fondo de Tierras* socio-economic study of the community conducted prior to the land sale labelled the group's "internal solidarity" as good (Fondo de Tierras 2004, 3). Bringing groups together to form a new community will not necessarily generate conflict – the case of San José La Pasión discussed in chapter 4 demonstrates that strong internal cohesion can be formed. If that unity has not been solidified and a dispute arises, however, the early stages of conflict can take place along previously existing community divisions.[27]

Another regrettable aspect of the Salvador Xolhuitz conflict lies in the oppositional participation of the campesino organizations representing the two groups. The CCDA continues to work with the large ADISC group, as they did during the *Fondo de Tierras* land purchase. After breaking off from ADISC, the smaller group strengthened their ties with the Kab'awil campesino organization that had brought them to Salvador Xolhuitz. While the CCDA and Kab'awil have worked together for years, having both been members of the CNOC campesino umbrella organization until 2008, the two groups also suffer from disputes of their own. As discussed in chapter 2, Guatemalan campesino organizations in the post-war period have often been divided by internal struggles over movement leadership and former guerrilla affiliation. In the case of the CCDA and Kab'awil, their previous respective ties to the FAR and ORPA guerrilla fronts position the two within a history of competition and non-cooperation. Of course, the distinct origins of CCDA and Kab'awil do not determine the actions of their representatives. But those origins have contributed to how the conflict has been dealt with. The two organizations each have allies within the *Fondo de Tierras* – the CCDA has Gilberto Atz, the campesino sector representative in the *Fondo de Tierras* Board of Directors, and Kab'awil works closely with Bonifacio Martín, the Indigenous sector representative –

which may explain the contradictory responses from FONTIERRAS to the two Salvador Xolhuitz groups. What is clear is that the two sparring community groups have received separate advice for advancing their positions, rather than having been brought together for dialogue and resolution.

After my research with Salvador Xolhuitz ended in early 2010, the conflict went through stages where sustained calm was broken by periodic violence, including the murder of one member of ADISC in October 2010. When I returned to visit the CCDA in 2015, I encountered the good news that an agreement had been made to end the conflict: the secretary for agrarian affairs had promised to purchase a piece of land on which to resettle the smaller ACROX group, leaving the majority ADISC as owners of Salvador Xolhuitz.[28] The conflict had drawn out much longer than it should have, partly influenced by outside actors. Three separate groups were brought together and forced to form a single community; an illegal negotiation was ignored by the *Fondo de Tierras*; and when financial differences turned into a serious dispute, the people of Salvador Xolhuitz were failed equally by the *Fondo de Tierras* and the campesino organizations representing them. The members of Salvador Xolhuitz I spoke with in 2009 remained hopeful about the future, and all of the people interviewed were actively working towards improving the coffee plots that had been neglected prior to the community purchase.[29] But their efforts have been held back significantly by the conflict that hangs over them. The case of Salvador Xolhuitz shows us once again how the act of attaining communal land ownership is only the first stage in the campesino struggle for community development and autonomy.

Don Pancho: "We're Used to Giving It Our All"[30]

Of the four community case studies visited for this project, Don Pancho is the most successful in strictly economic terms. Diversification of crops grown in good soil and on a variety of land types across the farm has allowed families in Don Pancho to count on a steady income throughout the year. Don Pancho is also the only one of the four communities that relies heavily on remittances sent from community members working in the United States, a factor that contributed substantially to the repayment of their *Fondo de Tierras* debt four years ahead of schedule. Those outside sources of income, however, do not fully explain this

Illustration 5.7. Don Efraín, a member of Don Pancho's governing council, tends to corn and coffee in his forest plot. His T-shirt, printed by the CCDA, reads, "If there isn't coffee for everyone, there won't be any for anyone."

highly productive and cohesive community, and Don Pancho stands out as a model of group unity and the innovative agricultural work that can allow newly landed communities to thrive. The group also has strong ties to the CCDA and a good relationship with the *Fondo de Tierras*, but the account that follows shows that these have been of secondary importance in comparison with the internal dynamics of the community itself.

I came to Don Pancho only in the final days of my 2010 fieldwork. Leocadio Juracán of the CCDA had mentioned the community as a good case study from our earliest meeting in 2009, but when a first visit to Don Pancho was prevented by scheduling obstacles I settled on Salvador Xolhuitz instead. When the conflict in Salvador Xolhuitz worsened and my research there was cut short, I looked back to Don Pancho as a last-minute addition to strengthen my case study with the CCDA. At the CCDA National Assembly held at the organization's Cerro de Oro coffee processing plant on 2 March 2010, in the wake of Leocadio's death threats and exile to Canada, I met with a group from Don Pancho. They were enthusiastic about the project and welcomed me to stay in the community shortly thereafter, and a plan was made for a week-long stay in three weeks' time. While I took only one five-day trip to Don Pancho, my time there was rich in experience. Three families in particular looked after me, and I managed to integrate into the community better in those few days than I had with the other three groups. In addition to the standard farm tour and door-to-door interviews, which I was left to conduct alone, I spent a day helping to repair a water collection tank and spent evenings with a number of families. I felt a strong bond with the community after those five days. My account of Don Pancho lacks the long-term observation across growing seasons present in the other case studies, but I nevertheless became close to the group and was able to grasp a sense of their community dynamics. The information presented here is based on my observations and interviews and is complemented by a community history written by the group in 2008.

Don Pancho is located in the southern piedmont department of Escuintla, a lush and sparsely populated region traditionally dominated by large sugar cane and coffee plantations. The 177-hectare property is easily accessible by a major unpaved road and has an abundance of quality land, fresh water, and forest. All of this is in contrast to the living conditions that the Maya Kaqchikel residents of Don Pancho endured before their purchase. Community members recounted in interviews how a shortage of basic resources drove them to undergo the search for land and ultimately leave their homes in San Martín Jilotepeque, Chimaltenango. "Back in San Martín we don't have land, there's nowhere to plant. We want to plant but there isn't anywhere, we're poor. There's no money to buy land and the land is very expensive. That is why we came here because there is no firewood, there is no water, the water runs out for drinking and for washing" (interview, Candelaria, 30 March 2010).

Don Efraín, the current treasurer for Don Pancho's *junta directiva*, the Junan Kusamuj Association (*Asociación Junan Kusamuj*), also points to a lack of jobs in the highlands. "We spent a lot of time in crisis there because there are no resources. There's no water, there's no land, there are no jobs. There are jobs, but I had to go to the *fincas* to work, to earn enough to sustain my family and my wife from day to day … I could only do that renting land on the *fincas*, on the coast" (interview, 31 March 2010).

A *Fondo de Tierras* socio-economic survey conducted before the Don Pancho land sale showed that just 68 per cent of the fifty-five families owned some agricultural land in San Martín Jilotepeque, and in every case that land made up less than half a *manzana*, or just under one acre (Fondo de Tierras 2002). Plantation work and rented land on the coast – which was paid for through sharecropping arrangements with landowners – provided some income, but water and firewood were always hard to come by.

Facing these shortages, people from the village of Estancia La Virgen in San Martín Jilotepeque came together to form a land committee. The search for land was initiated in 1997 by two men, and their efforts were originally concentrated within their home municipality. Land prices in San Martín were high, and the original plan to purchase a large property in the area that had previously been rented to campesinos proved unattainable. Over the following six years the group considered four more *fincas*, in 1997, 1999, 2002, and 2003. The second *finca*, after the original rental property, had no access to water and the quality of the soil was poor; the third, in the department of Guatemala, fell through because of difficult negotiations with the landowner; the fourth, which was the first farm the group looked at within the *Fondo de Tierras* system, had poor land and poor access; and on their fifth attempt the group purchased Don Pancho. By that time the group membership had turned over a few times, as families left in frustration after each failed attempt to acquire a new home (interviews, 30 and 31 March 2010; Asociación Junan Kusamuj 2008).

Much of the groundwork for a successful community was being laid even while the group searched for land. The membership may have been in flux due to difficult conditions, but the remaining members insisted on maintaining a close community of neighbours. Each new family was invited to the group by a member who knew them, and the emphasis was on acquiring hardworking and sober people. "'Take a look at the person,'" one man recalls instructing. "'Check that he is hard working, that if he comes with us he is going to listen. We don't want a person who is always drinking and drinking' … Every member brought someone, invited someone else, someone else, that's how we called them over. But we're all from the same village. We're not strangers, we all know each other" (interview, anonymous, 30 March 2010).

With the association holding onto a core group of neighbours from Estancia La Virgen and other nearby villages in San Martín Jilotepeque, the members also shared priorities when looking for land. Above all, the group insisted on locating a farm with fresh water sources, or "that vital liquid" as they describe water in their written community history (Asociación Junan Kusamuj 2008). They were also careful to buy land with good soil, and at least two prospective farms were turned down by the group for lacking water or having land of poor quality. These three elements – strong community cohesion, abundant fresh water, and land of good quality– were carefully monitored by the association, and we will see below that they turned out to be the deciding factors in the community's success.

The written community history describes the first contact with CCDA organizers as a turning point in the search for land (Asociación Junan Kusamuj 2008). With support and training from the CCDA, and a connection with the *Fondo de Tierras* in the form of CCDA ally and *Fondo de Tierras* board member Gilberto Atz, the Junan Kusamuj Association quickly advanced towards the Don Pancho purchase.[31] The association brought their numbers up to fifty-five families from just twelve, in order to meet FONTIERRAS requirements, and they were able to inspect potential land from the list of plantations offered through the institution. They also applied pressure tactics to push their application through the FONTIERRAS process once they had selected the Finca Don Pancho: the group staged a road blockade at Los Encuentros, protested in front of the *Fondo de Tierras* headquarters in Guatemala City, and occupied the plaza in front of the National Palace a number of times (Asociación Junan Kusamuj 2008). After joining forces with Atz and the CCDA in 2002, the Junan Kusamuj Association bought the Finca Don Pancho for Q2.86 million ($357,000) in 2003 and began moving to their new community on 20 October 2003.

Excitement about the purchase was short lived, and the first months and years on Don Pancho were extremely difficult. There was no housing on the farm and the families had to live in makeshift shacks. They were also surprised by two unexpected natural calamities: strong winds that blew down from the mountains and regularly destroyed their corn crops, and new lowland illnesses affecting their children, such as dehy-dration and intestinal parasites (Asociación Junan Kusamuj 2008). The first years were full of hard work, necessary in order to revive the aban-doned coffee plantation and establish the infrastructure for community life. As Maria Asución tells it, "We came here six years ago. When we came down here, it was all overgrown. You couldn't see the little road when we came down. And we made shacks out of plastic, that's what we were in. We lived a bit of a hard life. Thanks to God, little by little, step by step, we had our committee, they managed things, everything we have now – electricity, the roads, the houses … The *finca* looks very improved now, with help from God and our own hard work, and now here we are" (interview, 30 March 2010).

The improvements that Doña Maria mentions were managed through a communal labour system that may have been possible only as the result of the strong cohesion of the group. Labour for com-munity projects in Don Pancho is organized according to sets of 300 workdays. Each person in the community chooses when to participate in communal work, and anyone who reaches 300 days of labour is exempt from participation until everyone else has reached that same limit. As more people max out, those remaining are required to put in more frequent workdays. The count is reset once all have done their share (field notes, 30 March 2010). This system seems to have been implemented after some time on the land, however, and during at least the first year the communal work was more intensive. Every-one worked for no pay during the first two months after arriving on the farm, clearing overgrown areas and building temporary hous-ing. After that, the community worked together for a year and paid themselves a rate of Q40 per person per day. During that year, the group installed infrastructure for drinking water, distributed irriga-tion across the farm, fixed the roads, and built houses for all families (Asociación Junan Kusamuj 2008).

Farming was also organized according to a communal system dur-ing the first two years and included a cattle ranching project started through the *Fondo de Tierras* subsidy. After a change in elected com-munity leadership in 2005, however, the group decided to switch to individual farming plots, a move that interview respondents support strongly. The division of land orchestrated after two years of commu-nal farming again points to Don Pancho as a united and egalitarian community. Instead of asking for the technical assistance available from *Fondo de Tierras* engineers, community members measured and distributed plots on the basis of their own knowledge of the land. Six plots were given to each family, ensuring that each recipient had land in all areas of the geographically diverse farm. The plots were also drawn in non-uniform patterns, working their way around resources and land types so as to share those equally.[32] A lottery system was then held to distribute a set of six plots to each family. Tellingly, no conflicts over land distribution are mentioned in the community history or in any of my nineteen household interviews (Asociación Junan Kusamuj 2008).

The work schedule and land use mentioned were determined through a leadership and decision-making structure similar to that introduced in the other CCDA and CONIC case studies. Decisions in Don Pancho are made at community assemblies, and all accounts of the community point to high levels of participation by both men and women. The community leadership, elected by the assembly, falls under two councils, or *juntas directivas*. There is the *junta directiva* of the community association, and another *junta* for the Community Development Council (COCODE). The president of the association acts as the community's legal representative, and the president of the COCODE doubles as auxiliary mayor (*alcalde auxiliar*). According to my discussions with community members, community problem-solving tends to be taken care of within the COCODE, since the auxiliary mayor is embedded within that council, and oversight of communal labour and agricultural projects is conducted by the association council. Within the two councils there are just two committees, one for the school and another for security, with men from the community patrolling in shifts between 9:00 p.m. and 4:00 a.m. every night (field notes, 29 March 2010).

Of the two core elements of the CCDA land access strategy – accompanying communities to ensure good land and advising groups to use their FONTIERRAS subsidy to pay off their debt – Don Pancho declined to follow the latter. Rather than apply the subsidy against their debt, the Don Pancho community association invested the money in infrastructure improvement and economic projects. The community installed drinking water and an irrigation system; built a communal hall, community store, and shared corn mill; bought a tractor and sixty head of cattle; and paid for a period of salaries for communal work (field notes, 30 March 2010). Some of the money did make its way back to the debt, however: when the group switched from communal to

Illustration 5.8. *House provided under the FONTIERRAS "basic roof" program*   Illustration 5.9. *A FOGUAVI house*

individual farming, they sold the cattle and applied the full amount to their debt, which worked out to Q8,000 paid of the approximately Q59,000 owed by each family.

Outside institutions have also arranged for other projects in Don Pancho. The local congressional representative secured electricity for the community, the Ministry of Agriculture brought 100 orange trees for each Don Pancho family, the National Peace Fund (*Fondo Nacional para la Paz*, FONAPAZ) paid for construction materials for a school, and a waterwheel for irrigation was donated by a Rotary Club. Housing in Don Pancho came in waves of donations as well. After living in temporary shacks for the first two years, the *Fondo de Tierras* paid for basic houses made of tin siding under their *"techo mínimo"* (basic roofs) program for loan recipients. Following that, the Guatemalan Housing Fund (*Fondo Guatemalteco para la Vivienda*, FOGUAVI) state agency built sturdy concrete homes for some families in the community (see illustrations 5.8 and 5.9). The CCDA has also begun building houses in Don Pancho, with materials for the first four homes arriving while I was in the community. In addition, there are four large multistorey modern houses built by community members, presumably using funds sent home by family members working in the United States (field notes, 30 March 2010).

Of all the development projects and natural endowments at Don Pancho, community members expressed most pride in the abundance of fresh water. Using some of the twenty-two natural springs on the farm, the community has constructed a complicated system that brings water to all homes, to one area of the farm for irrigation, and to the cattle area on the side of the farm that is opposite the settlement. This is executed in part thanks to the natural slope of the property, which runs downhill from north to south. There was already a main water collection tank when the group bought the farm, and they installed pipes to run gravity-fed water downhill from the tank to their homes. At another collection tank, a waterwheel donated by the Rotary Club pushes water out to an irrigation system and uphill to a third tank in the cattle area. The irrigation system services an area where each family has a half-*manzana* plot. Since the pipes to the irrigated area were laid through the forest, some people have also tapped the pipes and run smaller hoses to irrigate their forest plots (see illustrations 5.10–5.11).

Each family in Don Pancho has six plots of land (see illustration 5.14). In addition to its housing lot, a family has plots in the four different terrain types across the farm: a quarter *manzana* in the irrigated area (*riego*), three *manzanas* in the former cattle field (*potrero*), half a *manzana* in the forest (*bosque*), and two plots of half a *manzana* each among the coffee trees (*cafetal*).[33] Across those four areas the campesinos have access to a number of growing conditions: open field in the cattle area, shaded jungle in the forest, coffee plots, and patches with constant irrigation. The forested area varies from plot to plot,

Illustration 5.10. *Waterwheel pumping water up to the cattle field*

Illustration 5.11. *Pipes carrying water through the forest for irrigation*

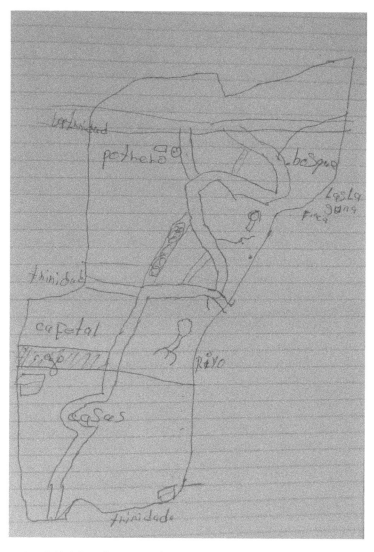

Illustration 5.12. Map of Don Pancho, Municipality of Escuintla, Department of Escuintla.
*This map was drawn from memory by a member of the community association of Don Pancho. The housing area is marked as the southern third of the property (*casas*), the area of irrigated plots is coloured dark and marked* riego, *the section filled with coffee trees is marked immediately north of that (*cafetal*), trees are drawn along the eastern side of the farm for the forest (*bosque*), and the open cattle grazing area is marked* potrero *in the northern half of the farm.*

depending on how many trees have been cut, with some families clearing the area and others farming under the original canopy (see illustrations 5.14–5.16).

Most families grow corn in the cattle field, but strong winds blow down from the mountain above and often ruin the crops there. Corn is also grown in the forest and irrigated area, but the agricultural focus lies less on basic grains and more on cash crops as well as fruit, vegetables, and herbs for household consumption.[34] Walking across Don Pancho for a few days I noticed an exceptional variety of crops: corn, beans, chillies, coffee, peanuts, green beans, oranges, mandarins, bananas, plantains, pineapples, lemons, limes, sugar cane, cardamom, cilantro, and the many greens referred to as *yierbitas*, pacaya, and chipilín.[35] Pacaya and chipilín are popular in Don Pancho as cash crops that earn decent rates in the market, with chipilín producing

Illustration 5.13. A chipilín patch, with firewood stacked in the upper left-hand corner. This plot produces chipilín worth Q100–200 every six weeks.

Illustration 5.14. Corn, coffee, and pacaya grown in the forest

year-round. Peanuts, green beans, and chillies all serve for selling in the market as well. But Don Pancho's residents have placed a lot of hope in their coffee. The farm produced 80,000–90,000 pounds of coffee cherries in 2009, and most families are still planting and tending to young trees to replace the older ones they inherited. People told me that their coffee harvests had been an important factor in paying back the *Fondo de Tierras* loan, and they looked forward to the coming harvests when the cash would be theirs to keep (field notes, 27–31 March 2010).

The community of Don Pancho is doing quite well in economic terms. The men report that they don't work on plantations anymore, or even away from the community in other jobs; irrigation, varied plots, and coffee trees make for a steady flow of agricultural income; and food staples are supplied through an emphasis on mixing many crops together in small plots.[36] But a non-agricultural factor has also helped many families in Don Pancho economically, especially in repaying their *Fondo de Tierras* loan by 2011, four years ahead of schedule (Fondo de Tierras 2011). Don Pancho is the only one of the four case study communities where a significant number of people have left to work in the United States. About a quarter of interview participants told me they have family working in the United States and sending money home, and others told me of their plans to leave for the United States soon. This was confirmed in an internal *Fondo de Tierras* letter. The letter, which was included in the file on Don Pancho made available to me by the community, prepares for the transfer of beneficiary status from ten men to their wives, since the men were away working for extended periods. The document details the location of the men in four different states, as well as Mexico; their work, from construction to gardening to a car wash; how long they have been away, ranging from six months to four years; and the amount of money they send home each month, between Q400 and Q2,000 (Fondo de Tierras 2007). Tension may have been created between those receiving remittances and those relying on their agricultural earnings, and some interview respondents expressed embarrassment at lagging behind in their debt repayment. Other people interviewed in the community said they had sold land in their home villages in San Martín Jilotepeque, with one man saying his house sold for Q7,000. Cutting their property ties back home gave people a chance to get ahead on their loan payments, including for those who didn't have family working in the United States. Whether through remittances, land sale, or other work, the residents of Don Pancho made their final payment to the *Fondo de Tierras* in October 2011, a year and a half after my visit to the community.

The prompt repayment and successful agricultural projects of Don Pancho must have kept the community on good terms with the *Fondo de Tierras*. After moving to the farm and making use of the subsidy, however, the group does not appear to have called on FONTIERRAS for assistance. In contrast, Don Pancho has maintained a working relationship with the CCDA. A number of people mentioned the CCDA in interviews and conversations, including Melecio, who was a Don Pancho community representative to CCDA events and who participated in CCDA-led protests, and Don Efraín, who told me that the CCDA has always helped the community with workshops and projects (interview, Melecio, 31 March 2010; field notes, 31 March 2010). Gumersinda summed up the general feeling in Don Pancho: "They've been with us since the beginning. There was a time when we didn't see them much, because the committees then didn't maintain contact with them. But then later we started visiting them again and they visited us ... Now they visit us, and they're helping us with some houses. It's the same as it was before [during the search for land]" (interview, 29 March 2010).

This is a more subtle relationship than seen in either of the CONIC case studies, where local activists maintain regular contact with communities to help guide them through their development plans. But it is perhaps the relationship that the CCDA hopes to have with the communities it has supported. As a community that isn't producing coffee for the CCDA direct trade project,[37] Don Pancho nevertheless stays in regular contact with its allies in the campesino movement. The CCDA helps train the group with agricultural techniques, and they look to Don Pancho when there is money for development projects – such as a day-care centre installed by the CCDA shortly before my visit, and the CCDA homes discussed above (see illustrations 5.15 and 5.16). In return, Don Pancho sends representatives to CCDA events and actions, helping the CCDA to strengthen its relationship with its rural base.

Illustration 5.15. *A day-care centre built by the CCDA*

Illustration 5.16. *Digging the foundation for one of the first CCDA houses*

These strong relationships between Don Pancho and both the CCDA and the *Fondo de Tierras*, when combined with the group's basic infrastructure attained through FONTIERRAS subsidies and their extra income from agriculture and remittances, leads to a sense of security, confidence, and autonomy among community members. Don Pancho also lacks the sense of *proyectismo*, the heavy emphasis on development projects that I felt in the CONIC case study communities.

Don Pancho is praised by both the CCDA and the *Fondo de Tierras*, which featured the group as a "successful project" in its November 2011 institutional bulletin (Fondo de Tierras 2011). Indeed, Don Pancho is exactly the kind of experiment that FONTIERRAS would want associated with its land sales. In place of any corruption, internal conflict, or loan default, Don Pancho appears as a united community whose hard work has led to community development and prompt repayment. However, it would be a mistake to contrast Don Pancho with more difficult FONTIERRAS situations such as Salvador Xolhuitz. Don Pancho was able to get ahead because of its own efforts, which in fact allowed it to avoid the pitfalls that many other communities are confronted with in the land access process. Because the group insisted on maintaining a close network of hardworking neighbours already known to one another, they avoided conflict between factions of a cobbled together new community. Because of their experience with a severe lack of resources in Chimaltenango, and thanks to the support of the CCDA, they held out for a farm with good soil and an abundance of water, both of which explain their agricultural success. And as a result of a trend of emigration to the United States, their loan was paid off more easily through income earned far from the FONTIERRAS farm. Don Pancho can undoubtedly be held up as a best-case scenario for a newly landed community, thanks to the group's hard work, determination, internal unity, and agricultural smarts. But this is not to say that other groups that experienced problems could have been just as successful. In many *Fondo de Tierras* land purchases, the cards are stacked against the beneficiary community. The case of Don Pancho shows us that exceptions are possible, given the right combination of factors.

Conclusion

As we see in the cases of Salvador Xolhuitz and Don Pancho, community experiences with *Fondo de Tierras* land sales vary widely. How is it possible that the community of Don Pancho has had such success with their new land while things have gone so poorly for Salvador Xolhuitz? Clearly the *Fondo de Tierras* is not a neutral party in this question. Established in order to promote a national land market in place of redistributive agrarian reform, FONTIERRAS has never operated with campesino interests in mind. Very little land has been sold through the institution, and many of the farms have been located in undesirable areas or were sold with depleted soil and resources. There has been little support for beneficiary communities in infrastructure or development projects, and the technical advice provided to the communities tends towards the promotion of export agriculture, and those projects often fail. And when problems arise within beneficiary communities, as in Salvador Xolhuitz, FONTIERRAS has no system to resolve them. Yet cases such as Don Pancho exist, in which campesino groups have established relatively comfortable and economically stable lives on land purchased through the *Fondo de Tierras*, and even repaid their loans according to the agency's terms.

The cases of Salvador Xolhuitz and Don Pancho show us that there is room for a community to make what it wants of the *Fondo de Tierras* experience. To follow *Fondo de Tierras* advice on land sales – jumble together a group of people, accept the landlord-arranged offer on the first farm presented, invest heavily in cash crops – may be to court failure. But if a community has enough foresight, patience, experience, and support to resist that approach, it is possible to end up with excellent conditions for resettlement and community development. Don Pancho serves as a best-case scenario of how to survive a *Fondo de Tierras* land purchase. Importantly, however, Don Pancho's success is based first on the group's internal dynamics – an insistence on a strong network of hardworking neighbours and on an abundance of natural resources on the new land – and also on the option to secure finances through international remittances. Sticking to the FONTIERRAS script would not have produced the same results.

The CCDA played something of a role in both the success of Don Pancho and the challenges faced by Salvador Xolhuitz. With Don Pancho, the CCDA helped to select an appropriate farm during the group's search, and the organization has maintained an open and supportive relationship with the community. In the case of Salvador Xolhuitz, while the CCDA has been attempting to resolve the community conflict, historical divisions within the campesino movement have only fuelled the conflict. It must be mentioned, however, that the CCDA approach to land access and community development is much more hands-off than that of CONIC. We saw with CONIC a campesino organization firmly dedicated to constant interaction with rural communities in order to facilitate development and to integrate the rural base into the organization's political project. The CCDA, on the other hand, has different modes of interaction with rural communities. The group is extremely active in political lobbying on behalf of campesinos, but this mainly takes place at the level of the core CCDA leadership. The group is also highly involved with the small number of communities that produce organic coffee for the *Café Justicia* direct trade coffee program. And then there are other rural communities that have some connection to the CCDA. In those cases, the CCDA is content to facilitate access to land and then step back and let the communities work out their own paths. We could even say that rather than attempting to implement a particular vision of alternative development in its allied communities, the CCDA facilitates spaces in which communities can live according to their own traditions. That space has allowed for the successful re-establishment of the Indigenous campesino lifestyle in some cases, but has done little to prevent conflict and hardship in others.

Overall, the CCDA is more willing to navigate the neoliberal terrain than are other campesino organizations such as *Plataforma Agraria* or CONIC. Whereas *Plataforma Agraria* has refused to participate in *Fondo de Tierras* projects since 2003, and CONIC emphasizes agrarian conflicts over land sales, and supports its communities in refusing to repay their FONTIERRAS loans, the CCDA has attempted to make what it can of the existing institutional framework. Given its decades of support for the guerrilla movement and peace negotiations, the CCDA tends to back the products of the peace accords and as such has insisted on taking advantage of the *Fondo de Tierras*.

Its critique of the market-based approach to agrarian reform is strong and genuine, but the CCDA nevertheless works with campesino communities to make the most of the resources available through FONTIERRAS. The *Café Justicia* project denotes a similar approach. Rather than rejecting cash crops and international trade altogether, the CCDA promotes their subversion. Working with campesinos who have been exploited by the coffee industry, they have created a scenario in which workers gain access to previously unattainable coffee land and processing equipment, as well as to international markets that will compensate them more fairly. The CCDA engagement with neoliberalism and capitalism, while less confrontational than an outright rejection, is nonetheless radical. It is an approach that fights tirelessly for structural change through political reform, while harnessing and altering the system to the advantage of campesinos wherever possible.

6 Beyond the Post-Conflict Period

The political history of Guatemala, at all times a heart-wrenching combination of tragedy and hope (Lovell 1995), has continued along its tumultuous path since the official end of war in 1996. The years since the bulk of research for this book was carried out have been no exception. When I returned to Guatemala in 2013 and 2015 to present findings and collect additional material, I found both tragedy and hope to be accelerating, and I witnessed the campesino movement countering heightened repression with an increase in organizational capacity. In this final chapter I assess my findings with campesino organizations and rural communities in light of current dynamics, showing how the shifting political context has led to different repercussions within the CONIC and CCDA campesino organizations.

Variation in the intensity of violence remains a reliable indicator of political dynamics in Guatemala (Brockett 2005). Rates of violent crime and homicide in Guatemala have actually dropped off recently, falling from a peak in 2009 and largely as the result of an aggressive campaign against organized crime and impunity kicked off by former attorney general Dr Claudia Paz y Paz Bailey, and backed by the *Comisión Internacional Contra la Impunidad en Guatemala* (International Commission against Impunity in Guatemala, CICIG) and by the country's human rights organizations (InSight Crime 2016a; Neier 2014; Tran 2013). If national rates are down, however, the situation faced by political organizers has only worsened, as evident in the constant escalation of military repression. President Alvaro Colom took the unprecedented move of declaring a "state of siege" in Alta Verapaz in 2010 and in the Petén in 2011, a category of martial law just one rung below a state of war (Granovsky-Larsen 2011; *Prensa* Libre 2011b). His successor, former general Otto Pérez Molina, enacted states of siege in Huehuetenango to curb protests against a hydroelectric project in 2012, and in protection of the El Escobal mining project in Santa Rosa and Jalapa in 2013 (Garcia Aupi and Ávila Gálvez 2013; Granovsky-Larsen and Weisbart, forthcoming; Solano 2015). Troops also committed the first military massacre since the end of the armed conflict in 2012, killing seven Indigenous protesters in Totonicapán (Amnesty International 2012). State violence against land claims continued as well, including in the March 2011 military, police, and paramilitary eviction of fourteen communities in the Polochic Valley (Batres 2011).

Alongside escalated remilitarization, the paramilitary threat had deepened against human rights and land defenders (a category including campesino and Indigenous activists) and journalists. Communities in resistance to mining projects were targeted with notable frequency; among high-profile cases were the 2012 attempted assassination of Yolanda Oqueli at the La Puya blockade of the El Tambor mine, and the wave of assassinations and shootings of community members protesting the Escobal mine in Santa Rosa and Jalapa (Amnesty International 2015, 2016; Pedersen 2014; Solano 2015). Communities organized in opposition to hydroelectric dams have also suffered heavy violence, with at least twenty-one murders related to anti-dam organizing between 2000 and mid-2016 (Finlay-Brook 2019; International Rivers 2016). Related to my research, Leocadio Juracán of the CCDA had been forced to flee the country under paramilitary threat, along with his family, shortly before the end of my fieldwork; one community member in Salvador Xolhuitz was shot and killed amid renewed intra-community tension in 2010; and the communities of Canlún and X'ya'al K'obe' discussed in chapter 3 were evicted violently in 2011. Overall the situation faced by grassroots activists in the country is grave, with the UDEFEGUA human rights organization recording over 650 threats and attacks against rights defenders in 2015 and 2016 alone, including twenty-two assassinations and another twenty attempted murders (UDEFEGUA 2016, 2017a, 2017b).

The varied nature of this repression – which is delivered by state forces, private security guards, and death squads alike – makes it easy to dismiss violent incidents as disconnected. Strong and active connections between the Guatemalan state, organized crime, and a variety of armed groups, however, are increasingly recognized as central to Guatemala's post-conflict political model and have been denounced since at least the early 2000s (Peacock and Beltrán 2003). With origins in the counter-insurgent state beginning in the late 1970s, a triple fusion of economic elites, armed forces officers, and organized criminal groups has moved out from the shadows and into the halls of power (Brands 2011; Briscoe and Rodríguez Pellecer 2010; InSight Crime 2016b; Solano 2017). This economic-military-criminal nexus had its most visible representation in the government of former general Otto Pérez Molina (2011–15), whose administration was filled with officers of the counter-insurgent-era armed forces, and whose active participation in organized crime was proven through the dismantling of sophisticated corruption schemes across a wide range of state institutions (CICIG 2016; InSight Crime 2016a).

In keeping with its counter-insurgent and paramilitary roots, the solidification of a military-criminal state has brought with it an increase in organized and repressive violence. A look at patterns of violence in fact suggests that the two forms of armed groups most commonly blamed for high murder rates – Mexican drug cartels and *mara* youth gangs, both of which are transnational in organization and activity – are quite likely scapegoats for less visible domestic groups with strong ties to the Guatemalan state.[1] In particular, two forms of non-state armed groups serve a paramilitary function and are apparently responsible for the majority of violent attacks on human rights defenders in Guatemala (Granovsky-Larsen forthcoming; UDEFEGUA 2015, 2016, 2017a). On the one hand, private security groups guard extractive projects and agricultural plantations aggressively and regularly use deadly force against protesters and campesino groups involved in agrarian conflicts. On the other, the majority of recent targeted attacks on rights defenders have been carried out by *sicarios*, or hired hitmen whose ranks, when exposed through rare cases of arrest, often involve the participation of active or former military and police officers (four anonymous interviews 2017; Argueta 2012; Solano 2015; UDEFEGUA 2016, 2017a).

While I had followed events in Guatemala from Canada and knew about the worsening organized criminal activity and the intensified repression against social movements, I was surprised to find, upon returning in 2013 and 2015, that a renewed spirit of organization and resistance had taken shape as well. This could be seen both in a reinvigorated energy within existing organizations and in new forms of community organizing against mega-development projects. Most notably, the *consulta*, or consultation, movement of communities organizing to hold plebiscites against mining projects had completely changed the national social movement scene. Begun in 2005 in the municipality of

Sipacapa, San Marcos, *consultas* had quickly become the newest form of community resistance to transnational capital, with at least seventy-eight consultations organized by affected communities themselves and carried out by the end of 2013 (Fulmer 2011; Laplante and Nolin 2014; Urkidi 2011). Where many rural communities had been slow to engage with the model of campesino and Indigenous social movement organizing inherited from the armed conflict era (discussed at length in chapter 2), the *consultas* provided a change in the available repertoire of contention that encouraged communities to organize themselves in response to immediate threats to their livelihoods (Tarrow 2011).

So successful was the new tactic, in fact, that it eventually breathed new life into some old organizations. To take our case studies as examples, CONIC and the CCDA both participated in *consultas* that drove off transnational projects: a proposed offshore iron extraction project in Champerico in the case of CONIC in 2012, and, with the CCDA, a plan to tap into geothermal energy from the depths of Lake Atitlán (field notes, 14 August 2013; CERIGUA 2011; Oxlajuj Tz'ikin 2012). Rather than a new strategy in an otherwise unchanged arena, however, the *consultas* reflected a renewed grassroots political engagement across Guatemala, evident in moments such as a 2012 campesino and Indigenous march from Alta Verapaz to Guatemala City, a student movement against neoliberal educational reforms in 2012–13, and a succession of massive protests against corruption that led to the arrest of President Otto Pérez Molina, Vice-President Roxana Baldetti, and many high-ranking officials from their administration (Batres 2012; Geglia 2012; InSight Crime 2016a).

This reinvigorated engagement was undeniable when I returned to spend time with the CCDA in 2013. The usual crowd of diehard supporters I had seen at CCDA events since 2003 were accompanied, and maybe even outnumbered, by new members from communities resisting mega-development projects including hydroelectric dams and expanding highways, and especially by young people eager to organize in their communities. When I returned again in late 2015, the CCDA had established a stronger presence across the country; the central offices were teeming with fresh faces from Huehuetenango and Alta Verapaz; and the CCDA general coordinator, Leocadio Juracán, had been elected to the Guatemalan Congress as a national representative for the social movement–based Convergencia political party. In the five years that had passed since my fieldwork in 2010, the grassroots political scene had changed dramatically, in response to the combined factors of intensified economic development, heightened militarization and repression, new organizational tactics, and persistence and adaptation of Guatemala's historical social movement organizations.

These recent changes to repression and resistance in Guatemala fit neatly with the path set by the peace accords. Negotiated peace and limited political and economic reform had been accepted by powerful local and transnational players partly in order to conceal major changes underway in the 1990s: a shift in power whereby investors in new economic sectors rose to the helm of an alliance with the traditional oligarchy and the military in order to pave the way for a transnational and neoliberal post-conflict order (Short 2007). Twenty years after the end of war, however, the form of neoliberalism that settled in Guatemala remains incomplete and far from hegemonic, in the Gramscian sense of the term. That is, the consensus for a neoliberal transition forged through the peace accords did not translate into hegemonic stability, or the acceptance across Guatemalan society that the post-conflict neoliberal state and its accompanying economic model were in the interest of the majority population rather than solely that of the elite (Gramsci 1971).

The return to reliance on repressive violence in order to force through economic projects, despite community opposition, points to an abandonment by the elite of the attempt to construct hegemony through the peace process. In place of consent, coercion has returned. This signals the end of the "post-conflict" period, or a temporal period lasting from 1996 to the return to military rule in 2011 as represented by the election of General Otto Pérez Molina.[2] Of course the labelling of any period after 1996 as "post-conflict" is problematic, given the continuation of violence, power structures, and impunity despite formal peace (Brett 2016; Knowlton 2017; McAllister and Nelson 2013). But there remains a point where the hegemonic project – the elite attempt to carry forward the old order through peace accord–based neoliberal reform, rather than through militarized repression – was abandoned, giving way to a new and yet unnamed period after the end of the post-conflict.

The period following the end of the "post-conflict" is also one in which corruption and organized crime have become the rule rather than the exception. As discussed above, the fusing of the economic elite, the military command, and organized crime – labels with increasingly blurred boundaries – has produced a political scenario in which corruption, organized crime, and extractive economic projects all go hand in hand. This scenario, in turn, is deeply saturated in the return to coercion over consent. Against this backdrop, Guatemala appears to support Tilly's theory of "war making and state making as organized crime" (1985). The Guatemalan state today operates in order to protect and enrich only those who are represented within its ranks, which squares with Tilly's depiction of the state as a collection of "coercive and self-seeking entrepreneurs [that] bears a far greater resemblance to the facts than do its chief alternatives: the idea of a social contract, the idea of an open market in which operators of armies and states offer services to willing consumers, the idea of a society whose shared norms and expectations call forth a certain kind of government" (Tilly 1985, 169).

The strongest counterweight to organized crime and corruption in Guatemala is posed by the International Commission against Impunity in Guatemala (CICIG), an autonomous, United Nations–backed investigative body that has rocked the country multiple times over its ten years of operations, by exposing details of high-level corruption and violence (InSight Crime 2016b). The work of the CICIG during the administrations of Otto Pérez Molina (2011–15) and Jimmy Morales (2016–present) helps show just how ingrained corruption and the economic-military-criminal nexus have become. In 2015 the CICIG presented an investigation into a criminal structure based within the Pérez Molina government that carried out systematic corruption operations. The CICIG made clear that this was not a case of corrupt individuals, but rather a "Mafioso criminal structure that had co-opted power through the ballot box in Guatemala and whose principal leaders were [former president and vice-president] Otto Pérez Molina and Roxanna Baldetti" (CICIG 2016).

Pérez Molina, Baldetti, and many members of their administration were jailed on corruption charges shortly before the presidential election of 2015, a context that allowed the comedian and political outsider Jimmy Morales to coast to victory. Subsequent revelations including a CICIG investigation into illicit campaign financing, however, have shown that President Morales himself is both deeply connected to military and organized criminal interests and a likely beneficiary of additional corruption schemes (Dudley 2017; Girón 2017).

What should be clear from the back-to-back administrations of presidents mired in accusations of corruption and connections to organized crime is that the Guatemalan state in its post-conflict form has become a shell for violently nefarious interests. This is the post-conflict neoliberal state in the period beyond the post-conflict: neoliberal in its dedication to a transnational, extractives-based economy, and violent in its abandonment of the peace accords–based project of hegemonic consent. What this new period means for the campesino movement, and how the movement was affected by the rise and fall of the attempted elite hegemonic project, are addressed in the remainder of this chapter.

CONIC and CCDA: Within and against the Market

The two organizations profiled in this study, the *Coordinadora Nacional Indígena y Campesina* (CONIC) and the *Comité Campesino del Altiplano* (CCDA), are two of the most established campesino groups in Guatemala, dating back to 1992 and 1982 respectively. They are also two of the organizations that have engaged most directly with neoliberal resources. While all other Guatemalan campesino organizations have participated in the neoliberal agrarian system to a certain extent, some have cut themselves off from engagement where possible. *Plataforma Agraria*, for example, withdrew from all interaction with the *Fondo de Tierras* as of 2003, and the *Comité de Unidad Campesina* (CUC) continues to insist on confrontational relations with governments, state institutions, and large landowners. If CONIC and the CCDA are more willing than some to engage with neoliberal agrarian institutions, however, they also show us that social movements are able to carry on resistance and alternative-building despite this engagement. In doing so, they also provide evidence that a neoliberal transformation in political subjectivity is not an automatic side effect of that engagement. The subjective element of neoliberal policies, CONIC and the CCDA show us, is an outcome that can be consciously rejected by social movement participants, despite an assumption within neoliberal theory to the contrary. As we will see over the following pages, the two campesino organizations have experienced a range of effects from their engagement with neoliberalism: CONIC has maintained its support for rural agrarian struggles even while its national leadership has reduced its willingness to resist established power, and the CCDA was eventually able to increase its ability to resist after a long engagement with neoliberal resources.

Both CONIC and the CCDA manage a wide variety of activities as social movement organizations with national reach. Each has one key program, however, that represents the group's best effort at building a socio-economic alternative to neoliberal policies, the agrarian status quo, and capitalism in general. For CONIC it is the Territorial

Collectives system that connects hundreds of rural communities with local Indigenous activists and national leadership. For the CCDA, the *Café Justicia* direct trade coffee project plays a similar role, bringing communities of coffee producers into an alternative model that flies in the face of the dominant coffee economy. These programs, which challenge the neoliberal transition by presenting functioning examples of what alternative socio-economic development could look like for rural Guatemalans, in fact are each tied inextricably with the organization's use of neoliberal resources.

CONIC: Territorial Collectives ... and a Collective Decline

The CONIC *Colectivos Territoriales*, or Territorial Collectives, together make up a national network of activists and communities that supports scores of land struggles, has led to an impressive number of successful cases of land access, and continues to nurture alternative socio-economic organization in recently landed communities. The network is made up of eleven regionally defined Territorial Collectives, each with a small number of local "promoters" (*promotores*) whose knowledge of local circumstances and languages allows them to work closely with each community organized in their area. A total of 619 communities are organized into the network across fifteen of Guatemala's twenty-two departments, and the way in which the system is organized leads to a fluid sharing of information both from the national leadership to the communities and from the communities up to CONIC's central organizing council in Guatemala City. This system has a particular ability to facilitate the maintenance of internal cohesion within groups struggling to access land or resettling on new land, which in turn is credited for the ability of many communities to survive and win land struggles and to later advance in socio-economic terms on new land. A review of our two CONIC case study communities highlights their continued anti-neoliberal organizing, despite the use of state resources.

The community of Victorias III in Retalhuleu, Champerico, purchased its land through the *Fondo de Tierras* in 1999. An insistence on communal living and solidarity, supported by local CONIC promoter Juventina López Vásquez, makes clear that the group has not accepted a neoliberal logic, despite making use of World Bank resources. Although each family in Victorias III works individual agricultural parcels, their development of community infrastructure is conducted exclusively through communal decision-making and an insistence that all families should benefit equally from any improvements. This became clear when, during one of my visits to the community, the group assembly aired a complaint to the CONIC promoter that a development agency wanted to set up a fish tank project that would support only a small number of families instead of the whole community. The group as a whole, including those who would benefit, insisted that the project should either be reformed to include all families, or be abandoned (field notes, 22 October 2009). Victorias III also displays strong solidarity with surrounding CONIC communities, especially through their participation in the *Oxlajuj Tz'iquin* program that brings representatives from eighteen nearby communities to collectively determine priorities for international development funding. Through the program, Victorias III and the other communities have also established inter-community networks of security and traditional health practices, among other efforts. The community has also demonstrated its willingness to continue resisting the state and neoliberalism in its insistence, backed by CONIC both locally and nationally, to refuse to make any payments on their FONTIERRAS loan. Victorias III held out and refused to pay their debt for sixteen years, until the debt was reduced by 75 per cent as part of a restructuring of the *Fondo de Tierras* in 2015 (research notes, 13 and 15 December 2015). This rejection shows the group's calculated decision to participate in the neoliberal *Fondo de Tierras* project only insofar as they would benefit from it, but to stop short of accepting an obligation to pay.

The community of San José La Pasión in Chahal, Alta Verapaz, has demonstrated a similar insistence on communalism and solidarity over individualism. After waging two land conflicts that lasted for many years and suffered violent repression, the families of San José La Pasión moved to land purchased by the Secretariat of Agrarian Affairs. Their experience of fighting for land together – surviving repression and eventually winning land through occupation – created a bond that would form a strong community and make the notion of individualism irrelevant. On their new land, the fifty-six families of San José worked together to build a house for each family and put in an equal number of hours each to build an elementary school with government funding. Despite the fact that the SAA funds that purchased their land came as part of the World Bank's land administration program and were probably routed through the *Fondo de Tierras* for the sale, residents of San José continue to support occupation and resistance. The community has been active in its new municipality of Chahal, speaking to other

CONIC communities to motivate them in demanding land and rights. Local CONIC promoter Hermelindo Chub Icó looks to the group as an example for others of how to access land and form new communities. People in San José La Pasión do not even discount the possibility of fighting for more land themselves in the future, to support their children's need for land of their own (interviews, anonymous, 23–4 January 2010). Not everyone in San José La Pasión sees another occupation as necessary, but it is clear that the spirit of resistance has not been extinguished in San José La Pasión, and neither have the strong sensibilities of communal practice and solidarity with communities facing similar situations.

CONIC's success with the Territorial Collectives, in supporting land struggles and accessing land, would not have been possible without using available neoliberal resources. First, many of the 144 cases of community land access facilitated by CONIC made direct use of neoliberal institutions. Forty-five CONIC communities purchased land through *Fondo de Tierras* loans, another four did so through its predecessor INTA, and six had titles granted by the FONTIERRAS regularization program. In addition to these more obvious engagements with a neoliberal institution, CONIC's strategy for land struggles relies significantly on the involvement of the Secretariat of Agrarian Affairs (*Secretaría de Asuntos Agrarios*, SAA). The SAA was created alongside the *Fondo de Tierras* as the conflict resolution branch of the World Bank's land administration package, and while it has had a positive impact in many communities, the institution nevertheless operates in a fashion that is entirely compatible with neoliberalism. Twenty-seven CONIC communities have been given land by the SAA, and many more of the nearly 100 ongoing agrarian conflicts CONIC works with are in regular negotiations with the same institution.

CONIC has also made use of neoliberalism by establishing a peace with various post-conflict neoliberal governments. Over its more than twenty-year history, CONIC has attempted to maintain a balance between direct action, political pressure, and negotiation as a strategy aimed at community land access. Since its last major protest in 2006, however, when CONIC organized a national Indigenous uprising, political pressure has given way to negotiation, and direct action has been limited to individual agrarian conflicts rather than more public or national protest. The organization has been accused by other social movement actors of cosying up to the governments of Alvaro Colom (2008–11) and Otto Pérez Molina (2012–15), but CONIC activists insist that staying on good terms with the administrations has allowed their community agrarian conflicts to avoid repression and often to end in land access.

As this research carried on in the years following the main round of fieldwork in 2009–10, however, it became increasingly clear that the CONIC national leadership had indeed been affected by its close relationship with the Colom and Pérez Molina administrations. The strongest evidence came in 2015, when CONIC first received a Q15-million budget directly from the government (Espina 2015) and then supported the Pérez Molina government during anti-corruption protests. In response to months of weekly protests that called for (and eventually achieved) the resignation of top politicians implicated in a major corruption scandal (Hernández Pico 2015) – protests larger and more sustained than any since the 1940s in Guatemala – CONIC released a statement condemning the protesters' attempted *"golpe de estado"*: "If we have to go the capital city, we will enter with thousands and thousands of men and women, Maya and campesinos, with their machetes sharpened and in hand, in order to defend the rule of law and the Constitution of the Republic" (Aguilar 2015).

For those who had long warned that CONIC had strayed from its values, as well as for some CONIC organizers, this was the last straw: CONIC had lost its willingness to resist following years of state funding and close ties to government.

The CONIC leadership is split on their own interpretation. Those who remain in key positions do not deny the facts mentioned above, but provide justification. César Bol, the CONIC general sub-coordinator, told me that the need for government funding became apparent as international financing has decreased in recent years. The Q15-million budget provided by the government is legitimate, Bol insists, because it was awarded by the Congress and not as a direct payment by the president or any other functionary. As for CONIC's opposition to the anti-corruption protests, Bol says that the group was defending the constitutional order and not the government (research notes, 15 December 2015).

But these decisions also produced internal turmoil, and at least one resignation: Juan Tiney, a CONIC co-founder, left the organization in protest in 2015 (Tiney 2015). Tiney agrees that decreased funding led CONIC close to the government but holds that – in contrast to open debate within CONIC over state funding during the Colom years – this produced a scenario where a select few CONIC leaders would negotiate behind closed doors and then require organizational support for the government (interview, Tiney 2015). In his letter of resignation, Tiney writes, "It is true that [CONIC] privileges dialogue and negotiation, but this does not imply silencing our voice against the non-compliance or political errors of institutions and government officials" (Tiney 2015). Tiney explained to me that even the organizational structure of CONIC had changed, from a directive council (*consejo de dirección*) that took its mandate from the national assembly of CONIC communities, to a more centralized governing council (*junta directiva*). "CONIC has a legal structure now, a *junta directiva* that isn't politically belligerent ... They are obedient, they are simply there to fulfil requirements" (interview). The position to maintain open dialogue and negotiation with governments, a position upon which CONIC was founded and that guided the group's successful agrarian struggles over more than two decades, eventually led the organization to abandon resistance and support governments in order to receive preferential access to resources.

Overall, CONIC's engagement with neoliberalism is varied. On the one hand, Charles R. Hale's position, introduced in chapter 1, appears to hold: that the acceptance of neoliberal resources leads to a decline in an organization's ability to resist or to initiate socio-economic transformation. And yet, neoliberal resources have been used by a variety of CONIC actors – not only the national leadership, but also rural communities that have accessed land, and the Territorial Collectives system that bridges the national and the rural. The Territorial Collectives network, CONIC's strongest program, continues to function, and the rural communities that have engaged in agrarian struggles carry on the organization's past spirit of resistance. This presents us with an interesting scenario, a paradox of resistance and pacification within the single organization of CONIC. It remains to be seen to what extent the communities and the Territorial Collective system can continue to build and resist within the new, weakened CONIC.

CCDA: Café Justicia ... and Renewed Resistance

In contrast to CONIC, the Campesino Committee of the Highlands (*Comité Campesino del Altiplano*, CCDA) has remained true to its roots, gaining strength over the same recent period as CONIC's decline. The group has managed to avoid the pacifying intentions of neoliberalism, but it has not avoided participation in neoliberal programs or acceptance of neoliberal resources. This paradoxical relationship to neoliberalism is encapsulated in the *Café Justicia* direct trade coffee project that is the engine of the CCDA's impressive demonstration of socio-economic and agrarian alternatives. Following over fifteen years of work as a social movement organization defending campesino and Indigenous rights beginning in 1982, the CCDA launched its coffee program in 1999, entering a second phase in the group's organizational history (Martínez 2006). CCDA organizers had helped three campesino communities to access land in 1998. With the coffee produced on two of these former plantations they began to build their international exports, with Canadian solidarity activists transporting and selling the first shipment of just 100 pounds. Five years later, 30,000 pounds of coffee from the 2004 harvest were sent to two distributers in British Columbia and Nova Scotia, a number that more than doubled to 67,600 pounds in 2008. The *Café Justicia* project involves just thirteen communities, but the impact of its sales extends into every aspect of the CCDA's work. Funds generated by coffee sales not only go to higher wages and additional benefits in producer communities, as is standard in direct trade and fair trade models, they also finance CCDA efforts in other arenas. Most importantly, the CCDA has used coffee funds to support, on the one hand, protest and lobbying aimed at national political reform, and, on the other, the implementation of alternative agricultural projects in rural communities across Guatemala.

As with CONIC's system of Territorial Collectives, the *Café Justicia* project formed alongside the CCDA's extensive use of neoliberal resources. In the CCDA's case, engagement with neoliberalism has come mainly through participation in the *Fondo de Tierras*. As a campesino organization that formed during the armed conflict in 1982 and participated in the peace process through guerrilla connections, the CCDA has promoted the implementation of accord promises and the utilization of the resulting institutions. The group encourages campesino communities to use FONTIERRAS loans for land access, and communication with the institution has been made more fluid through the participation of a close CCDA ally in the FONTIERRAS governing council. As state funding dwindled for the institution after eight years of operation, the CCDA continued to promote other state institutions and programs proposed in or created by the Socio-Economic Accord, such as the Cadastral Information Registry project and a proposed Agrarian Tribunal. While the entire approach to rural reform proposed in the Socio-Economic Accord must be understood as part of the neoliberal agrarian regime promoted by the World Bank and the Guatemalan elite, the CCDA and other campesino organizations that formed during the war view it as laying a foundation necessary for eventual agrarian reform. As such, the CCDA has relied almost exclusively on the *Fondo de Tierras* for communal land access: of the twenty-two farms accessed by communities together with the CCDA between 1998 and 2009, thirteen were bought with FONTIERRAS loans, and another three were secured through its regularization program.

While the CCDA has consistently participated in the *Fondo de Tierras* and promoted other elements of the neoliberal agrarian regime proposed in the peace accords, they have at the same time maintained a strong rejection of neoliberalism. This resistance has gathered momentum, especially since 2012, in a series of events that have seen the CCDA take on such a central role within the campesino movement as to become its main protagonist. The decisions by and impact on the CCDA are discussed in detail later in this chapter, but a brief listing of events is necessary at this point. The major event that catapulted the CCDA to national attention was a 216-kilometre, nine-day march from Cobán, Alta Verapaz, to Guatemala City in March 2012, organized in coordination with the CUC. In similar fashion to Padre Andrés Girón's 1986 campesino march, the 2012 Indigenous, Campesino, and Popular March for the Defence of Mother Earth (*Marcha Indígena Campesina y Popular por la Defensa de la Madre Tierra*) aimed to return agrarian politics to the political agenda (Hernández 2012). Demands were presented to the Guatemalan government in support of both a comprehensive agrarian reform and specific community agrarian struggles, as well as other demands concerning militarization, rights violations, mining and other mega-projects, and the passage of laws being considered by Congress (Marcha Indígena Campesina y Popular 2012). Some of the concrete demands were met after negotiation with President Otto Pérez Molina, including the restructuring of *Fondo de Tierras* loans to reduce campesino debt in most cases by 75 per cent (Gobierno de Guatemala 2012; Hernández 2015). The heavy participation of campesinos from Alta and Baja Verapaz in the march brought the CCDA into closer contact with Maya Q'eqchi' communities that were waging agrarian struggles and facing severe repression. The CCDA began to support many such struggles – in a shift from their post-conflict emphasis on market-based land access – and even opened regional offices in Alta and Baja Verapaz. Participation in these alternative agrarian struggles led the CCDA in March 2015 to establish an occupation camp with 400 Q'eqchi' families near the National Palace in Guatemala City, dubbed the Q'eqchi' Community (*Comunidad Q'eqchi'*). The occupation pressured for the resolution of agrarian conflicts and again was met with concrete concessions by the government (CCDA 2015; Gobierno de Guatemala 2015).

Between the 2012 march and the 2015 occupation, the CCDA had positioned itself as the most active campesino organization in the country, and communities began to flock to the group for assistance. That support, along with a national upswell of protest against corrupt politicians, was capitalized on by the CCDA during the 2015 general elections: Leocadio Juracán of the CCDA was elected to the Congress of the Republic along with two other social movement leaders for the new political party, Convergence for the Democratic Revolution (*Convergencia para la Revolución Democrática*, CRD). Once in Congress, Juracán and his CRD associates became a voice for campesinos and Indigenous Guatemalans, drafting or supporting twenty-nine legal proposals within their first four months in office, including initiatives backing labour rights, gun control, dignified migration, and the search for missing women (S. Morán 2016). Laws to curtail mining and hydroelectric damn projects, and to protect community access to water in the face of increasing commercial use, would follow in 2016. The CCDA, which had based its approach to land access even more thoroughly within neoliberal institutions than did CONIC, has shown that continued – and even amplified – resistance is possible following the acceptance of neoliberal resources.

The CCDA's path to becoming a more central grassroots political actor on the national scene was not disassociated from its work in rural communities. The support that the organization enjoys is based significantly in its many projects to build alternative socio-economic programs, especially in its home departments of Sololá and Chimaltenango. The strongest of these programs, the CCDA *Café Justicia* project, makes direct use of neoliberal resources and global capitalism to support the CCDA's social movement alternatives. Most of the communities producing the organic coffee exported to Canada as *Café Justicia* are not recently landed or FONTIERRAS projects, but rather are made up of small producers who already held coffee plots. At least three new *Fondo de Tierras* communities do export coffee with the project, however, and more are participating in the lengthy process to convert their soil to organic production and meet other requirements for inclusion in the *Café Justicia* project. So while we cannot say that the project as such relies on neoliberal funds, especially since the first two farms to produce coffee for export were acquired through international donations, the CCDA coffee project nevertheless incorporates a number of communities that do owe their current state to FONTIERRAS loans.

In addition to the inclusion of FONTIERRAS communities, the coffee project also relies on the global market to function. The CCDA has made a consistent and self-reflective effort to subvert the profit-generating aspects of its business to the socially and politically transformative goals of the organization, even deciding to distance the project from the Fairtrade International certification label in favour of direct trade with a solidarity group and a workers' cooperative. Nevertheless, export quantities, sales, and coffee prices depend on global economic trends, and the anti-capitalist coffee project of the CCDA relies directly on participation in the global capitalist market. This participation does not contradict the CCDA's core values and goals, however, since the organization enters the market in order to protect the non-capitalist social relations practised for production of its export coffee. The CCDA has not created a productive system isolated from capitalism, but rather a strong instance of the social economy akin to the Mondragón cooperatives in the Basque Country or the worker-recovered factories in Argentina – projects that harness the global market for funds but insist on using them to protect non-capitalist social relations of production and to foster broader projects of alternative socio-economic organization (Reed and McMurtry 2009). The CCDA represents another excellent example alongside Mondragón and the factories in Argentina, navigating trade and sales within the international capitalist market while ensuring the continuation of its non-capitalist social relations of production. As *Café Justicia* exports grow, the CCDA has also managed to remove itself incrementally from market relations. As of the 2017–18 harvest, for example, the CCDA no longer sends its coffee internationally through Guatemala's centralized and oligarchy-controlled export service but as part of the Guatemalan Federation of Coffee Cooperatives (FEDECOCAGUA).

The CCDA's qualified resistance to neoliberalism is best exemplified in the *Café Justicia* project and the promotion of agrarian sovereignty.[3] The coffee project has allowed small producers to take hold of a crop that was once based in exploitation and reserved for the accumulation of elite profit and power, and to produce and sell it on the basis of cooperative principles, using their share of sales to improve living conditions. The CCDA as an organization, for its part, has funnelled a share of coffee earnings into anti-neoliberal protest and the promotion of political reform. *Café Justicia* funds have also allowed the CCDA to promote an array of alternative agrarian practices that break the dependence of producers and communities on capitalist agriculture, ranging from mixed-cropping and organic fertilizer to fish ponds and local markets. There is no evidence to suggest that the ideals of the CCDA, its energy to resist, or the transformative potential of its work have been diluted through its acceptance of neoliberal resources. Instead, the CCDA as an organization has remained politically belligerent and increased its penchant for protest and direct action in recent years. Its programs such as *Café Justicia* and the many elements of agrarian sovereignty have continued to grow as well and the examples of alternative production and socio-economic organization promoted by the CCDA have become the reality in many rural communities. We can see an example of these alternatives built upon neoliberal resources in the case study community of Don Pancho.

Don Pancho is made up of fifty-five families from the highland department of Chimaltenango who resettled in the southern piedmont, on a plantation rich in water and other resources. Their experience provides us with a clear case of a strategic engagement with neoliberalism, through a community that has at once fully embraced the *Fondo de Tierras* model of land access and rejected the neoliberal approach to agrarian production. After an extensive search in which they insisted on a farm with abundance of water, quality soil, and a reasonable price, the members of Don Pancho purchased their land through a *Fondo de Tierras* loan. However, the community not only made use of the World Bank–funded institution and accepted its obligation to repay debt; many members paid off their share of the land ahead of schedule through international migration and remittances. At the time of my research, one quarter of interview participants reported having a family member working in the United States and sending money back to pay off the loan. So many members of the community worked in the United States, in fact, that the *Fondo de Tierras* took the step, unprecedented in my experience, of changing the names of many officially recognized heads of households to the women who stayed on the farm while their husbands worked abroad. Family remittances have become a common economic strategy across Latin America in the neoliberal period, and authors such as Robinson (2008, 158–60) interpret the trend as functional to neoliberalism for their pacifying effect on an otherwise desperate economic landscape.

Despite embracing the neoliberal model to gain access and title to land, however, the community of Don Pancho has rejected neoliberal agricultural production. Interview participants ignored the advice of *Fondo de Tierras* technicians who promoted a grid-based distribution of land and reliance on cattle and coffee. Instead, the community worked collectively to measure and distribute six oddly shaped, small plots of land per family, ensuring equal access to every type of terrain and resources for all. Across those six plots, most families have implemented an agricultural system that draws heavily from the CCDA's model of agrarian sovereignty: a diversity of crops that prioritize subsistence and local market sales, organic production and mixed cropping, and participation in the CCDA-promoted projects of organic coffee production and community fish ponds. The result that I witnessed after the community had been on their land for six years was unparalleled economic security as well as a sense of independence from outside groups and development projects. This was the CCDA community model in action: assistance in acquiring top-quality land at a reasonable price, regardless of its neoliberal flavour, demonstration of alternative community agriculture, then a hands-off approach to fostering community subsistence and autonomy without intervening with a development plan.

Unfortunately, my second CCDA case study with the community of Salvador Xolhuitz does not provide another example of the subversion of neoliberal resources. Rather, the violent conflict that erupted within the community highlights the destructive potential in the neoliberal model of market-led agrarian reform. The *Fondo de Tierras* insisted on working with a certain number of beneficiaries per land area rather than focusing on the internal cohesion of community members, and its representatives turned a blind eye to the illegal sale of additional land by the former owner. These two elements combined to drive a fissure through the community, and that division eventually turned lethal. The conflict has consumed the efforts and resources of both sides of the community, and all members of Salvador Xolhuitz have been prevented from realizing their potential or establishing economic, political, or agrarian autonomy. While Don Pancho presents us with an example of the successful working of the CCDA approach to land access and community development, the case of Salvador Xolhuitz reminds us that not all cases end well for community members. The CCDA and CONIC, along with other campesino organizations, have proven adept at making use of neoliberal resources, accepting offers of inclusion in the neoliberal agrarian system with underlying intentions to subvert that system for pre-existing anti-neoliberal goals. Such subversion is not always possible, however, and the case of Salvador Xolhuitz – as well as that of CONIC's national leadership in recent years – points clearly to the many risks associated with stepping into the land market or other aspects of the neoliberal agrarian order.

The Neoliberal Temptation

The first chapter of this book argued for the need to assess the engagement of social movements with neoliberalism on the basis of long-term impact, rather than dismissing movements automatically for that engagement. The case studies outlined here and explored in detail throughout the book show that acceptance of neoliberal resources does not necessarily lead to the creation of neoliberal subjects. While warnings of the pacifying effect of neoliberalism proved true over the long run with CONIC, our other case studies – including the CCDA, as well as rural communities organized within CONIC – show that some campesino groups have engaged with neoliberalism without weakening their transformative potential. Even taking into account CONIC's difficulties, both campesino organizations built and sustained socio-economic alternatives to neoliberal restructuring by intentionally and effectively using those very resources against neoliberalism in order to mount challenges to the new political-economic order. If CONIC has strayed from a path of resistance recently, its Territorial Collectives network – which was built on the use of World Bank–funded institutions and a truce with neoliberal governments – continues to function in the rural areas, promoting collective organizing and a politicized indigeneity to fight for territorial control. And the CCDA *Café Justicia* program has consciously managed participation in the neoliberal land market and the global coffee market in order to protect non-capitalist social relations of production and to promote anti-neoliberal political reform.

These cases demonstrate the potential of all Guatemalan campesino organizations to maintain their focus on structural change in a postconflict political arena that posits the neoliberal agrarian order as propoor and pro-campesino. Realizing this potential despite relentless pressure is an ongoing challenge for social movement organizations, as we have seen. Clearly the warnings about the limiting effects of participation in neoliberalism contain important truths. Charles R. Hale, whose work with Central American Indigenous, Black, and campesino movements led to a grounded and nuanced set of such warnings, provides us with some precautions that are substantiated in the present study and others that I question here. To recap those warnings (introduced in more detail in chapter 1), we can read Hale's position as follows: the recognition of Indigenous rights and the granting of territorial autonomy for Indigenous groups in neoliberal-era Central America, while beneficial for the cultural recognition and immediate material satisfaction of recipients, works in tandem with the transnational neoliberal political-economic project. The support of transnational bodies and local elites suggests that these reforms complement the neoliberal transition, by bringing traditional Indigenous territories into the formal land market and by pacifying potentially rebellious populations through their incorporation in the neoliberal model. This process generates two widespread examples of such pacification, according to Hale. On the one hand, the recognition of Indigenous cultural rights alongside the violent repression of movements with economic demands creates what Hale calls the *indio permitido*, or "authorized Indian," grassroots actors whose demands do not challenge the key tenets of economic or political power (Hale 2002, 2004; Hale and Millamán 2006). And on the other hand, Hale observes the creation of "empty spaces," wherein retreat of state services from areas of land granted or sold for Indigenous autonomy or agrarian distribution is accompanied by reliance on the internalization of the state's task of subject formation (Hale 2011). In both scenarios Hale relies on a core assumption that recipients of neoliberal resources will comply with the task of neoliberal subject formation, since they will have been bound by the constraints associated with the special rights and resources granted by the state. Two passages, published nine years apart, demonstrate the centrality of this position to Hale's analysis: "Neoliberal doctrine is predicated not on destroying the Indigenous community in order to remake the Indian as citizen, but rather, re-activating the community as effective agent in the reconstitution of the Indian citizen-subject ... [T]he state does not merely 'recognise' community, civil society, Indigenous culture and the like, but actively re-constitutes them in its own image, sheering [*sic*] them of radical excesses, inciting them to do the work of subject-formation that otherwise would fall to the state itself" (Hale 2002, 496).

These two principles together – special rights and reinforcement of a capitalist market for land and resources – converge to yield an especially compelling logic: states devolve authority to far-flung spaces, recognize the inhabitants' rights and let them govern themselves, which has the effect of constraining their political participation beyond the local level, especially in relation to broader structures of political-economic inequity (Hale 2011, 195).

One of Hale's observations held true throughout my study, that the local and transnational proponents of neoliberalism benefit from the current model of land registration and redistribution (Hale 2011, 194–5). The location of farms sold through the *Fondo de Tierras* in undesirable regions, the abundance of poor-quality land sold, the often unreasonably high debt taken on by campesino communities, and the predatory acquisition by large landowners of newly titled land in areas of economic growth, all strongly support the widely held opinion that the *Fondo de Tierras* model benefits *terratenientes* first and foremost. Elite support for land titling, market-based land distribution, and limited Indigenous territorial autonomy is essentially self-serving rather than benevolent. In addition, we can argue that the participation of social movement organizations in the *Fondo de Tierras*, and in peace accord reforms more generally, helped facilitate the transition to a transnationalized economy and a neoliberal post-conflict state by directing grassroots energy into extracting the best possible outcome from the new order rather than exclusively opposing it.

I also agree with Hale that, alongside the material goal to bolster the power of capital, neoliberal transitions include the intention to affect political subjectivity. Foucault's lectures on neoliberal governmentality make clear the assumption inherent in neoliberal theory that any change to economic conditions will alter patterns of social behaviour, given the supposed economic rationality of all people. "Whereas in the classic liberal conception, *homo oeconomicus* forms an external limit and the inviolable core of governmental action, in the neo-liberal thought of the Chicago School he becomes a behaviouristically manipulable being and the correlative of a governmentality which systematically changes the variables of the 'environment' and can count on the 'rational choice' of the individuals" (Lemke 2001, 200).

But has the market-based approach to agrarian change produced a rural population that is satisfied with the current model and unwilling to challenge the dominant political economic order? The answer here is qualified. The community of Salvador Xolhuitz, mired in violent internal conflict that stemmed from structural flaws within neoliberal land institutions, points to the dangers that accompany funding. CONIC presents an even more severe case, its national leadership increasingly cosy with successive governments to the point of being granted an official budget line. These two cases highlight the very real negative effects that can stem from participation in neoliberalism. The other four cases explored in this book, however, contain examples of three communities –

two of them aligned with CONIC – and an organization that have based their strength on the strategic use of neoliberal resources and have managed to build and sustain alternative socio-economic models.

The continued resistance to established power, and an ongoing experimentation with the construction of alternatives, are thus possible and have been accomplished by some campesino groups – even if others have not had the same success. A necessary question, then, stems from the capacity of some – but not all – social movement actors to realize this possibility: how did the CCDA resist the malicious intent of neoliberalism's invitation to participate, while CONIC slipped into its folds?

CCDA and the Re-articulation of Resistance

CONIC took a sharp turn in 2015 towards what Hale calls the *indio permitido*, setting aside dissent in return for privileged access to state resources. At around the same time, the CCDA experienced tremendous growth, both internally and in the scope and influence of the organization: between 2012 and 2015 the CCDA opened regional offices across Guatemala, established itself as a central group leading national campesino resistance, and amassed widespread support to elect a CCDA activist to the Guatemalan Congress. The recent divergence between the CCDA and CONIC came despite the fact that, as expanded on above, both groups embraced the market model and accepted neoliberal resources in order to assist with community land access. This section charts the rise of the CCDA. As CONIC narrowed its decision-making circle, allowing for critical dialogue with governments to give way to a negotiation of resources in exchange for obedience, the CCDA took a number of turns that led the group to stronger grassroots connections and more defiant resistance. A series of major events between 2008 and 2015 is outlined below, each of which represents strategic decisions by CCDA leadership that led the group to rise to prominence within the same neoliberal context that saw CONIC shed much of its strength.

CCDA activists themselves trace the group's turning point to the split within the CNOC national umbrella organization in 2008. As explained in chapter 2, by 2008 CNOC – Guatemala's first coordinating alliance of campesino organizations, founded in 1992 – had lost the unity and presence it had commanded in the early 2000s, mainly as a result of internal divisions over resources and tactics. Along with other groups, the CCDA pulled out of CNOC in 2008. When asked about the CCDA's current increased visibility, long-time core members Lesbia Morales and Marcelo Sabuc both marked the withdrawal from CNOC as the beginning of a new period (interviews 2015). Where the CCDA had previously worked in communities as the CCDA but appeared in national campesino politics as part of CNOC, the group slowly began to present themselves as the CCDA.

The CCDA transition to national attention did not happen all at once, as the group first helped to found another umbrella organization, the National Indigenous-Campesino and Popular Council (Consejo Nacional Indígena-Campesina y Popular, CNAIC-P). A complete turnabout came only after threats and attacks on the CCDA in 2010. The CCDA's long preference to shy from the spotlight stemmed from repression against the group in its early days, when emerging at the height of conflict in 1982 led to the assassination and exile of the original CCDA leadership. Ironically, the CCDA embraced widespread attention under its own name only after renewed attacks between 2008 and 2010. Although this decision wasn't mentioned in interviews, I have noticed, as a long-time observer of the CCDA, that since CCDA General Coordinator Leocadio Juracán and his family returned from paramilitary-driven exile in 2010, all of the group's political protest and proposal has been done under the name of the CCDA. The decision was presumably strategic: to gain public and media attention in order to shield the group from attacks, especially within a climate in which decreased funding for international human rights accompaniment was followed by constant threats and attacks since 2008.[4] National recognition, noted CCDA Sub-Coordinator Lesbia Morales, means both more and less protection for the CCDA: protection from some threats as discussed here, but also the assumption of risk tied to the many agrarian conflicts the CCDA now works with as the group has attracted new rural communities (interview 2015).

The first two steps towards strengthening the CCDA occurred in 2008 and 2010, as the group left CNOC and increased its public presence. These led towards the most important turning point for the CCDA: the 2012 Indigenous, Campesino, and Popular March for the Defence of Mother Earth. The march – which the CCDA organized in collaboration with the CUC, and that covered the 216 kilometres between Cobán and Guatemala City over nine days in March 2012 – was conceived of as a creative tactic to return agrarian issues to national political concern. This was achieved, along with concrete concessions from the government such as the reduction of debt for Fondo de Tierras communities. Importantly, the march also had a major impact on the CCDA organization. First, since the march began in Alta Verapaz, the CCDA connected with a region that is central to contemporary agrarian issues but had been mostly outside the scope of CCDA work before 2012. Lesbia Morales describes the nine days of walking as a learning together with all the participants. "With all the demands that were brought forward from different parts of the country, to be able to have the capacity to prioritize and present these was very interesting. It was a learning process. We believe that it was a school for us, too, to walk for nine days, because there was everything: there was harmony, there was food, there was communication. We didn't ever lose anything. In other words, it was a question of living in community" (interview 2015).

The CCDA as an organization was changed as its core leadership came into close cooperation and dialogue with community members from Alta Verapaz. The group began to expand. Where CCDA community accompaniment had focused on assisting highland communities through Fondo de Tierras land purchase, after the 2012 march the organization began to support agrarian conflicts to defend or reclaim Indigenous land (struggles that had fallen more within the work of CONIC, as described in chapters 3 and 4). So many communities approached the CCDA after the march that the group opened regional offices in the departmental capitals of Cobán, Alta Verapaz and Purulhá, Baja Verapaz.[5] By 2015 support for communities engaged in alternative agrarian struggles and defence of territory – particularly in communities resisting imposition of hydroelectric dams and diversion of rivers – had become a central aspect of the CCDA's work (interviews, Chic 2015; and Sabuc 2015).

The new focus on supporting agrarian conflicts snowballed for the CCDA, attracting more communities to this now prominently visible campesino organization and leading to creative protests – such as the 2015 Comunidad Q'eqchi' tent city described above – that have highlighted the group even further. It should be mentioned, however, that this new focus has not come at the cost of the CCDA's traditional work with alternative agrarian programs and *Café Justicia*. If anything, those programs have grown as well, with coffee exports increasing along with the number of full-time workers, facilities, and programs associated with the CCDA's agrarian initiatives (field notes, 7 and 12 December 2015). This has led to a doubling of the CCDA's strength: the support garnered through agrarian community development work has continued to grow, and there is now fresh backing from across the country for a campesino organization that supports agrarian struggles and pushes for political change at the national level.

If the CCDA could sense its increased support before 2015, it was demonstrated concretely in national elections that September. Following at least three prior campaigns in which CCDA candidates were not elected to office, Leocadio Juracán, the general coordinator and most public face of the CCDA, was elected to the Guatemalan Congress with the CRD party. In Guatemala 31 of the 158 Congressional representatives are elected as national representatives rather than for a particular district. Juracán ran successfully for the national list, meaning that he had to be supported nationwide in order to be elected – and he was, with over 170,000 votes, including support within every one of Guatemala's 336 municipalities (interview, Chic 2015). Juracán's election can be attributed in part to the rejection of establishment parties that accompanied a vibrant wave of anti-corruption protests in 2015. However, José Chic, a recent addition to the CCDA leadership who worked closely with the election campaign, notes that the distribution of votes points to hard support for Juracán rather than soft support for candidates not affiliated with major parties. Around 110,000 of the votes for Leocadio Juracán came from rural areas across all twenty-two Guatemalan departments, which Chic understands as "recognition that Leocadio can channel many social movement demands – [demands] to attend to the communities – and we believe that the communities have a lot of hope for Leocadio" (interview 2015). Juracán sees the campaign in similar light: "One of the points that made it so that the CCDA could place and see elected a congressional representative, I believe, was the constant struggles and the identification and accompaniment that we have had, not only with members of the CCDA [bases], but with the social movement in general in the country. The CCDA is a visible organization, an important organization in Guatemala. And that definitely helped us, in this occasion, to win some congressional seats, at least three" (interview 2015).[6]

Leocadio Juracán's election to Congress can be understood as a pinnacle moment for the CCDA. After more than thirty years of working as an innovative but relatively small and little-known campesino organization, the CCDA had gathered enough support to send one of its own to represent Guatemala's social movements and Indigenous peoples in the national legislature. How was this achieved? Importantly for our consideration of the impact of neoliberal resources on social movement organizations, it was not achieved through an unqualified rejection of neoliberalism. The CCDA was strengthened through the continued deliberate use of neoliberal resources including land purchases through the *Fondo de Tierras*. And while the group branched out to begin supporting alternative land access struggles through agrarian conflicts, especially in the Verapaz region, it did not denounce its past support for Guatemala's heavily neoliberal agrarian institutions. Juracán, for example, mentioned that within the work to be done to improve the agrarian situation in Guatemala is the revision – not elimination – of the *Fondo de Tierras*, as well as the creation of the peace accords–mandated agrarian code and agrarian tribunals (interview 2015).

The CCDA remains an example of how a social movement organization can accept resources from neoliberal institutions and then use them strategically to strengthen its efforts to resist and to build alternatives. What we saw with the recent divergence between the CCDA and CONIC, however, was that it was important for an organization to remain aware that such engagement with neoliberalism remains strategic. CONIC appears to have given in to the temptation to trade acquiescence for a funding windfall, a move that brought the organization into the state fold and away from grassroots opposition. The CCDA, by contrast, made several important decisions between 2008 and 2015, each of which reaffirmed the group's willingness and ability to resist the dominant order, while continuing to use state agrarian resources in its efforts to build strength among rural communities. This contrast shows us that there is a fine line to be walked continuously, but that the path can be maintained.

While Charles Hale warns of the dangers associated with land struggles in the neoliberal era, and cautions that movements face a choice between acceptance or refusal of land granted for autonomous governance, he also contemplates the direction that Indigenous activism could take within this context (Hale 2004, 19–21, 2011, 201–5). Perhaps the CCDA in its current phase of action has embodied that possible direction, what Hale calls a re-articulation of resistance.

Hale imagines a direction for the re-articulation of Indigenous and Afro-descendent movements, one that he has not seen carried out but could begin to counter the limiting effects of the neoliberal multicultural project on transformative agendas. Reading across two of Hale's articles (2004, 2011), a re-articulated resistance would appear to draw from two principles. The first is to build bridges between the categories of Indigenous activism that neoliberal multiculturalism created: the *indio permitido* or authorized Indian, and its Other, the condemned Indian. Where exclusion of Indigenous politics that challenge the power of the state and capital is made possible through encouragement of pacified, culturally focused movements, the importance and impact of both would only be strengthened by their (re-)unification (Hale 2004, 19–21). Second, Hale hopes that a reassessment of land struggles will come about in such a way that state sanctioned autonomy-for-autonomy's-sake is replaced by a less dependent and more productive use of territory. "The new emphasis is less on improving the terms of devolution of authority from the state to autonomous unit and more on reducing these ties of dependency and tutelage altogether. It is less about incrementally improving the terms of economic relations and more about finding ways to achieve an ever increasing measure of self-sustaining production. In regard to political horizons, this radicalized notion of autonomy is adamantly local, but also potentially more transnational in scope" (Hale 2011, 204).

This approach to Indigenous political activism would presumably occur outside the venues of territorial governance granted by the state and the World Bank, since Hale insists (2011, 202, 206) that a continuation – and presumably a re-articulation, as well – of transformative goals is incompatible with the short-term material achievement of land through neoliberal concession.

The CCDA, especially in its current phase, does all of this. And it does so while continuing to accept neoliberal resources, including land. First, the CCDA builds bridges across movements. This has been accomplished recently in two directions: upwards into the state through the election of Leocadio Juracán to Congress and the negotiation that this implies, with other Indigenous activists, as well as politicians and bureaucrats of all stripes; and outwards to rural communities engaged in unsanctioned agrarian struggles. From a more local and limited form of organizing, the CCDA has recently built ties to other Indigenous movements that engage in a politics both more and less radical than that of its previous self – in other words to both condemned and authorized groups. Second, the CCDA has always focused on productive projects and self-sufficiency. The core of the group's activities since 1987 has been the construction of socio-economic alternatives in rural communities, especially through direct or secondary involvement in the *Café Justicia* project.

The interpretation and expression of Indigenous identity has also played a significant role in the diverging politics of the CCDA and

CONIC and today informs the CCDA's unique resurgence. While the varying interpretation of indigeneity between the CCDA and CONIC cannot explain the divergence between these groups on its own, the two organizations' incorporation of expressed Indigenous identity into strategic decision-making certainly has played a role over the years. Responding to the perceived shunning of the concerns of rural Indigenous communities by the URNG guerrilla command – concerns that placed first the defence of Indigenous territory and resolution of agrarian conflicts, even through direct negotiation with the state – CONIC formed as an Indigenous-campesino organization in rebellion against the CUC and URNG in 1992 (Velázquez Nimatuj 2008; see also chapter 4 above). CONIC's position that the defence of Indigenous community land requires dialogue with those in power has informed the group's unwavering willingness to compromise with government administrations of any stripe.

In comparison, the expression of Indigenous identity within the CCDA has been more subdued and has taken a back seat to a primarily class-based analysis of Guatemalan politics. The group's leadership and membership have always been predominantly Indigenous (until recently, mainly Maya Kaqchikel from Sololá and Chimaltenango; more recently, including Indigenous activists from across the country). The design and explanation of its economic and political projects have also been based in the needs of Guatemala's Indigenous populations, as demonstrated consistently in CCDA publications reaching back to its formation in 1982 and its early community development projects in 1987. However, as noted, this is a more subtle indigeneity, one that sits at the core of the CCDA's collective identity but is expressed as complementary to an economic analysis. This balance has helped to lead the CCDA to the position in which it finds itself today: strongly rooted in solidarity with Indigenous peoples across the country, but with a perspective on Guatemalan politics that refuses to let go of demands for structural economic change, and even revolution.

Ultimately, then, we can interpret the current phase of the CCDA as one of a re-articulation of resistance: from a middle position of compliance – but not complacence – with the neoliberal agrarian order, to one that has connected across movements, increased its radical demands, and continued to nurture its productive alternatives. In doing so, the CCDA itself also bridges the terrain between authorized and condemned Indian. Authorized in its acceptance and use of neoliberal funds, but condemned in acting upon the two principles barred by neoliberal multiculturalism: posing challenges to the productive regime (through agrarian conflicts, contentious legal proposals, and alternative production) and accumulating political power in order to challenge the dominant order (Hale 2004, 18–19). While not all Indigenous or campesino organizations will manage this re-articulation – and none in Guatemala has done so as successfully as the CCDA – this one group shows us that participation in the neoliberal agrarian system and continued insistence on transformation are not incompatible. The CCDA has carried on, and now re-articulated, its resistance not only despite participation in neoliberalism, it flourished as an organization and launched its re-articulation using resources claimed through that participation.

This assessment is tentative, given the enormous uncertainty ahead. The biggest question is whether the CCDA will be able to maintain its position and continue to harness grassroots support for political power. Importantly, the group seeks these goals within a context of two new difficulties: staying the course within a social movement that has attached itself to elected positions, and the increased repressive violence that comes with a decision to back radical demands for land and territory.[7] Another question is whether the re-articulation apparent in CCDA organizing will spread beyond that organization and into the broader campesino movement. The two are deeply tied, with the CCDA taking cues for its growth from communities engaged in resistance, while CCDA productive projects bring more communities into the movement. Parallel community organizing outside of campesino organizations, especially through the *consulta* movement against mining and other mega-projects, is also connected, drawing from and contributing to the ongoing politics of the campesino movement.

The post-conflict period is over and Guatemala has entered a new era. The elite attempt to construct hegemony around a neoliberal peace has been abandoned and replaced with a return to violent coercion that stems from a state apparatus fused with military and organized criminal power. But as this book has highlighted, resistance and alternative building not only have remained active throughout the post-peace period, they have continued to gather momentum. The rejuvenation of grassroots organizing owes much to the campesino movement, which has maintained a constant presence through its protest and proposal, direct action in defence of land and territory, and alternative community-based agrarian programs. And while these efforts have coincided with an invitation for organized campesinos to participate in the neoliberal restructuring of agrarian projects – participation that campesino organizations navigated to their advantage with varying success – overall the movement held onto its visions of a different Guatemala, along with its potential to bring them to life. As has been the scene at so many points in Guatemala's history, campesinos and Indigenous people today continue to move forward through violence, with hope and strength.

Glossary

alcalde auxiliar. Auxiliary mayor. In rural Guatemalan villages, this person serves as an intermediary to the municipal mayor, representing the community.

asamblea. Community assembly. Made up of all adults in a community, this is the highest decision-making body of campesino groups resettled on communal land.

bajío. In the Victorias III community, the low marshy area of the farm.

baldío. Unused state land. Under Guatemalan law, *baldíos* should be turned over to farmers and made productive.

beneficio. Coffee-processing plant. A *beneficio* can vary in size and sophistication, from a concrete platform for drying beans in the sun through to a collection of heavy machinery.

caballería. Measurement of land equal to forty-five hectares.

campesino. Peasant. Small-scale or landless rural farmers, mainly Indigenous.

colonato. Economic institution of large-scale farming using resident workers, or *mozos colonos*.

compañero/a. Comrade.

conflictividad agraria. Unequal economic, social, and political conditions that together give rise to specific agrarian conflicts.

consulta. Community consultation. *Consultas*, which involve secret ballots or show-of-hands polls, are usually organized in order to challenge a large resource extraction project, such as mining.

cuerda. Measurement of land. Exact size varies by region within Guatemala, but a *cuerda* is consistently small. In parts of Alta Verapaz, for example, a *cuerda* is equal to one-sixteenth of a *manzana*.

desalojo. Eviction, usually of a land occupation or other agrarian conflict.

derechos históricos. Historical rights to traditionally used lands, whether recognized legally by the state or perceived by a community.

finca. Plantation. The word is used to describe commercial plantations as well as the communal land owned by resettled campesino groups.

finquero. Large landowner. Synonymous with *terrateniente*.

Fondo de Tierras. Land Fund. A Guatemalan institution of market-led agrarian reform funded by the World Bank that has become the cornerstone of state agrarian policy in the post-conflict period.

junta directiva. Governing council. In the context of rural communities, the *junta directiva* is the elected leadership.

lucha revindicativa. Struggle to recover the resources (especially land) and rights historically denied to Indigenous campesinos.

manzana. Measure of land equal to 1.7 acres.

milpa. Traditional campesino agricultural plot of corn, beans, squash, and *yierbita* herbs. *Milpa* can also refer to a plot with just corn.

mozos colonos. Farm workers residing permanently on a plantation. The system of housing *mozos colonos* as labourers on plantations (especially coffee plantations), which began in the nineteenth century and had mostly ended by the early 2000s, is equated with slavery by many campesinos.

prestaciones. Payment owed to workers by bosses if fired without cause, *laborales* mandated under the Guatemalan Constitution.

proyectismo. "Project-ism." An over-emphasis on development funding for agriculture and infrastructure projects by members of a rural community.

quintal. Bag of crops weighing 100 pounds.

terrateniente. Large landowner. Synonymous with *finquero*.

tierra fría. The cold land. A reference to villages in cold mountain climates.

yierbitas. Herbs. The term refers to the variety of edible herbs and plants grown in corn plots or harvested wild in forests.

List of Interview Participants and Research Sites

Interviews

Anonymous

Four interviews with government officials and human rights activists, on paramilitary violence.
Guatemala City, September 2017

Cristina Ardón Simón

Women's Program coordinator, Campesino Committee of the Highlands (*Comité Campesino del Altiplano*, CCDA)
Aldea Quixayá, Sololá, 5 January 2010

Gilberto Atz

Campesino Sector representative to the Directive Council, *Fondo de Tierras*
Guatemala City, 27 October 2009

Candelaria Beb Tut

Member of Alta Verapaz Territorial Collective, National Indigenous and Campesino Coordinator (*Coordinadora Nacional Indígena y Campesina*, CONIC)
El Estor, Izabal, 19 November 2009

César Bol

General sub-coordinator of National Directive Council; coordinator of Communications, Relations, and Propaganda Program; and coordinator for Accompaniment of Territorial Collectives in the Q'eqchí Region, CONIC
Guatemala City, 4 March 2010

Celso Caal
Alta Verapaz departmental coordinator, CONIC
Cobán, Alta Verapaz, 2 February 2010

Miguel Angel Cardona
Coordinator of Regional Offices, Secretaría de Asuntos Agrarios (SAA)
Guatemala City, 1 December 2009

José Chic
Member of Political Commission, CCDA
Aldea Quixayá, Sololá, 14 December 2015

Hermelindo Chub Icó
Coordinator of Izabal Territorial Collective, CONIC
Guatemala City, 26 March 2010

Sergio Funes
CNP-Tierra and CEIDEPAZ
Guatemala City, 17 March 2010

Luis Galicia
Member of Political Commission, *Plataforma Agraria* and researcher in the
Campesino Studies section of the Association for the Advancement of
Social Sciences in Guatemala (*Asociación para el Avance de las Ciencias
Sociales en Guatemala*, AVANCSO)
Guatemala City, 22 March 2010

Abisaias Gómez Hernández
Coordinator of Executive Committee, *Plataforma Agraria*
Guatemala City, 10 March 2010

Rafael González
General coordinator, Committee for Campesino Unity (*Comité de Unidad
Campesina*, CUC)
Guatemala City, 9 March 2010

Moisés Guzmán Grijalva
Member of Directive Council, *Comunidad Indígena Xinka de Jutiapa*
Guatemala City, 8 March 2010

Leocadio Juracán
General coordinator, CCDA
San Lucas Tolimán, Sololá, 29 September 2009, and Aldea Quixayá, Sololá,
10 December 2015

Juventina López Vásquez
Coordinator of Retalhuleu Territorial Collective and member of National
Directive Council, CONIC; Coordinator of *Oxlajuj Tz'ikin* Comprehensive
Rural Development Program
Retalhuleu, Retalhuleu, 9 February 2010, and Nueva Cajolá, Retahuleu,
13 December 2015

Israel Macario
Representative to ADRI, *Plataforma Agraria*
Guatemala City, 10 March 2010

Bonifacio Martín
Indigenous Sector representative on Directive Council, *Fondo de Tierras*
Guatemala City, 23 March 2010

Maria Mateo Francisco
Coordinator, Alliance of Rural Women (*Alianza de Mujeres Rurales*, AMR)
Guatemala City, 26 March 2010

Rigoberto Monteros
Member of National Directive Council and Legal Program coordinator,
CONIC
Guatemala City, 28 October 2009.

Carlos Morales
General coordinator, National Coordinator of Campesino Organizations
(*Coordinadora Nacional de Organizaciones Campesinas*, CNOC), and
general coordinator, Verapaz Union of Campesino Organizations (*Unión
Verapacense de Organizaciones Campesinas*, UVOC)
Guatemala City, 29 October 2009 and 4 March 2010

Lesbia Morales
Sub-coordinator, CCDA
Aldea Quixayá, Sololá, 14 October 2009, and 10 December 2015

Luis Fernando Peña de León
General manager, *Fondo de Tierras*
Guatemala City, 2 November 2009

Virgilio Pérez Calderón
Legal representative, Civil Society for the Development of Colomba
(*Sociedad Civil para el Desarrollo de Colomba*, SCIDECO)
Guatemala City, 10 March 2010

Eliseo Pérez Mejía
Indigenous Sector representative to the Directive Council, *Fondo de Tierras*,
and member, Kab'awil
Guatemala City, 23 March 2010

Lorenzo Pérez Mendoza
Treasurer of Executive Committee, Guatemalan National Committee of the
Displaced (*Consejo Nacional de Desplazados de Guatemala*, CONDEG)
Guatemala City, 10 March 2010

Marcelo Sabuc
Legal representative, CCDA
Aldea Quixayá, Sololá, 14 October 2009, and 14 December 2015

Basilio Sanchez Trieles
Member of Political Council, Campesino Development Committee (*Comité
de Desarrollo Campesino*, CODECA)
Mazatenango, 12 March 2010

Juan Tiney
Treasurer of National Directive Council and co-founder, CONIC
Guatemala City, 26 March 2010, and 15 December 2015

Emilio Tzib Quej
Coordinator of Baja Verapaz Territorial Collective, CONIC
El Estor, Izabal, 19 November 2009

Ingrid Urízar
Legal advisor, Interdiocesan Land Pastoral of San Marcos (*Pastoral de la
Tierra Interdiocesana de San Marcos*, PTSM)
Guatemala City, 25 March 2010

Hélmer Velásquez
  Executive director, Coordinator of NGOs and Cooperatives (*Coordinadora de ONG y Cooperativas*, CONGCOOP)
  Santiago Atitlán, Sololá, 2 March 2010

Sebastian Velásquez
  Sub-coordinator of Executive Committee, CONDEG
  Guatemala City, 10 March 2010

Marta Cecilia Ventura
  Sub-secretary of National Directive Council, CONIC
  Guatemala City, 25 March 2010

Case Study Communities

Don Pancho
  Escuintla, Escuintla – March 2010
  Nineteen survey interview participants

Salvador Xolhuitz
  Nuevo San Carlos, Retalhuleu – July 2009 to January 2010
  Eleven survey interview participants

San José La Pasión
  Chahal, Alta Verapaz – July 2009 to January 2010
  Twenty-eight survey interview participants

Victorias III
  Champerico, Retalhuleu – September 2009 to February 2010
  Thirty-eight survey interview participants

Other Communities Visited

Canlún
  Panzós, Alta Verapaz – 19–20 January 2010
  CONIC community in land occupation, reclaiming land lost during 1960s

Xya'al K'obe'
  Cobán, Alta Verapaz – 2–3 February 2010
  CONIC community in agrarian conflict within a Laguna Lachuá National Park

Anonymous communities
- Alta Verapaz, Chahal municipality (1) – July 2009
  CONIC community in occupation of unused state land
- Alta Verapaz, Chahal municipality (2) – October 2009
  CONIC community evicted from a land occupation
- Alta Verapaz, Chahal municipality (3) – October 2009
  CONIC community in agrarian conflict, a border dispute with
  neighbouring communities
- Alta Verapaz, La Tinta municipality – January 2010
  UVOC community with land from Secretaría de Asuntos Agrarios
- Alta Verapaz, Panzós municipality – January 2010
  CONIC community with land from the *Fondo de Tierras*
- Chimaltenango, Patzún municipality (1) – June and July 2009
  CCDA community with land from *Fondo de Tierras*
- Chimaltenango, Patzún municipality (2) – July and September 2009
  CCDA community with coffee land from the *Fondo de Tierras*

Recorded Testimony

Canlún
19–20 January 2010
Community assembly, on agrarian conflict with sugar cane company

Salvador Xolhuitz
13 January 2010
Local elected authorities, on internal community conflict

San José La Pasión
22 July 2009
Local elected authorities, on land occupation carried out before gaining
land

Xya'al K'obe'
2 February 2010
Community assembly, on land conflict with national park

Anonymous community 1
July 2009
Community assembly, on land purchase process

Anonymous community 2

July 2009
Association president, on land purchase process

Anonymous community 3

January 2010
Community authorities, on agrarian conflict as *mozos colonos* before
gaining land

Notes

1. Strategic Engagements with Neoliberalism

1 The astronomical rates of economic inequality produced under neoliberalism provide the clearest indication of the returned power of economic elites: the top 0.1 per cent of income earners in the United States tripled their share of national income between 1978 and 1999; in the United Kingdom the top 1 per cent of earners doubled theirs between 1982 and the early 2000s; and in global terms, the richest 20 per cent of countries more than doubled their share of world income as compared to the poorest 20 per cent between 1960 and 1997 (Harvey 2005, 16–17; McNally 2011, 44–5).

2 While there is still friction between factions of the Guatemalan elite, cooperation between neoliberal elites, the traditional oligarchy, and the military is more common than during the counter-insurgency or the peace process. The economic interests of all factions have coalesced around neoliberalism and transnational mega-projects, and the participation of multiple factions within presidential administrations has become common. Traditional sugar barons such as the family of former president Óscar Berger (2004–7), for example, have invested together with Nicaraguan and U.S. capital in cane and African palm for agro-fuel exports, and the administration of former general Otto Pérez Molina (2012–15) regularly exercised military force in support of mining and hydroelectric projects (Girón 2010a; Solano 2012, 2015).

2. The Guatemalan Campesino Movement: Organizing through War and Peace

1 These figures do not include land expropriated from the United Fruit Company, which would bring the total to 526,465 hectares (Handy 1994b 94, 197). Handy cites the original figures as 529,939 and 765,233 *manzanas*, respectively; the amounts listed in hectares above are calculated on the basis of 1.7 acres to the *manzana* and 2.471 acres to the hectare.

2 When the phenomenon was at its height in the mid-1970s, 57 per cent of cooperatives were found in the Western Highlands, especially in the department of Chimaltenango, and many others had been established in the northern region of the Ixcán and the department of El Petén (Davis 1983, 162; May 2001, 95; Schwartz 1987).

3 An essay by Juan Carlos Mazariegos, "Theories about the Campesino Social Movement in Guatemala, 1962–2006," highlights the importance of academic knowledge production in the emergence of the movement. Mazariegos argues that Marxist political theory provided local social scientists and rural organizers with an analysis of Guatemalan society that would influence the structure and goals of the CUC and other early "popular organizations" as movements focused on class struggle.

4 The CCDA provides an exception, organizing in Chimaltenango and Sololá during 1982, before being forced underground between 1983 and 1987 (see chapter 5).

5 Among the new farm purchases were at least two given to occupations organized by Padre Andrés Girón. Handy (1994a, 43–4), argues that the Cerezo administration tolerated, and even encouraged, a certain minimally provocative campesino activism while repressing occupations that posed more serious challenges. Girón, Handy notes, "clearly fit the Christian Democrats' agrarian plan" by being open to the settlement of land occupations and agrarian conflicts through the provision of INTA land.

6 Market-based land access had been gaining steam as an alternative to land distribution since the early 1980s. USAID was especially active in promoting what they called "commercial land markets," funding the Penny Foundation Land Market Project (*Fundación del Centavo*) pilot project between 1984 and 1987. INTA experimented with market-based land access, but, from 1987 onwards, CONATIERRA was the first government land program based exclusively in the "willing seller, willing buyer" land market model (*Central America Report* 1986b, 1987a, 1987b; Stewart, Fairhurst, and Pedroni 1987; USAID 1982).

7 While ties to guerrilla armies were ubiquitous during the 1980s, the guerrillas were not the only factors influencing the resurgent social

movements. In an assessment of "Social Movements, Indigenous Politics, and Democratisation in Guatemala, 1985–1996," Brett shows that factors combined to shape Guatemalan movements in the wake of the 1986 transition, including an atmosphere of reduced state terror; the decline of the Soviet Union; a shift from a struggle against the state to an effort to transform it; the rising importance of transnational advocacy networks; and the emergence of mainly Indigenous- and gender-based identity politics (Brett 2008, 9–19).

8 CNOC quickly expanded to include many more campesino organizations, including the CCDA, CODECA, Kabawil, and others (CNOC 1999, 25).

9 A coalescence of multiple neoliberal transitions is at play here, as the "coffee crisis" of the early 2000s came about as a result of the neoliberal decision to abandon the International Coffee Agreement on coffee quotas (Fridell 2007a).

10 In a process resembling Guatemala's peace process, efforts to have ADRI's law adopted came a long way but were ultimately stalled. The government agreed to a policy blueprint and cooperated on a draft law in 2008, but the bill has since been stalled in Congress. Chances of the law passing have been reduced further as the result of a lobbying campaign and parallel proposal by the organized agri-business sector (ADRI et al. 2009; ADRI and Gobierno de Guatemala 2008; Congreso de la República de Guatemala 2008; Girón 2010b; Plan Visión de País n.d.; interview, Galicia 2010).

11 Notably CONIC withdrew from ADRI and has been present as an independent organization at discussion sessions alongside ADRI, government representatives, and the MOSGUA pro-government umbrella organization of social organizations. With the exception of CONIC, however, ADRI includes every major campesino organization in the country.

12 Although it is not explored in this study, the Guatemalan campesino movement also counts with an important transnational dimension. Guatemalan groups participated in the Central American Association of Campesino Organizations for Cooperation and Development (*Asociación Centroamericana de Organizaciones Campesinas para la Cooperación y el Desarrollo*, ASOCODE) in the1990s and continue to be active in the Latin American Coordinator of Rural Organizations (*Coordinadora Latinoamericana de Organizaciones del Campo*, CLOC) as well as the *Vía Campesina* global peasant network (Desmarais 2007; Edelman 1998, 2008). As a result of this participation, some key positions and proposals advanced by Guatemalan campesino organizations, such as the CNOC *Proposal for Integral Agrarian Reform*, align neatly with work by *Vía*

Campesina or other transnational groups. Strong connections with campesino organizations outside of Guatemala also lead to regular interaction and exchange of ideas, such as in CONIC's exchange between members of Guatemalan agrarian communities and Brazilian MST activists, and in the CCDA's participation in Central American regional solidarity economy markets and workshops.

13 In some cases non-campesino social organizations or NGOs such as the *Pastoral de la Tierra* or the *Fundación Guillermo Toriello* played the same role, but accompanying groups are usually campesino organizations.

14 The original name of the ANN was the Alliance for a New Nation (*Alianza Nueva Nación*) but changed to the Alternative for a New Nation after the 2007 elections. Both names use the acronym ANN.

15 The community of Salvador Xolhuitz, discussed in chapter 5, provides an example of the harm that can be caused when two campesino organizations – in this case, CCDA and Kab'awil – support opposing sides of a local conflict.

16 The *Fondo de Tierras* governing council includes two positions each for the campesino, cooperative agricultural, and Indigenous sectors, who steer the fund alongside six representatives from the Ministry of Agriculture, Cattle, and Food and the Ministry of Public Finance and six from the private sector. Attempts to gain or hold onto these seats are rumoured to be responsible for some of the recent fracturing of CNOC.

17 A notable exception is presented by the Verapaz Union of Campesino Organizations (*Unión Verapacense de Organizaciones Campesinas*, UVOC). Across the accompaniment of over two hundred communities in agrarian conflict and sixteen successful cases of land access, UVOC has never dealt with the *Fondo de Tierras* (interview, Morales 2009, 2010; UVOC 2007).

18 Decentralization was set out in the Decentralization Law, Municipal Code, and Law of Urban and Rural Development Councils, all passed in 2002. For discussion of these laws, see Silva (2010) and FUNCEDE (2002).

19 While campesino demands entered Guatemalan national politics through grassroots activism beginning in the 1970s and 1980s, those same demands were also expressed in numerous rebellions in the late nineteenth century against liberal land laws, and also through the agrarian reform of the "democratic spring" in the 1950s (Handy 1994b; Martínez Peláez 2011; McCreery 1994).

3. Between the Bullet and the Bank: Campesino Access to Land

1 While complete data are available only to 2009, reports indicate that by July 2013 the number of farms had reached 273, or an additional eight farms per year (Hernández 2013).

2 Instead of the standard eight regions used officially in Guatemala, which divide the country by mainly topographically related groups of departments (states), AVANCSO has proposed five agrarian regions determined by land use and whose borders run between municipalities (AVANCSO 2008). The latter allows for a more nuanced view of regions based on local social and economic dynamics, but the terminology employed may be confusing for those unfamiliar with the system. For example, the region of "Alta Verapaz" does not coincide with the borders of the department of the same name, instead including much of Alta Verapaz and Izabal as well as parts of Baja Verapaz and El Quiché, whereas the "Northern Highlands" includes a great deal of the department of Alta Verapaz as well as all of the Petén and parts of Izabal, El Quiché, and Huehuetenango.

3 I arrived at this assessment over the course of my fieldwork, during which time I visited FONTIERRAS-purchased farms and spoke with local campesino activists and community members in all five agrarian regions. The position is confirmed when looking at the distribution of farms by municipality. For example, fifty-three farms were sold in Alta Verapaz through *Fondo de Tierras* between 1998 and 2009, but none were from the municipalities of Chisec or Fray Bartolomé de las Casas, where the agrofuel industry is booming and a major highway is under construction (Fondo de Tierras 2009a).

4 Groups that purchased land through the *Fondo de Tierras* receive a subsidy to invest in productive projects and technical assistance by agronomists over three years, but neither aspect has functioned properly. Communities and campesino organizations report that in some cases the agronomists never arrive and in many more they give inappropriate advice. For example, a community I visited in Chimaltenango was advised by a *Fondo de Tierras* technician to cut down all of the trees on its forested property, sell the lumber, and invest the earnings in non-traditional agricultural crops, despite the fact that the forest grew on a steep mountain slope in a landslide-prone area (field notes, June and July 2009). Many groups also lose their subsidies to mismanagement or internal corruption (see the case study of Salvador Xolhuitz in chapter 5).

5 Agrarian debt held by campesino communities was greatly relieved in 2012, when the Guatemalan government responded to campesino pressure by allowing for significant reduction of debt in most cases. The campesino actions leading to debt reduction are discussed in chapter 6.

6 I arrived at these categories through conversations and interviews with campesino activists and others involved in dispute settlement. My fieldwork also brought me to seven communities engaged in agrarian

conflict in Alta Verapaz and Izabal, and included extensive research with two communities that came to own land through agrarian conflict (see case studies of Victorias III and San José La Pasión in chapter 4). My assessment is further confirmed by a large set of studies of Guatemalan agrarian conflicts (Amnesty International 2006; CALDH and CONIC 2009; Camacho Nassar 2003; CUC 2002; Hurtado Paz y Paz 2008; Santa Cruz 2006; Universidad Rafael Landívar 2009; Alonzo 2009; van Leeuwen 2006, 2010). These studies concur in their depiction of agrarian conflict and its many causes, but the subcategorization of conflicts used here is my own.

7 The role of new economic activities in generating agrarian conflicts since the 1960s should be emphasized. A study by the Universidad Rafael Landívar (2009) highlighted such conflicts, pointing to those stemming from a northern mega-highway project (*Franja Transversal del Norte*), protected natural areas, agro-fuels, mineral extraction, petroleum activity, hydroelectric production, and drug-related activity.

8 An overlapping context for these evictions should be noted. Guatemalan President Álvaro Colom declared martial law in the department of Alta Verapaz between December 2010 and February 2011. This was the first such order since the end of the armed conflict in 1996, decreed ostensibly in the fight against Mexican drug cartels. While the evictions described here were carried out after martial law ended, they were preceded by aggression during the period of military control: Felix Cuc Xo, a Xya'al K'obe' community leader, was beaten and arrested on 8 February, and communities surrounding Canlún, also within the land used by Chabil Utzaj, were evicted during the martial law period (Granovsky-Larsen 2011).

9 The Finca Chitocán and Finca La Moca occupations are documented in Amnesty International (2006, 25–9) and GHRC (2006).

10 This number increased nearly three-fold between 2010, when data on agrarian conflicts were first accessed for this research, and the figures presented here from early 2016. In that timespan, the number of cases in the SAA database grew from 4,883 to 7,690; broken down by the stage of conflict, cases grew from 2,326 to 4,251 (resolved), from 1,047 to 1,964 (closed or concluded), and decreased slightly from 1,511 to 1,475 (outstanding). That the number of outstanding cases remained similar five years later suggests that although many conflicts are being resolved, the rate of overall conflictivity remains unaddressed. The 2016 data are also more accurate than those provided in 2010, since the percentage of cases presented without accompanying hectare amounts dropped from 15 per cent to 1 per cent.

11 The SAA database does not include details of the conditions under which
    individual conflicts end, beyond the categories of "resolved," "closed," or
    "concluded." Files on each case recorded by the SAA are available through
    the agency's main office in Guatemala City, however, and a review of cases
    could provide more precise figures on land access.

12 Field research visit to Canlún, including recorded community testimony,
    19–20 January 2010. The group also provided me with a copy of a land
    registration map showing the area owned by the Cooperativa Samilhá
    R.L. in the 1960s. For more information on Chabil Utzaj and contemporary
    conflicts in the Polochic Valley, see Hurtado Paz y Paz (2008, 336–45),
    Frajedas, Alberto, and Dürr (2008), and Universidad Rafael Landívar
    (2009).

13 Two other communities – Michbil Rix Pu and Sak'opur – also branched
    out from Salacuín into land that was later claimed by the Laguna Lachuá
    park. The three communities, while all engaged in the Lachuá conflict, are
    represented by different campesino organizations (CONIC and CUC) and
    have followed different paths in their respective struggles for land (SAA
    2009a; Universidad Rafael Landívar 2009, 74–6).

14 Field research visit to Xya'al K'obe', including recorded community
    testimony, 2–3 February 2010. The group provided me with a folder of
    documents demonstrating the conflict negotiation process, including the
    SAA satellite study, *Estudio fotogramétrico: caso comunidades Michbil Rix Pu,
    Xya'alko'be, Se'quixpur, Cobán, Alta Verapaz* (SAA 2009a). More information
    on the Laguna Lachuá conflicts can be found in a study by the Universidad
    Rafael Landívar (2009, 74–6), and conflicts within other natural reserves are
    discussed at length by Hurtado Paz y Paz (2008) and Grandia (2009, 2012).

15 The position equating *colonato* with slavery was also formed by interviews
    and discussions with former *mozos colonos* on the Finca Salvador Xolhuitz
    in Nuevo San Carlos, Retalhuleu (see chapter 5).

16 The cited numbers of *fincas* and *mozo colono* communities varied slightly
    across interview accounts, but all placed the number of farms before
    recent struggles at between seventy and seventy-eight and the number
    of remaining farms at either two or three. The figures here match a
    commentary published by the Indigenous researcher of campesino
    struggles Irma Alicia Velásquez Nimatuj (2010), who described the
    transformation of San Miguel Tucurú as its own agrarian reform.

17 The amount of registered farmland owned by individuals was calculated
    at 88.5 per cent in 1979, 85.1 in 2004, and 92.8 in 2008. The share of all
    farms owned by individuals was counted as 99.6, 97.9, and 92.8 per cent,
    respectively, for the same years.

18 I thank Eugenio Incer and Luis Galicia of AVANCSO for explaining SAA land purchases to me in this way. Their assessment was backed up in my conversations with community leaders and campesino activists working with land conflict resolution.

19 Important exceptions to this generalization can be found in a critical analysis of the *Fondo de Tierras* and SAA by Garoz, Alonso, and Gauster (2005), and in a reflection on agrarian social movement strategy in post-conflict Guatemala by van Leeuwen (2010).

4. CONIC: A Campesino Organization Apart

1 For the purpose of our brief introduction I rely mainly on the account provided by Irma Alicia Velásquez Nimatuj (2008, chap. 3), whose dissertation research included interviews on these events with key members of both CONIC and CUC.

2 CONIC's self-identification as an Indigenous organization has grown even stronger over its history. Long-time observer and ally Santiago Bastos quoted a CONIC activist as referring to the "Mayanization" (*mayanización*) of the organization, which Bastos worried has led to a "neglect of mobilization as campesinos" (2010, 29).

3 Of the twenty-two founding members of CONIC, seventeen were Indigenous and all but four came from rural communities involved in agrarian conflicts over land titles (Bastos and Camus 2003, 38; Brett 2008, 122). The strong initial representation of Indigenous campesinos who themselves struggled for land helps to explain the emphasis that CONIC has placed on land access.

4 CONIC has assisted cases of land access in Alta Verapaz (fifty cases), Baja Verapaz (thirteen), Chimaltenango (ten), Escuintla (five), Huehuetenango (five), Izabal (thirteen), El Progreso (one), Quetzaltenango (five), El Quiché (seven), Retalhuleu (ten), San Marcos (seven), Santa Rosa (two), Sololá (two), and Suchitepéquez (fourteen).

5 Another CONIC document lists just thirty-three communities with debt for land purchase as of 2009, suggesting that other CONIC-FONTIERRAS communities have paid their debts entirely (CONIC 2009b).

6 This section on CONIC's organizational structure is based on observation and conversation in the Alta Verapaz and Retalhuleu Territorial Collectives, including interviews with five Territorial Collective Promoters (Candelaria Beb, Celso Caal, Hermelindo Chub Icó, Juventina López Vasquez, and Emilio Tzib Quej), and a discussion on Territorial Collectives with César Bol, the coordinator for Accompaniment of Q'eqchi' Region

Territorial Collectives (El Estor, Izabal, 19 November 2009). CONIC's organizational structure is also discussed by Bastos and Camus (2003, 54–60).

7 "*Estamos bien jodido pero contento*" (interview, Rigoberto, Victorias III, 10 February 2010).

8 My account of Victorias III is based on six visits to the community of between one and four days each over the course of six months; survey interviews with members of thirty-eight households (half of the total seventy-four families); an interview and discussions with Juventina López Vasquez, the coordinator of CONIC's Territorial Collective in Retalhuleu; documentation compiled by the Cooperación Galega development organization; and the full file on the community kept by the *Fondo de Tierras* in Guatemala City.

9 The community was founded with ninety-four families, but twenty left the farm early on. New members of the community are now accepted when someone decides to leave, but the number has been capped at seventy-four (field notes, 15 January 2010).

10 At the time of research in 2010, a lack of legal ownership of their land was a source of anxiety that came up frequently in interviews. At the meeting discussed here, a CONIC representative explained that the land title should not be on the list of community priorities, but the group insisted on placing their land title at the top. The community later qualified for a 75 per cent reduction in debt following the *Fondo de Tierras* restructuring discussed in chapter 6, and when I visited in 2015 the group was set to pay off the remaining amount that year.

11 "*Hay que hacer en conjunto: tanto como comunidad, tanto como organización también*" (Domingo, speaking in group testimony, San José La Pasión, 22 July 2009).

12 Chahal will quite likely be more connected to the rest of Guatemala very soon. A controversial highway project initiated in the 1970s, the *Franja Transversal del Norte*, was recently boosted through renewed funding. During my research in Chahal, construction was underway on a section of the highway that passed through the town of Chahal, an hour's drive from San José La Pasión.

13 My work in San José La Pasión was somewhat limited by a language barrier. Very few people in the community speak Spanish, meaning that I relied on the local CONIC activist and a handful of community volunteers to translate all of my interactions with members of the Maya Q'eqchi' community. While the depth of my engagement with the community was doubtlessly lessened by speaking through translators, I felt privileged

to be able to research with this very remote, monolingual village twelve hours from Guatemala City and six hours' travel from the highway town of Rio Dulce, Izabal. The information presented here is based entirely on my time in the community. I paid four visits to San José La Pasión between July 2009 and January 2010, staying for between one and three days each trip, and conducted survey interviews with half of all households, or twenty-eight people.

14 See chapter 3 for more on struggles for *prestaciones laborales* labour rights.

15 None of the accounts of the conflict explain why the group occupied land owned by a cooperative instead of a private farm.

16 The Guatemalan Secretariat of Agrarian Affairs sponsored the purchase of twenty-one farms for conflict resolution between 2007 and 2010 (see chapter 3).

17 FONAPAZ apparently also took pride in the school. As I sat in the FONAPAZ office in Guatemala City one day, waiting to request access to documents, I saw San José La Pasión community members and their school flash across a large-screen TV advertising FONAPAZ projects.

18 The price of corn varies by region and fluctuates by month, but I use the approximate rate of Q100/*quintal* that was frequently cited in discussion with community members. A publication by Guatemala's MAGA agricultural ministry (2013) provides similar numbers, with national average prices of Q104 in 2008, Q128 in 2009, and Q115 in 2010.

5. CCDA: A Revolutionary Enterprise

1 "Direct trade" refers to a model similar to fair trade, but one that opts to bypass the fair trade certification program. A growing number of producer cooperatives in the Global South and importers and roasters in the North have chosen direct trade over fair trade for what is perceived as a dominance of the traditional fair trade market by corporate players such as Starbucks and Dunkin' Donuts. Under direct trade, producers establish direct relationships with their northern partners and agree to terms that are similar to those of the fair trade agreement but generally exceed fair trade minimum standards (Fridell 2007a, 2007b, 2009; Stenzel 2013).

2 The major portion of this chapter, including the two community case studies, discusses the CCDA using data collected through 2010. Some mention is made of the substantial changes to the organization between 2010 and 2015, however, and these changes are expanded upon in more detail in the book's final chapter.

3 The organizational history repeated by members of the CCDA today
holds that the group's original name was the Campesino Committee in
Defence of the Highlands (*Comité Campesino en Defensa del Altiplano*), but
that the word *defence* was dropped following severe repression. However,
documents produced by the CCDA to announce its formation in 1982
make no mention of any name other than the current one.

4 The CUC had been forced underground in 1980 following a successful
labour campaign and a subsequent round of retaliatory state violence.
While campesinos have organized for centuries, and other types of formal
groups have played important historical roles in Guatemala – including
the peasant leagues and other community-based campesino groups
organized by labour organizations during the 1944–54 era of democratic
reform (Handy 1994b) – CUC and the CCDA were the first of the social
movement organizations founded and led by campesinos that we see
today.

5 The list of CCDA projects from the 1980s and 1990s was compiled from
primary documents collected in the archives of the Latin America Working
Group housed at York University's Centre for Research on Latin America
and the Caribbean, and of the Guatemalan News and Information Bureau
maintained online by Princeton University. The list of projects is almost
certainly incomplete.

6 In interviews and documents, people in some CCDA communities even
confuse CNOC and the CCDA, with Gilberto Atz straddling the line
between the two.

7 The first CCDA annual operating plan was written in 2005 for 2006
operations and did not include an introductory analysis of the national
political and agrarian situations as did the subsequent plans cited here
(CCDA 2005).

8 Of those farms that still owe money for land purchase, however, most still
owe the majority of the cost, and many have been noted by the *Fondo de
Tierras* as suffering from significant productive or organizational problems
(Fondo de Tierras 2009a, 2009b). This is telling of the CCDA problem of
losing touch with those communities that are not integrated into their
direct trade coffee program.

9 CCDA communities produced 36,646.5 *quintales* of coffee cherries, or *uva*,
the fruit picked from coffee trees that contains the bean. After two stages
of drying and processing the beans, first to *pergamino* and then to *oro*, with
around 5.5 pounds of *uva* resulting in 1 pound of *oro* for export, the final
product would be approximately 6,663 100-pound bags. A total of 676

quintales of *oro* was actually exported (CCDA 2009a, 14–15; field notes, 15 December 2009). By the 2014–15 harvest, exports had increased to seven shipping containers, each carrying 288 *quintales* of *oro*, or just over 200,000 pounds of dried coffee.

10 BC-CASA paid US$150 per 100-pound bag of *oro* in 2008, as opposed to the $121 minimum set by the Fair Trade Labeling Organization.

11 The names and emphasis of CCDA programs change slightly from year to year. The five programs named above were the focus of CCDA work in 2009 (CCDA 2009a, 7).

12 The concerns brought up in 2010 are interesting for our discussion of the CCDA's evolution, but it should be noted that that *visión grande* clearly was re-established and adhered to in the years ahead, as discussed below.

13 In 2010 the CCDA received funding from Catholic Committee against Hunger and for Development (*Comité Catholique Contra la Faim et pour le Développement*, CCFD-Terre Solidaire), American World Jewish Service, German Development Service (*Deutscher Entwicklungsdienst*, DED), *Trócaire*, the Canadian International Development Agency's Project for Rural Economic Development in the Department of Sololá (PROSOL), Rights Action, and Veterinarians without Borders, and received group visits from other solidarity organizations and North American schools.

14 In 2008, CNAIC was composed of the CCDA, *Defensoría Indígena las Verapaces* (DIV), Asociación Nuevo Amanecer Maya Chuj, Asociación Integral de Servicios Comunitarios de Salud (AICSECO), Unión Campesina del Sur (UCS), and Asociación Maya Sin Tierra (CCDA 2008b, 38).

15 The departments and numbers of communities, in 2010, were: Sololá (forty-eight communities), Chimaltenango (thirteen), Quiché (7), Huehuetenango (twenty-four), San Marcos (four), Retalhuleu (three), Suchitepéquez (six), Escuintla (three), Santa Rosa (four), Baja Verapaz (six), and Alta Verapaz (six) (CCDA 2009b). By 2015, with the expansion of the CCDA's work discussed below, the group had established a presence in twenty of Guatemala's twenty-two departments.

16 These snippets were offered within responses to other questions. The interview, conducted early in my research, unfortunately did not touch directly on shaky CCDA-community relations.

17 The CCDA's relationship with the CUC had been strengthened since 2007 through a six-year joint project sponsored by the German *Deutscher Entwicklungsdienst* (DED) development agency. The project aimed to harness the specializations of the two organizations to resolve agrarian conflicts by strengthening alternative community agricultural projects (conversation with Elisabeth Giesel of the DED, 7 January 2010; CCDA et al. 2006).

18 When I returned to the CCDA in 2013 and 2015, I was surprised at the number of new faces and the contingent of young CCDA workers. I discuss the CCDA's successful renovation in more detail in chapter 6.

19 Xolhuitz is pronounced "shole-oo-ITZ."

20 I wasn't able to speak with Salvador Xolhuitz community members from the ACROX side of the conflict, but I did speak with campesino activists in Kab'awil and the *Fondo de Tierras* who work with ACROX and support them in negotiations.

21 Documents produced by the community and by FONTIERRAS list as the campesino organization accompanying ADISC in their search for land the *Consejo Nacional Indígena y Campesino Kut Bal Bey*, which was a short-lived campesino umbrella group that the CCDA joined.

22 The ethnic composition of Salvador Xolhuitz is 80 per cent Ladino, or non-Indigenous, with 10 per cent Maya Mam and 10 per cent Maya K'iche' (Fondo de Tierras 2004).

23 Extra pieces of land that are not registered in an official land title, known as *excesos*, are quite common in Guatemala, and were a major concern of the World Bank–sponsored Cadastral Information Registry project (Grandia 2012, chap. 4; Funes 2010). As Grandia points out (2012, 127), the cadastral process also allowed for arbitrary and questionable resolution of *exceso* ownership. On the *prestaciones laborales* system, see chapter 3 of this volume.

24 I have refrained from including the names of individuals on either side when referring to accusations, threats, or illegal acts.

25 In early January 2010, it appeared that the conflict would only intensify and that more violence could erupt. After a final visit on 10 January to talk to the ADISC governing council, I stopped my fieldwork with Salvador Xolhuitz. The conflict did erupt again in October 2010, when a member of the ADISC group died of a gunshot wound to the eye (CCDA, e-mail messages to author, 14 and 17 October 2010).

26 According to the CCDA's Marcelo Sabuc, members of the group that split off from the main association all came from the latecomer third group (interview, Aldea Quixayá, Sololá, 14 October 2009).

27 I also have personal connection to another case where internal conflict arose out of the FONTIERRAS insistence on community composition as dictated by land extension. Finca Concepción in the department of Santa Rosa is so large, at 1,980 hectares, that for its sale to go ahead FONTIERRAS had to hastily pull together 580 families into a single group. When I spent close to two months as a human rights observer at Finca Concepción in 2004, an internal coup within the *junta directiva* had led to expulsion of one group, the subsequent occupation in protest of one

area of the farm by the expelled group, and the frequent use of firearms against that protesting group. One member of the small group was killed in 2005, ending the occupation. By 2009, when Finca Concepción came up in conversation with a FONTIERRAS representative during an interview, multiple armed groups were reportedly fighting for control of the enormous plantation and its revenue (Atz 2009; Fondo de Tierras 2009a).

28 The SAA had promised to buy the land, running the purchase through the *Fondo de Tierras*. CCDA representatives noted that the SAA and FONTIERRAS were worried that the ACROX group was not large enough for a new piece of land and, in a troubling potential repetition of Salvador Xolhuitz's history, they were considering adding additional families for the new community (field notes, 9 December 2015).

29 Members of Salvador Xolhuitz also expressed pride in having their own land. Ancelmo, the ADISC treasurer, told me, "Things are a little better here, because in the plantations I used to work so hard, but the earnings were more for the rich. Here, on the other hand, every person is their own boss, every person has to figure out how to make their lands more productive because the earnings are going to be your own. So things are a little better when it comes to work, because I'm not living under a boss anymore, I'm not enslaved by a boss" (interview, Salvador Xolhuitz, 17 September 2009).

30 "*Estamos acostumbrados a darle*" (interview, Hipólito, Don Pancho, 30 March 2010).

31 Gilberto Atz, the campesino representative on the *Fondo de Tierras* Board of Directors, is a close collaborator with the CCDA. Atz and the members of Don Pancho are also from San Martín Jilotepeque in Chimaltenango, the municipality where the CCDA announced its formation in 1982.

32 This system is similar to the customary management of lowland Q'eqchi' villages in Alta Verapaz, Izabal, and Petén described by Grandia (2012, chap. 3). Grandia contrasts the customary management distribution of multiple non-uniform plots according to terrain type, with the grid system encouraged under private property regimes. When land is handed out according to a grid, some farmers have access to good land and water and are close to roads, while others may have to put up with long walks, swampy land, or steep hills (90–7).

33 Two smaller plots of coffee land were given to each family instead of one larger one, in order to more evenly distribute the coffee trees of varying quality. One *manzana* is equal to 1.7 acres.

34 Interview participants reported growing an average of eleven *quintales* (100-pound bags) of corn and a maximum of thirty *quintales*.

35 Pacaya is an edible forest palm; chipilín is a leafy green vegetable.
36 Don Efraín told me proudly that he produces all of his own food now, and only buys non-food items in the market such as salt, sugar, and lime for tortillas (cal).
37 At 732 metres above sea level, Don Pancho produces a low-grade coffee that doesn't meet the Café Justicia standards.

6. Beyond the Post-Conflict Period

1 Some clarification on categories of armed groups is in order. While domestic drug-trafficking organizations – many with ties to counter-insurgent-era military officers – control the drug trade in Guatemala, they are deeply connected to Mexican groups (Brockett 2012). Sicario hitmen, it should also be noted, do not necessarily serve a paramilitary function. Many sicario groups are based in street gangs, but those that target human rights defenders, often with sophisticated logistics and military-grade hardware, should be considered closer in operation to paramilitary death squads than gangs (three anonymous interviews 2017).
2 I thank Charles R. Hale for his role in thinking through the end of the "post-conflict" period. At my doctoral defence, Dr Hale led the discussion in this direction, and our conversation lingered on the question of the post-conflict and what lies beyond. There is also a general sense in Guatemala that the post-conflict period has come to a close, as alluded to in the work of Yagenova and Véliz (2011), who mark the end of the period as 2003.
3 I borrow the concept of "agrarian sovereignty" from Haroon Akram-Lodhi (2013, 157–70), who suggests the term as one that would broaden the idea of food sovereignty to include land redistribution and other aspects of agrarian reform measures necessary for its realization.
4 Juracán survived an assassination attempt in 2008 and was driven out of the country by death threats from a paramilitary group in 2010. As part of the threats in 2010, the CCDA's coffee-processing plant was ransacked, and part of its coffee harvest was stolen; after Juracán left Guatemala in 2010, masked and armed men had a regular presence around the CCDA main offices in the village of Quixayá. More details are included in Granovsky-Larsen (forthcoming).
5 A fourth CCDA office – following the headquarters in the village of Quixayá in San Lucas Tolimán, Sololá, and the two new offices in Alta and Baja Verapaz – was opened in Santa Cruz del Quiché. The Quiché office was the result of a project, funded by the German Development Service (Deutscher Entwicklungsdienst, DED), to bring the CCDA and the CUC

together for productive projects in communities with recently resolved agrarian conflicts (field notes, 7 January 2010).

6 Two other activists were elected to Congress with the CDR: Sandra Morán, a feminist and Guatemala's first openly gay congressperson; and Alvaro Velásquez, a professor of sociology.

7 On 8 June 2016, Daniel Choc Pop, a community organizer from San Juan Tres Ríos, Alta Verapaz, was murdered. Choc Pop had been active with his community's struggle to have their historical land title recognized, a case that was backed by the CCDA and has generated intimidation and violence against the community (Front Line Defenders 2016).

References

Abbott, Jeff. n.d. "The Fourth Invasion: Capitalism's New Wars in Central America." Unpublished.

ACROX (Asociación Campesina Rosario Xolhuitz). 2008. *Hechos cronológicos registrados en la comunidad agraria Xolhuitz, en el municipio de Nuevo San Carlos, en el departamento de Retahuleu.* City: Publisher.

ADISC (Asociación de Desarrollo Integral Santa Cruz). 2006. *Memoria histórica sobre hechos reales de la asociación ADISC en la pre y pos adquisición de la finca Salvador Xolwitz.* Community document.

– 2009. *Estatuto interno* Community document.

ADRI, CONADUR, MOSGUA, CONIC, UNAC-MIC (Alianza de Desarrollo Rural Integral, Consejo Nacional de Desarrollo Urbano y Rural, Movimiento de Organizaciones Sociales de Guatemala, Consejo Nacional Indígena y Campesina, Mesa Indígena y Campesina), and Gobierno de Guatemala. 2009. *Política nacional de desarrollo rural integral.* Guatemala City: Presidencia de la República.

ADRI, and Gobierno de Guatemala. 2008. "Anteproyecto de ley del sistema nacional de desarrollo rural integral." Draft of proposed law.

Aguilar, María. 2015. "Excusan la corrupción y fomentan la mentira gubermental." *elPeriódico,* 25 April.

Akram-Lodhi, A. Haroon. 2013. *Hungry for Change: Farmers, Food Justice and the Agrarian Question.* Halifax: Fernwood.

Allison, Michael E. 2016. "The Guatemalan National Revolutionary Unit: The Long Collapse." *Democratization* 23 (6): 1042–58. https://doi.org/10.1080/135 10347.2016.1159557.

Alonzo, Fernando. 2009. *Conflictividad agraria en Alta Verapaz: Un mal negocio para todos.* Guatemala City: CONGCOOP.

Alonso Fradejas, Alberto, Fernando Alonzo, and Jochen Dürr. 2008. *Caña de azúcar y palma africana: Combustibles para un nuevo ciclo de acumulación y dominio en Guatemala*. Guatemala City, Guatemala: CONGCOOP.

Álvarez, Lorena. 2009. "La figura del mozo colono que se niega a desaparecer." *elPeriódico*, 14 July. http://www.albedrio.org/htm/noticias/ep140709.htm.

Amnesty International. 2006. *Guatemala: Land of Injustice?* City, Guatemala: AI.

– 2012. "Guatemala: After Massacre, Real Dialogue Must Follow Investigation and Prosecutions," 26 October. https://www.amnesty.org/en/news/guatemala-after-massacre-real-dialogue-must-follow-investigation-and-prosecutions-2012-10-26.

– 2014. *Mining in Guatemala: Rights at Risk*. London: Amnesty International.

– 2016. *We Are Defending the Land with Our Blood: Defenders of the Land, Territory, and Environment in Honduras and Guatemala*. London: Amnesty International.

Andrés, Asier. 2011. "Desalojos de campesinos: Una política de estado." *elPeriódico*, 22 March.

Aragón, Andrea. 2006. *Guatemala de mis dolores*. Antigua Guatemala, Guatemala: Ediciones del Pensativo.

Archibold, Randal C. 2012. "Guatemala Shooting Raises Concerns about Military's Expanded Role." *New York Times*, 20 October. https://www.nytimes.com/2012/10/21/world/americas/guatemala-shooting-raises-concerns-about-militarys-expanded-role.html.

Argueta, Otto. 2012. "Private Security in Guatemala: Pathway to Its Proliferation." *Bulletin of Latin American Research* 31 (3): 320–35. https://doi.org/10.1111/j.1470-9856.2012.00734.x.

Asociación Junan Kusamuj. 2008. "Breve historia Don Pancho." Community document.

AVANCSO (Asociación para el Avance de las Ciencias Sociales en Guatemala). 2008. *Regiones y zonas agrarias de Guatemala: Una visión desde la reproducción social y económica de los campesinos*. Guatemala City: AVANCSO.

BANRURAL (Banco de Desarrollo Rural). 1999. "Resolución no. CA-081-0-99." Guatemala City: BANRURAL.

Barrios, Yassmin. 2013. "Transcripción de la lectura de sentencia por genocidio Ixil, 10 de Mayo 2013." HIJOS Guatemala. hijosguate.blogspot.ca/2013/05/lectura-de-sentencia-por-genocidio-10.html.

Bastos, Santiago. 2010. "La política maya en la Guatemala posconflicto." In *El movimiento maya en la década después de la paz (1997–2007)*, edited by Santiago Bastos and Roddy Brett, 3–54. Guatemala City: F&G Editores.

Bastos, Santiago, and Manuela Camus. 2003. *CONIC: 11 años de lucha por la madre tierra, la vida y la paz*. Guatemala City: CONIC.

Batres, Rodrigo. 2011. "Ocupaciones de fincas: La expresión de la histórica concentración de la tierra en Guatemala." *Enfoque* 17:2–27.

– 2012. "El gobierno de Otto Pérez Molina, el discurso del cambio y la problemática agraria." *El observador* 7 (36–7): 80–116.

Brands, Hal. 2011. "Crime, Irregular Warfare, and Institutional Failure in Latin America: Guatemala as a Case Study." *Studies in Conflict and Terrorism* 34 (3): 228–47. https://doi.org/10.1080/1057610X.2011.545937.

Braudel, Fernand. 1980. *On History*. Translated by Sarah Matthews. Chicago: University of Chicago Press.

Brett, Roddy. 2008. *Social Movements, Indigenous Politics and Democratisation in Guatemala, 1985–1996*. Leiden: Brill. https://doi.org/10.1163/ej.9789004165526.i-229.

– 2016. "Guatemala: The Persistence of Genocidal Logic beyond Mass Killing." In *How Mass Atrocities End: Studies from Guatemala, Burundi, Indonesia, the Sudans, Bosnia-Herzegovina, and Iraq*, edited by Bridget Conley-Zilkic, 29–55. Cambridge: Cambridge University Press.

Briscoe, Ivan, and Martín Rodríguez Pellecer. 2010. *A State under Siege: Elites, Criminal Networks, and Institutional Reform in Guatemala*. The Hague: Netherlands Institute of International Relations Clingendael.

Brockett, Charles D. 2005. *Political Movements and Violence in Central America*. New York: Cambridge University Press. https://doi.org/10.1017/CBO9780511614378.

2012. "The Consequences of Expanding Domestic and Transnational Drug Trafficking Organizations for Guatemala and for Hemispheric Drug Policy." Paper presented at the 2012 Congress of the Latin American Studies Association, San Francisco, 23–6 May.

Brown, Wendy. 2015. *Undoing the Demos: Neoliberalism's Stealth Revolution*. Brooklyn: Zone Books.

CALDH (Centro para la Acción Legal en Derechos Humanos), and CONIC (Coordinadora Nacional Indígena y Campesina). 2009. *Conflictividad de la tierra: Evidencias de violaciones a los derechos humanos en Guatemala*. City, Guatemala City: CALDH.

Camacho Nassar, Carlos, ed. 2003. *Tierra, identidad y conflicto en Guatemala*. Dinámicas agrarias 5. Guatemala City: FLACSO, MINUGUA, and CONTIERRA.

Cambranes, J.C., ed. 1992a. *500 años de lucha por la tierra*. 2 vols. City, Guatemala City: FLACSO.

– 1992b. "Democratización y movimientos campesinos pro-tierra." In *In 500 años de lucha por la tierra*, edited by J.C. Cambranes, 2:39–72. Guatemala City: FLACSO.

Carr, Matthew. 1991. "Guatemala: State of Terror." *Race & Class* 33 (1): 31–56. https://doi.org/10.1177/030639689103300102.

CCDA (Comité Campesino Del Altiplano). 1982a. *Denuncia*.

– 1982b. *Documento de denuncia internacional acerca del heróico pueblo del altiplano de Guatemala y los refugiados internos*. Self-published.

– 1982c. *Informe*. Self-published.

– 1987a. Letter from Francisco Calí on the CCDA "capacitación de jóvenes" project, 9 October.

– 1987b. Letter from Francisco Calí on the CCDA "producción de candelas" project, 9 October.

– 1989a. *Proyecto: tiendas comunales*, 15 August. Self-published.

– 1989b. *Proyecto de ayuda de emergencia a población campesina indígena de Chimaltenango en el altiplano central*, August. Self-published.

– 1990. Untitled flyer.

– 2005. *Plan operativo anual del Comité Campesino del Altiplano 2006*. Internal report.

– 2006. *Plan operativo anual del Comité Campesino Del Altiplano CCDA 2007*. Internal report.

– 2007. *POA integrado 2008*. Internal report.

– 2008a. *El comercio justo plus. Un aporte a la economía campesina en resistencia al T.L.C.* Guatemala City: CONGCOOP.

– 2008b. *Plan estratégico del CCDA. 2009–2013*. Internal report.

– 2009a. *Plan de negocios*. Asociación, Comité Campesino Del Altiplano. Empresa, Servicios Campesinos Del Altiplano. Internal report.

– 2009b. *Provenientes de 122 comunidades*. Internal report.

– 2010. "El Comité Campesino del Altiplano CCDA informa sobre el asesinato del compañero José María López Ventura en la comunidad Salvador Xolhuitz," email 17 October.

– 2015. Letter from the CCDA to President Otto Fernando Pérez Molina, 20 April.

– n.d. "Project Funding Proposal: For Traditional Mayan Crafts Production in the *Altiplano*."

CCDA, CUC, CONGCOOP, and DED (Comité de Unidad Campesina, Coordinación de ONG y Cooperativas de Guatemala, and Deutscher Entwicklungsdienst). 2006. *Documento estratégico del proyecto: "Tierra, conflictividad y desarrollo rural."* Internal publication.

CEH (Comisión para el Esclarecimiento Histórico). 1999. *Guatemala memoria del silencio*. 12 vols. Guatemala: UNOPS.

Central America Report. 1986a. "Private Sector Bristles at Land Demands." *Central America Report*, 18 July.

– 1986b. "Special Report. Girón Lights the Fuse: The Land Problem in Guatemala." *Central America Report*, 11 July.

– 1987a. "Land Crunch Gets Noisier." *Central America Report*, 3 April.

– 1987b. "Land Distribution in 1987: A Piecemeal Approach." *Central America Report*, 4 December.

– 1988. "Church Addresses Land Question." *Central America Report*, 25 March.

– 1991a. "Violent Eviction from Occupied Land." *Central America Report*, 22 March.

– 1991b. "Workers Occupy Plantations." *Central America Report*, 13 December.

– 1992a. "The Eternal Crises of Land and Labor." *Central America Report*, 10 April.

– 1992b. "Massive Land Takeovers." *Central America Report*, 27 March.

– 1994a. "Land Conflicts." *Central America Report*, 29 April.

– 1994b. "Land Occupation Rekindles Anti-Foreigner Sentiment." *Central America Report*, 5 August.

CERIGUA (Centro de Reportes Informativos sobre Guatemala). 2011. "Realizan consulta comunitaria en Champerico sobre exploración de hierro en las playas del Pacífico." *CERIGUA*, 8 June. https://cerigua.org/article/realizan-consulta-comunitaria-en-champerico-sobre-/.

CEUR (Centro de Estudios Urbanos y Regionales). 1990. "Invasiones de tierras (1986–1990). Un desborde popular en tiempos de democrácia." *CEUR boletín* 9:1–16.

CICIG (Comisión Internacional Contra la Impunidad en Guatemala). 2016. *Caso cooptación del estado*, 2 June.

CIIDH (Centro Internacional para Investigaciones en Derechos Humanos) y El Observador. 2014. "Violencia y seguridad en Guatemala: Un informe de derechos humanos."

CNOC (Coordinador Nacional de Organizaciones Campesinas). 1999. *II Congreso Nacional Campesino: Memoria*. Guatemala City: CONGCOOP.

– 2004. *Propuesta de desarrollo rural. Plataforma política de la Coordinadora Nacional de Organizaciones Campesinas*. 3rd ed. Guatemala City: Magna Terra Editores.

– 2005a. *Propuesta de desarrollo alternativo de la agricultura indígena y campesina*. Guatemala City: Editorial Rukemik Na'ojil.

– 2005b. *Propuesta de reforma agraria integral*. Guatemala City: Magna Terra Editores.

– 2008. *Actualización de nuestra estrategia y acciones de lucha*. Guatemala City: CNOC.

– 2011. "Historia." *CNOC*. http://www.cnoc.org.gt/historia.html (site discontinued.

Comisión de Tierras. 2008. "Propuesta de soluciones operativas y funcionales del Fondo de Tierras para un mejor cumplimiento de sus atribuciones." Legal reform proposal created in Congress.

Congreso de la República de Guatemala. 2008. *Iniciativa que dispone aprobar ley de desarrollo rural integral*. Guatemala City: Congreso de la República de Guatemala.

– n.d. *Código de comercio*. http://www.wipo.int/edocs/lexdocs/laws/es/gt/gt010es.pdf.

CONIC (Coordinadora Nacional Indígena y Campesina). 2009a. "Colectivos territoriales: Conceptos y obligaciones." Internal document.

– 2009b. "Comunidades con deuda por obtención de tierras." Internal spreadsheet.

– 2009c. "Comunidades organizadas en CONIC 2009." Spreadsheet circulated internally.

– 2009d. "Plan estratégico 2009–2013. Por la vida, la madre tierra y los derechos colectivos del pueblo maya." Internal report.

– 2009e. *Problemas agrarios en comunidades organizados en CONIC año 2009*. Internal document.

– 2009f. "Tierras entregadas 1991–2009." Spreadsheet.

– 2010. "18 años de lucha." *CONIC*, 15 December. http://www.mayaconic.org.

– 2011a. "Desalojo en comunidades indígenas para instalar destacamentos militares." *CONIC*, 7 March. http://www.mayaconic.org.

– 2011b. "Guardia privada de la empresa cañera Chabil Utzaj / Ingenio Guadalupe asesina a un campesino." *CONIC*, 21 May. http://mayaconic.org.

– 2015. "Tierras entregadas 1992–2014." Spreadsheet.

Copeland, Nicholas. 2011. "'Guatemala Will Never Change': Radical Pessimism and the Politics of Personal Interest in the Western Highlands." *Journal of Latin American Studies* 43 (3): 485–515. https://doi.org/10.1017/S0022216X11000411.

Cox, Robert W. 1981. "Social Forces, States, and World Orders: Beyond International Relations Theory." *Millenium* 10 (2): 126–55. https://doi.org/10.1177/03058298810100020501.

Cramer, Christopher, and Paul Richards. 2011. "Violence and War in Agrarian Perspective." *Journal of Agrarian Change* 11 (3): 277–97. https://doi.org/10.1111/j.1471-0366.2011.00312.x.

Creelman, Matthew. 2010. "Desalojo violento en la finca Salvador Xolhuitz deja 10 familias campesinas en desamparo." Albedrio, 10 February. http://www.albedrio.org/htm/articulos/m/mcreelman-009.htm.

Crowell, Erbin, and Darryl Reed. 2009. "Fair Trade: A Model for International Co-operation among Co-operatives?" In *Co-operatives in a Global Economy: The Challenges of Co-operation Across Borders*, ed. Darryl Reed and J.J.

McMurtry, 141–177. Newcastle upon Tyne: Cambridge Scholars Publishing. https://doi.org/10.5848/CSP.0255.00005.

CUC (Comité de Unidad Campesina). 2002. "Información de 10 conflictos de tierra en los cuales se llevan procesos judiciales, asesorados por la oficina jurídica del Comité de Unidad Campesina." Paper presented at "Foro sobre conflictividad agraria" conference, Guatemala City, 17–18 April.

Dale, Peter, and John McLaughlin. 1999. *Land Administration*. Oxford: Oxford University Press.

Davis, Shelton H. 1983. "State Violence and Agrarian Crisis in Guatemala: The Roots of the Indian-Peasant Rebellion." In *Trouble in Our Backyard: Central America and the United States*, ed. Martin Diskin, 156–71. New York: Pantheon Books.

Deininger, Klaus, and Hans Binswanger. 1999. "The Evolution of the World Bank's Land Policy: Principles, Experience, and Future Challenges." *World Bank Research Observer* 14 (2): 247–76. https://doi.org/10.1093/wbro/14.2.247.

Deininger, Klaus, and Gershon Feder. 2009. "Land Registration, Governance, and Development: Evidence and Implications for Policy." *World Bank Research Observer* 24 (2): 233–66. https://doi.org/10.1093/wbro/lkp007.

de León, Luis. 2006. "Irregularidades en el manejo del Fontierras." *elPeriódico*, 27 February. https://www.elperiodico.com.gt/es//investigacion/25093 (site discontinued).

Desmarais, Annette Aurélie. 2007. *La Vía Campesina: Globalization and the Power of Peasants*. Halifax: Fernwood Publishing and Pluto.

Dinerstein, Ana C. 2015. *The Politics of Autonomy in Latin America: The Art of Organizing Hope*. New York: Palgrave Macmillan. https://doi.org/10.1057/9781137316011.

Dosal, Paul J. 1995. *Power in Transition: The Rise of Guatemala's Industrial Oligarchy, 1871–1994*. Westport, CT: Praeger.

Dudley, Steven. 2017. "With Bold Move against CICIG, Guatemala President Calling Trump's Bluff." *InSight Crime*, 27 August. https://www.insightcrime.org/news/analysis/with-bold-move-against-cicig-guatemala-president-calling-trump-s-bluff./

Duménil, Gerard, and Dominique Lévy. 2004. *Capital Resurgent: Roots of the Neoliberal Revolution*. Translated by Derek Jeffers. Cambridge, MA: Harvard University Press.

Edelman, Marc. 1998. "Transnational Peasant Politics in Central America." *Latin American Research Review* 33 (3): 49–86.

– 1999. *Peasants against Globalization: Rural Social Movements in Costa Rica*. Stanford: Stanford University Press.

– 2008. "Transnational Organizing in Agrarian Central America: History, Challenges, Prospects." *Journal of Agrarian Change* 8 (2–3): 229–57.

– 2009. "Synergies and Tensions between Rural Social Movements and Professional Researchers." *Journal of Peasant Studies* 36 (1): 245–65. https://doi.org/10.1080/03066150902820313.

Erazo, Juliet S. 2013. *Governing Indigenous Territories: Enacting Sovereignty in the Ecuadorian Amazon.* Durham, NC: Duke University Press. https://doi.org/10.1215/9780822378921.

Espina, Cindy. 2015. "El presidente y la CONIC confirman alianza." *elPeriódico*, 15 July.

Farmer, Paul. 1996. "On Suffering and Structural Violence: A View from Below." *Daedalus* 125 (1): 261–83.

Figueroa Ibarra, Carlos. 2003. "Protesta popular y cooptación de masas en Guatemala." *Observatorio social de América Latina* 4 (11): 143–70.

Finlay-Brook, Mary. 2019. "Extreme energy injustice and the expansion of capital." In *Organized Violence: Capitalist Warfare in Latin America,* ed. Dawn Paley and Simon Granovsky-Larsen. Regina: University of Regina Press.

Fledderjohn, David. 1976. *Terminal Report: Agricultural Cooperative Project in Guatemala. Agricultural Cooperative Development International Task Order #2, AID/Pha/BOA 1078.* Washington: USAID.

Flores Alvarado, Humberto. 2003. *Los compromisos de paz: Sinopsis de su cumplimiento.* Secretaría de la Paz de la Presidencia de la República Guatemala City: SEPAZ.

Fondo de Tierras. 2002. "Dictamen socioeconómico y organizativo Asociación Junan Kusamuj." Internal document.

– 2004. "Dictamen socioeconómico y organizativo Asociación de Desarrollo Integral Santa Cruz -ADISC-." Internal document.

– 2007. Letter from Laura Soto, socio-economic analyst, to Eddy Flores Molina, coordinator of the Socio-economic Branch. Fondo de Tierras.

– 2008. Letter from Miguel Antonio López Quiñónez, director of access to land, to Sergio Francisco Morales Suárez, Fondo de Tierras itinerary general manager, 6 August.

– 2009a. "Fincas entregadas, 1998–2009." Excel spreadsheet created for the author in compliance with an Access to Public Information request.

– 2009b. *Identificación y caracterización de la cartera del Fondo de Tierras.*

– 2010. "Fondo de Tierras programa de regularización de tierras del estado, escrituras individuales y colectivas 2000-2009." Excel spreadsheet created for the author in compliance with an Access to Public Information request.

– 2011. "Finca 'Don Pancho': Proyecto exitoso." *Fondo de Tierras Informativo Boletín,* November.

Fraser, Nancy. 2009. "Feminism, Capitalism and the Cunning of History." *New Left Review* 56:97–117.

Fridell, Gavin. 2007a. *Fair Trade Coffee: The Prospects and Pitfalls of Market-Driven Social Justice.* Toronto: University of Toronto Press. https://doi.org/10.3138/9781442684331.

– 2007b. "Fair-Trade Coffee and Commodity Fetishism: The Limits of Market-Driven Social Justice." *Historical Materialism* 15 (4): 79–104. https://doi.org/10.1163/156920607X245841.

– 2009. "The Cooperative and the Corporation: Competing Visions of the Future of Fair Trade." *Journal of Business Ethics* 86 (S1): 81–95. https://doi.org/10.1007/s10551-008-9759-3.

Front Line Defenders. 2016. "Case History: Daniel Choc Pop." https://www.frontlinedefenders.org/en/case/case-history-daniel-choc-pop.

Fulmer, Amanda M. 2011. "La consulta a los pueblos indígenas y su evolución como herramienta de negociación política en América Latina. Los casos de Perú y Guatemala." *Apuntes (Lima)* 38 (68): 37–62. https://doi.org/10.21678/apuntes.68.619.

FUNCEDE (Fundación Centroamericana de Desarrollo). 2002. *La descentralización en Guatemala en una perspectiva histórica en el marco de la legislación del 2002.*

Gaia, Elena. 2010. "Mi Familia Progresa: Change and Continuity in Guatemala's Social Policy." *Social Policy Report* 22:199–223.

Garcia Aupi, Ana, and Ruben Ávila Gálvez. 2013. "Santa Cruz Barrillas: Criminalización y presos políticos." *Enfoque* 4 (26): 2–60.

García-Ruiz, Jesús. 1998. "Rupturas, continuidades y recomposiciones en las sociedades rurales: El rol de lo religioso en las dinámicas sociales de los grupos mayas de Guatemala." In *Los retos de la globalización: Ensayos en homenaje a Theotonio Dos Santos,* ed. López Segrera, 767–816. Caracas: UNESCO.

Garoz, Byron, Alberto Alonso, and Susana Gauster. 2005. *Balance de la aplicación de la política agraria del Banco Mundial en Guatemala, 1996–2005.* ed. López Segrera, 767–816. Guatemala City: CONGCOOP.

Gauster, Susana, and S. Ryan Isakson. 2007. "Eliminating Market Distortions, Perpetuating Rural Inequality: An Evaluation of Market-Assisted Land Reform in Guatemala." *Third World Quarterly* 28 (8): 1519–36. https://doi.org/10.1080/01436590701637375.

Geglia, Beth. 2012. "Student Eviction Does Not Stop Guatemalan Movement against Privatization." *Waging Nonviolence*, 4 July. https://wagingnonviolence.org/feature/student-eviction-does-not-stop-guatemalan-movement-against-privatization.

GHRC (Guatemala Human Rights Commission – USA). 2006. Tensions Rise on Finca in Alta Verapaz. http://www.ghrc-usa.org/Resources/2006/LandViolence.htm.

Gill, Stephen. 2003. *Power and Resistance in the New World Order*. New York: Palgrave Macmillan.

Girón, Crosby. 2010a. "Entrevista con Fernando Solís, investigador de El Observador: de Guatemala." *Inforpress centroamericana*, 13 August.

– 2010b. "Ley de desarrollo rural con pocas posiblidades." *Inforpress centroamericana*, 3 September 3.

– 2017. "De la ofensa contra la CICIG a la Caja de Pandora." *Envío* 429 (December).

Gobierno de Guatemala. 1996. *Acuerdo sobre aspectos socioeconómicos y situación agraria*. Peace accord between the Guatemalan government and guerrillas.

– 2008. *Ley de acceso a la información pública*. Decreto número 57-2008.

– 2012. "Respuestas del ejecutivo a las demandas de la marcha indígena, campesina y popular. "Document detailing agreements reached between the Guatemalan government protesters.

– 2015. *Acuerdos y compromisos entre el Comité Campesino del Altiplano*. CCDA- y el Gobierno de la República.

Gould, Kevin A. 2014. "Everyday Expertise: Land Regularization and the Conditions for Land Grabs in Petén, Guatemala." *Environment & Planning* 46 (10): 2353–68. https://doi.org/10.1068/a140188p.

Grajales, Jacobo. 2011. "The Rifle and the Title: Paramilitary Violence, Land Grab and Land Control in Colombia." *Journal of Peasant Studies* 38 (4): 771–92. https://doi.org/10.1080/03066150.2011.607701.

Gramsci, Antonio. 1971. *Selections from the Prison Notebooks*. Translated by Quintin Hoare and Geoffrey Nowell Smith. New York: International Publishers.

Grandia, Liza. 2009. "Raw Hides: Hegemony and Cattle in Guatemala's Northern Lowlands." *Geoforum* 40 (5): 720–31. https://doi.org/10.1016/j.geoforum.2009.01.004.

– 2012. *Enclosed: Conservation, Cattle, and Commerce among the Q'eqchi' Maya Lowlanders*. Seattle: University of Washington Press.

Grandin, Greg. 2011. *The Last Colonial Massacre: Latin America in the Cold War*. 2nd ed. Chicago: University of Chicago Press. https://doi.org/10.7208/chicago/9780226306896.001.0001.

– 2013. "Five Hundred Years." In *War by Other Means: Aftermath in Post-Genocide Guatemala*, ed. Carlota McAllister and Diane M. Nelson, 49–70. Durham, NC: Duke University Press. https://doi.org/10.1215/9780822377405-002.

Granovsky-Larsen, Simon. 2011. "Martial Law, Repression, and Remilitarization in Guatemala." NACLA Online, 17 February. https://nacla.org/node/6879.

– 2017. "Guatemalan Water Protectors Fight to Free Their Rivers." Upside Down World, 18 September. http://upsidedownworld.org/archives/guatemala/guatemalan-water-protectors-fight-to-free-their-rivers/.

– 2018. "Terror in Guatemala" NACLA Online, 21 June. https://nacla.org/news/2018/06/21/terror-guatemala.

– Forthcoming. "Institutionalized Terror: Paramilitaries and the Guatemalan State." In *The Political Violence of Capital: Paramilitary Formations in Global Perspective*, ed. Jasmin Hristov, Jeb Sprague-Silgado, and Aaron Tauss.

Granovsky-Larsen, Simon, and Caren Weisbart. Forthcoming. "Violent Norms in the Implementation of Tahoe Resources' San Rafael Mine." In *Mining in a Time of Impunity in the Aftermath of Guatemala's Genocide: The Violence of Contemporary Predatory Mineral Exploitation*, ed. Catherine Nolin and Grahame Russell. Springer Briefs in Latin American Studies.

Green, Duncan. 2003. *Silent Revolution: The Rise and Crisis of Market Economics in Latin America*. New York: Monthly Review.

Hale, Charles R. 2002. "Does Multiculturalism Menace? Governance, Cultural Rights and the Politics of Identity in Guatemala." *Journal of Latin American Studies* 34 (3): 485–524. https://doi.org/10.1017/S0022216X02006521.

– 2004. "Rethinking Indigenous Politics in the Era of the 'Indio Permitido.'" *NACLA Report on the Americas* 38 (2): 16–21. https://doi.org/10.1080/10714839.2004.11724509.

– 2006a. "Activist Research v. Cultural Critique: Indigenous Land Rights and the Contradictions of Politically Engaged Anthropology." *Cultural Anthropology* 21 (1): 96–120. https://doi.org/10.1525/can.2006.21.1.96.

– 2006b. *Más Que Un Indio: Racial Ambivalence and Neoliberal Multiculturalism in Guatemala*. Santa Fe, NM: School of American Research Press.

–, ed. 2008a. *Engaging Contradictions: Theory, Politics, and Methods of Activist Scholarship*. Berkeley: University of California Press.

– 2008b. "Introduction." In *Engaging Contradictions: Theory, Politics, and Methods of Activist Scholarship*, ed. Charles R. Hale, 1–28. Berkeley: University of California Press.

– 2011. "*Resistencia Para Qué?* Territory, Autonomy and Neoliberal Entanglements in the 'Empty Spaces' of Central America." *Economy and Society* 40 (2): 184–210. https://doi.org/10.1080/03085147.2011.548947.

Hale, Charles R., and Rosamel Millamán. 2006. "Cultural Agency and Political Struggle in the Era of the Indio Permitido." In *Cultural Agency in the Americas*, ed. Doris Sommer, 281–304. Durham, NC: Duke University Press.

Handy, Jim. 1984. *Gift of the Devil: A History of Guatemala*. Toronto: Between the Lines.

– 1994a. "Demilitarizing Community in Guatemala." *Canadian Journal of Latin American and Caribbean Studies* 19 (37–8): 35–60.

– 1994b. *Revolution in the Countryside: Rural Conflict and Agrarian Reform in Guatemala, 1944–1954*. Chapel Hill: University of North Carolina Press.

– 2017. "The Violence of Dispossession: Guatemala in the Nineteenth and Twentieth Centuries." In *Politics and History of Violence and Crime in Central America*, ed. Sebastian Huhn and Hannes Warnecke-Berger, 281–323. London: Palgrave Macmillan.

Harvey, David. 2005. *A Brief History of Neoliberalism*. Oxford: Oxford University Press.

Helwege, Ann, and Melissa B.L. Birch. 2007. *Declining Poverty in Latin America? A Critical Analysis of New Estimates by International Institutions*. Medford, MA: Global Development and Environment Institute, Tufts University.

Hernández, Oswaldo J. 2012. "Los pasos del campesinado." Plaza Pública, 29 March.

– 2013. "Fontierras: Arrendamientos en lugar de créditos para favorecer a los mismos." Plaza pública, 15 July. https://www.plazapublica.com.gt/content/fontierras-arrendamientos-en-lugar-de-creditos-para-favorecer-los-mismos.

– 2015. "Fontierras: Arrendamientos en lugar de créditos para favorecer a los mismos." Plaza Pública, 13 July.

– 2016. "El clan Mendoza Matta: El agro según el crimen organizado." Plaza pública, 22 April. https://www.plazapublica.com.gt/content/el-clan-mendoza-matta-el-agro-segun-el-crimen-organizado.

Hernández Pico, Juan. 2015. "Some Pointers to Understanding the 'Guatemalan Spring.'" *Envío* 410, September.

Huet, Alfonso. 2008. *Nos salvó la sagrada selva: La memoria de veinte comunidades q'eqchi'es que sobrevivieron al genocidio*. Guatemala City: ADICI Wakliiqo.

Humphries, Beth, Donna M. Mertens, and Carole Truman. 2000. "Arguments for an 'Emancipatory' Research Paradigm." In *Research and Inequality*, ed. Carol Truman, Donna M. Mertens, and Beth Humphries, 3–23. London: University College London Press.

Hurtado Paz y Paz, Laura. 2008. *Dinámicas agrarias y reproducción campesina en la globalización: el caso de Alta Verapaz, 1970–2007*. Guatemala City: FyG Editores.

Hussey, Ian. 2012. "'Political Activist as Ethnographer' Revisited." *Canadian Journal of Sociology* 37 (1): 1–23.

INAB (Instituto Nacional de Bosques). 2007. *Informe del Instituto Nacional de Bosques sub-región IX-3 Retalhuleu, al Organismo Judicial de Nuevo San Carlos.* Retahuleu.

INE (Instituto Nacional de Estadísticas). 1979. *III censo nacional agropecuario.* Guatemala City: INE.

– 2004. *IV censo nacional agropecuario.* Guatemala City: Instituto Nacional de Estadística.

– 2008. *Encuesta nacional agropecuaria.* Guatemala City: Instituto Nacional de Estadística.

Inforpress centroamericana. 2006. *"Fondo de Tierras*: Entre la crisis y el abandono." *Inforpress centroamericana*, 30 June.

– 2009. "Organizaciones campesinas e indígenas impulsan ley de desarrollo rural integral." *Inforpress centroamericana*, 20 November.

InSight Crime. 2016a. "Guatemala fuera de control: La CICIG y la lucha contra la impunidad." *Nueva sociedad* 263: 81–95.

– 2016b. "Guatemalan Elites and Organized Crime: Introduction." InSight Crime, 1 September. Intro. Edgar Gutiérrez. https://www.insightcrime.org/investigations/guatemala-elites-and-organized-crime-introduction/.

International Rivers. 2016. "Murdered for Their Rivers: A Roster of Fallen Dam Fighters." International Rivers, 20 June. https://www.internationalrivers.org/resources/murdered-for-their-rivers-a-roster-of-fallen-dam-fighters-11499.

Jonas, Susanne. 1997. "The Peace Accords: An End and a Beginning." *NACLA Report on the Americas* 30 (6): 6–10. https://doi.org/10.1080/10714839.1997.11722821.

– 1998. "Can Peace Bring Democracy or Social Justice? The Case of Guatemala." *Social Justice (San Francisco, Calif.)* 25 (4): 40–74.

– 2000. *Of Centaurs and Doves: Guatemala's Peace Process.* Boulder, CO: Westview.

Kading, Terrance W. 1999. "The Guatemalan Military and the Economics of *La Violencia*." *Canadian Journal of Latin American and Caribbean Studies* 24 (47): 57–91. https://doi.org/10.1080/08263663.1999.10816776.

Kay, Cristóbal. 1989. *Latin American Theories of Development and Underdevelopment.* New York: Routledge.

– 2001. "Reflections on Rural Violence in Latin America." *Third World Quarterly* 22 (5): 741–75. https://doi.org/10.1080/01436590120084584.

– 2006. "Rural Poverty and Development Strategies in Latin America." *Journal of Agrarian Change* 6 (4): 455–508. https://doi.org/10.1111/j.1471-0366.2006.00132.x.

Kelly, Alice B. 2011. "Conservation Practice as Primitive Accumulation." *Journal of Peasant Studies* 38 (4): 683–701. https://doi.org/10.1080/03066150.2011.607695.

Knowlton, Autumn. 2017. "Q'eqchi' Mayas and the Myth of 'Postconflict' Guatemala." *Latin American Perspectives*, 12 May. https://doi.org/10.1177/0094582X16650179.

Konefal, Betsy. 2010. *For Every Indio Who Falls: A History of Maya Activism in Guatemala, 1960–1990*. Albuquerque: University of New Mexico Press.

Lahiff, Edward, Santurnino M. Borras Jr, and Cristóbal Kay. 2007. "Market-Led Agrarian Reform: Policies, Performance and Prospects." *Third World Quarterly* 28 (8): 1417–36. https://doi.org/10.1080/01436590701637318.

Laplante, J.P., and Catherine Nolin. 2014. "*Consultas* and Socially Responsible Investing in Guatemala: A Case Study Examining Maya Perspectives on the Indigenous Right to Free, Prior, and Informed Consent." *Society & Natural Resources* 27 (3): 231–48. https://doi.org/10.1080/08941920.2013.861554.

Lemke, Thomas. 2001. "'The Birth of Bio-Politics': Michel Foucault's Lecture at the College de France on Neo-liberal Governmentality." *Economy and Society* 30 (2): 190–207. https://doi.org/10.1080/03085140120042271.

Loeb, David. 1995. "Campesinos Taking Back Their 'Mother Earth': 'We Are Here on Our Own Land'." *Report on Guatemala* 16 (2): 8–11.

Lovell, W. George. 1992. *Conquest and Survival in Colonial Guatemala: A Historical Geography of the Cuchumatán Highlands, 1500–1821*. 2nd ed. Montreal and Kingston: McGill-Queen's University Press.

– 2000. *A Beauty That Hurts: Life and Death in Guatemala*. 2nd ed. Toronto: Between the Lines.

MAGA (Ministerio de Agricultura, Ganadería, y Alimentación). 2006. "Vulnerabilidad: Programa para el desarrollo para la población." *MAGActual* 3 (21): 26–8.

– 2013. "Informe de la mesa del sistema de monitoreo de cultivos," Boletín no. 1, March. http://web.maga.gob.gt/wp-content/uploads/bol/smc/boletin_1_smc_marzo.pdf.

Manz, Beatriz. 1988. *Refugees of a Hidden War: The Aftermath of Counterinsurgency in Guatemala*. Albany: State University of New York Press.

Marcha Indígena Campesina y Popular. 2012. *Planteamientos concretos al Sr. Otto Perez. Molina, Presidente de Guatemala.*

Margheritis, Ana, and Anthony W. Pereira. 2007. "The Neoliberal Turn in Latin America: The Cycle of Ideas and the Search for an Alternative." *Latin American Perspectives* 34 (3): 25–48. https://doi.org/10.1177/0094582X07300587.

Martí i Puig, Salvador. 2010. "The Emergence of Indigenous Movements in Latin America and Their Impact on the Latin American Political Scene: Interpretive Tools at the Local and Global Levels." *Latin American Perspectives* 37 (6): 74–92. https://doi.org/10.1177/0094582X10382100.

Martínez, Daniel E. 2006. "Reinterpreting the Tool of Domination: Fair Trade and the CCDA's Political Struggle." MA thesis, University of Calgary.

Martínez Peláez, Severo. 2009. *La Patria Del Criollo: An Interpretation of Colonial Guatemala.* Edited by Christopher H. Lutz. Translated by Susan M. Neve and W. George Lovell. Durham, NC: Duke University Press. https://doi.org/10.1215/9780822392064.

– 2011. *Motines de indios: La violencia colonial en Centroamérica y Chiapas.* City, Guatemala City: FyG Editores.

Marx, Karl. 1976. *Capital: A Critique of Political Ecomomy,* vol. 1. London: Penguin Books.

May, Rachel. 2001. *Terror in the Countryside: Campesino Responses to Political Violence in Guatemala, 1954–1985.* Athens: Center for International Studies, Ohio University.

Mazariegos, Juan Carlos. 2007. "Teorizando la pugna: Las teorías sobre el movimiento campesino en Guatemala, 1962–2006." In *Aproximación a los imaginarios sobre organización campesina en Guatemala: Ensayos sobre su construcción histórica,* 115–71. Textos para Debate 19. Guatemala City: AVANCSO.

McAllister, Carlota, and Diane M. Nelson, eds. 2013. *War by Other Means: Aftermath in Post-Genocide Guatemala.* Durham, NC: Duke University Press. https://doi.org/10.1215/9780822377405.

McCleary, Rachel M. 1999. *Dictating Democracy: Guatemala and the End of Violent Revolution.* Gainesville: University Press of Florida.

McCreery, David. 1983. "Debt Servitude in Rural Guatemala, 1876–1936." *Hispanic American Historical Review* 63 (4): 735–59. https://doi.org/10.2307/2514903.

– 1994. *Rural Guatemala, 1760–1940.* Stanford: Stanford University Press.

McMurtry, J.J. 2009. "Ethical Value-Added: Fair Trade and the Case of Café Feminino." *Journal of Business Ethics* 86 (S1): 27–49. https://doi.org/10.1007/s10551-008-9760-x.

McNally, David. 2011. *Global Slump: The Economics and Politics of Crisis and Resistance.* Oakland: PM.

Miethbauer, Thomas. 2005. *Reporte final de la consultaría para el Banco Mundial. Proyecto Apoyo al Fondo de Tierras (PAFT, BIRF 4432-GU)..*

Milian, Byron, and Liza Grandia. 2013. "Inheriting Inequality: Land Administration and Agrarian Structure in Petén, Guatemala." Annual World Bank conference on land and poverty, Washington DC, 8–11 April.

Ministerio de Gobernación. 1998. "Reglamento de inscripción de asociaciones civiles."

Molyneux, Maxine. 2008. "The 'Neoliberal Turn' and the New Social Policy in Latin America: How Neoliberal, How New?" *Development and Change* 39 (5): 775–97. https://doi.org/10.1111/j.1467-7660.2008.00505.x.

Moore, Barrington Jr. 1993. *Social Origins of Dictatorship and Democracy: Lord and Peasant in the Making of the Modern World*. Boston: Beacon.

Morán, Rolando. 2002. *Saludos revolucionarios. La historia reciente de Guatemala desde la óptica de la lucha guerrillera (1984–1996)*. Guatemala City: Fundación Guillermo Toriello.

Morán, Sandra. 2016. Personal communication, 15 June.

Mukherjee Reed, Ananya. 2008. *Human Development and Social Power: Perspectives from South Asia*. New York: Routledge. https://doi.org/10.4324/9780203895238.

Murphy, Edward. 2004. "Developing Sustainable Peripheries: The Limits of Citizenship in Guatemala City." *Latin American Perspectives* 31 (6): 48–68. https://doi.org/10.1177/0094582X04269911.

Neier, Aryeh. 2014. "Guatemala's Shameful Repudiation of Justice." *New York Review of Books NYR Blog*, 10 February. https://www.nybooks.com/blogs/nyrblog/2014/feb/10/guatemala-shameful-repudiation-justice.

Nolin, Catherine, and Jaqui Stephens. 2010. "'We Have to Protect the Investors': 'Development' and Canadian Mining Companies in Guatemala." *Journal of Rural and Community Development* 5 (3): 37–70.

North, Liisa L. 1998. "Reflections of Democratization and Demilitarization in Central America." *Studies in Political Economy* 55 (1): 155–71. https://doi.org/10.1080/19187033.1998.11675304.

Noticias del Istmo. 1982. "Asesinato masivo y silencioso." 15 December.

ODHAG (Oficina de Derechos Humanos del Arzobispado de Guatemala). 1998. *Guatemala: Nunca más*. 4 vols. Guatemala City: ODHAG.

Oxlajuj Tz'ikin. 2012. "Pobladores de Champerico presentan resultados de las consultas comunitarias ante diferentes entidades del estado." Oxlajuj Tz'ikin, 26 April. http://oxlajujtzikin.blogspot.com/2012/04/pobladores-de-champerico-presentan.html.

Pallister, Kevin. 2013. "Why No Mayan Party? Indigenous Movements and National Politics in Guatemala." *Latin American Politics and Society* 55 (3): 117–38. https://doi.org/10.1111/j.1548-2456.2013.00205.x.

Palma Murga, Gustavo. 1997. "Promised the Earth: Agrarian Reform in the Socio-economic Agreement." *Accord: An International Review of Peace Initiatives* 2:74–80. https://www.c-r.org/downloads/02_Guatemala.pdf.

PDH (Procuraduría de Derechos Humanos). 2007. Memorandum REU 205-2006, "Informe de acompañamiento."

Peacock, Susan C., and Adriana Beltrán. 2003. *Hidden Powers in Post-Conflict Guatemala: Illegal Armed Groups and the Forces behind Them*. Washington, DC: Washington Office on Latin America.

Pearce, Jenny. 1998. "From Civil War to 'Civil Society': Has the End of the Cold War Brought Peace to Central America?" *International Affairs* 74 (3): 587–615. https://doi.org/10.1111/1468-2346.00036.

Pedersen, Alexandra. 2014. "Landscapes of Resistance: Community Opposition to Canadian Mining Operations in Guatemala." *Journal of Latin American Geography* 13 (1): 187–214. https://doi.org/10.1353/lag.2014.0018.

Pedroni, Guillermo. 1992. "Crisis rural y programas de acceso a la tierra en Guatemala. Continuidad y discontinuidad de una política." In *In 500 años de lucha por la tierra en Guatemala*, vol. 2, ed. J.C. Cambranes, 39–72. City, Guatemala City: FLACSO.

Peluso, Nancy Lee, and Christian Lund. 2011. "New Frontiers of Land Control: Introduction." *Journal of Peasant Studies* 38 (4): 667–81. https://doi.org/10.1080/03066150.2011.607692.

Pérez, Regina. 2013. "Ambientalistas y defensores de recursos naturales bajo asedio; activismo les puede costar la vida." *La Hora*, 10 July. https://lahora.gt/hemeroteca-lh/ambientalistas-y-defensores-de-recursos-naturales-bajo-asedio-activismo-les-puede-costar-la-vida/.

Peters, Krijn, and Paul Richards. 2011. "Rebellion and Agrarian Tensions in Sierra Leone." *Journal of Agrarian Change* 11 (3): 377–95. https://doi.org/10.1111/j.1471-0366.2011.00316.x.

Pimple, Minar, and Manpreet Sethi. 2005. "Occupations of Land in India: Experiences and Challenges." In *Reclaiming the Land: The Resurgence of Rural Movements in Africa, Asia and Latin America*, ed. S. Moyo and P. Yeros, 235–56. London: Zed Books.

Plan Visión de País. n.d. Ley marco de desarrollo rural.

Plataforma Agraria. 2004. "Una visión crítica de FONTIERRAS." Paper presented at the Foro Mundial sobre Reforma Agraria, Valencia, Spain, 5–8 December.

– 2010. "La trampa del Fondo de Tierras." Albedrío, 23 December. http://www.albedrio.org/htm/otrosdocs/comunicados/plataformaagraria-022.htm.

PNC (Policía Nacional Civil). 2007. *Informe sobre investigación según causa número MP157/2,007/1532. Agencia 2. Sub-estación 43–31*. Nuevo San Carlos, Retahuleu.

Polanyi, Karl. 2001. *The Great Transformation: The Political and Economic Origins of Our Time*. Boston: Beacon.

Ponciano, Karen. 2009. "Experiencias pastorales y lucha campesina 1970-1980." In *Glosas nuevas sobre la misma guerra: Rebelión campesina, poder pastoral y genocidio en Guatemala*, ed. AVANCSO, 69–121. Textos para Debate 23. City, Guatemala City: AVANCSO.

Portes, Alejandro, and Kelly Hoffman. 2003. "Latin American Class Structures: Their Composition and Change during the Neoliberal Era." *Latin American Research Review* 38 (1): 41–82. https://doi.org/10.1353/lar.2003.0011.

Potter, Brian. 2007. "Constricting Contestation, Coalitions, and Purpose: The Causes of Neoliberal Restructuring and its Failure." *Latin American Perspectives* 34 (3): 3–24. https://doi.org/10.1177/0094582X07300586.

Prashad, Vijay. 2007. *The Darker Nations: A People's History of the Third World*. New York: W.W. Norton.

Prensa Libre. 2011a. "Al menos un muerto y cinco heridos en ataque armado a indígenas." *Prensa Libre*, 22 May.

Prensa Libre. 2011b. "Presidente Colom decreta estado de sitio en Petén." *Prensa Libre*, 16 May. http://www.prensalibre.com/noticias/politica/Presidente-Colom-decreta-Sitio-Peten_0_481752130.html (site discontinued).

– 2017. "La impunidad supera el 97% en Guatemala." *Prensa Libre*, 3 April. https://www.prensalibre.com/guatemala/politica/la-impunidad-supera-el-97-en-guatemala.

Reed, Darryl, and J.J. McMurtry, eds. 2009. *Co-operatives in a Global Economy: The Challenges of Co-operation across Borders*. Newcastle upon Tyne: Cambridge Scholars Publishing.

Remijnse, Simone. 2001. "Remembering Civil Patrols in Joyabaj, Guatemala." *Bulletin of Latin American Research* 20 (4): 454–69. https://doi.org/10.1111/1470-9856.00025.

Resistencia de los Pueblos. 2014. "De tierras, territorios, y soberanías." *Resistencia de los Pueblos*, December.

Robinson, William I. 1996. *Promoting Polyarchy: Globalization, US Intervention, and Hegemony*. Cambridge, UK: Cambridge University Press. https://doi.org/10.1017/CBO9780511559129.

– 2003. *Transnational Conflicts: Central America, Social Change, and Globalization*. London: Verso.

– 2008. *Latin America and Global Capitalism*. Baltimore: Johns Hopkins University Press.

Rueschemeyer, Dietrich, Evelyne Huber Stephens, and John D. Stephens. 1992. *Capitalist Development and Democracy*. Chicago: University of Chicago Press.

SAA (Secretaría de Asuntos Agrarios). 2009a. *Estudio fotogramétrico: Caso comunidades Michbil Rix Pu, Xya'alko'be*. Se'quixpur, Cobán, Alta Verapaz.
– 2009b. "Registro de casos SAA – octubre 2009." Excel spreadsheet created for the author in compliance with an Access to Public Information request.
– 2010a. "Departamento de atención a crisis: Listado de fincas entregadas, 2007–2009." Document created for the author in compliance with an Access to Public Information request.
– 2010b. "Información de conflictos agrarios." Document created for the author in compliance with an Access to Public Information request.
– 2011. "Fincas compradas en el 2010 y 2011 por medio del programa de atención a crisis." Document created for the author in compliance with an Access to Public Information request.
– 2016. "Registro de casos SAA – enero 2016." Excel spreadsheet created for the author in compliance with an Access to Public Information request.
Saad-Filho, Alfredo, and Deborah Johnston, eds. 2005. *Neoliberalism: A Critical Reader*. London: Pluto.
Sandoval Villeda, Leopoldo. 1992. "El problema agrario guatemalteco: Evolución y opciones." In *500 años de lucha por la tierra en Guatemala*, edited by J.C. Cambranes, 2:211–62. Guatemala City: FLACSO.
Santa Cruz, Wendy. 2006. *Una aproximación a la conflictividad agraria y acciones del movimiento campesino*. Guatemala City: FLACSO.
Schirmer, Jennifer. 1998. *The Guatemalan Military Project: A Violence Called Democracy*. Philadelphia: University of Pennsylvania Press.
Schneider, Aaron. 2014. "The Great Transformation in Central America: Transnational Accumulation and the Evolution of Capital." In *Handbook of Central American Governance*, ed. Diego Sánchez-Ancochea and Salvador Martí i Puig, 25–44. New York: Routledge.
Schneider, Pablo R., Hugo Maul, and Luis Mauricio Membreño. 1989. *El mito de la reforma agraria: 40 años de experimentación en Guatemala*. Guatemala City: Centro de Investigaciones Económicas Nacionales (CIEN).
Schwartz, Norman B. 1987. "Colonization of Northern Guatemala: The Petén." *Journal of Anthropological Research* 43 (2): 163–83. https://doi.org/10.1086/jar.43.2.3630223.
– 1990. *Forest Society: A Social History of Petén*. Philadelphia: University of Pennsylvania Press.
Segovia, Alexander. 2004. "Centroamérica después del café. El fin del modelo agroexportador tradicional y el surgimiento de un nuevo modelo." *Revista centroamericana de ciencias sociales* 2 (1): 5–38.
– 2005. *Integración real y grupos de poder económico en América Central: Implicaciones para el desarrollo y la democracia de la región*. San José, Costa Rica: Fundación Friedrich Ebert.

Serrano López, Claudia Carolina. 2008. *Los pobres ante la irrenunciabilidad de las prestaciones laborales mínimas.* Estudios sobre pobreza 8. Guatemala City: FLACSO.

Short, Nicola. 2007. *The International Politics of Post-Conflict Reconstruction in Guatemala.* New York: Palgrave Macmillan. https://doi.org/10.1007/978-1-137-04084-8.

Silva, Lanuza Edwin W. 2010. "Consejos de desarrollo: Espacios de participación democrática o de mediatización? Impacto de las decisiones de los COCODE en los municipios Santa Lucia Cotzumalguapa y Nuevo Progreso." Undergraduate thesis, Universidad de San Carlos, Guatemala.

Simon, Jean-Marie. 1987. *Guatemala: Eternal Spring, Eternal Tyranny.* New York: W.W. Norton.

Sinclair, Minor. 1995. "Faith, Community and Resistance in the Guatemalan Highlands." In *The New Politics of Survival: Grassroots Movements in Central America*, ed. Minor Sinclair, 75–106. New York: Monthly Review.

Smith, Carol A. 1990a. "Class Position and Class Consciousness in an Indian Community: Totonicapán in the 1970s." In *Guatemalan Indians and the State: 1540 to 1988*, ed. Carol A. Smith, 205–29. Austin: University of Texas Press.

–, ed. 1990b. *Guatemalan Indians and the State, 1540 to 1988.* Austin: University of Texas Press.

– 1990c. "The Militarization of Civil Society in Guatemala: Economic Reorganization as a Continuation of War." *Latin American Perspectives* 17 (4): 8–41. https://doi.org/10.1177/0094582X9001700402.

Smith, Linda Tuhiwai. 1999. *Decolonizing Methodologies: Research and Indigenous Peoples.* London: Zed Books.

Solano, Luis. 2005. *Guatemala: Petróleo y minería en las entrañas del poder.* City, Guatemala City: Inforpress centroamericana.

– 2012. "Gobierno del PP: Elites militares y económicas se reparten el control del estado." *El observador* 7 (34–5): 4–54.

– 2015. *Under Siege: Peaceful Resistance to Tahoe Resources and Militarization in Guatemala.* https://miningwatch.ca/sites/default/files/solano-underseigereport2015-11-10.pdf.

– 2016. "De narcotráfico, agronegocios y la justicia para campesinos despojados." *El Observador Informe Especial*, 18 April. https://cmiguate.org/de-narcotrafico-agronegocios-y-la-justicia-para-campesinos-despojados/.

– 2017. "El estado guatemalteco, la contrainsurgencia, y el crimen organizado." *El Observador – Informe Especial* 8, 16 March.

Stahler-Sholk, Richard, Harry E. Vanden, and Marc Becker, eds. 2014. *Rethinking Latin American Social Movements: Radical Action from Below.* Lanham, MD: Rowman & Littlefield.

Stenzel, Paulette L. 2013. "Mainstreaming Fair Trade and Resulting Turmoil: Where Should the Movement Go from Here?" *William and Mary Environmental Law and Policy Review* 37 (3): 617–73.

Stewart, Steven O., Peter Fairhurst, and Guillermo Pedroni. 1987. *Final Report: Evaluation of Commercial Land Market Project.* PIO/T No. 520-0000. 1-3-70030. Washington, DC: USAID.

Stiglitz, Joseph. 2003. "Whither Reform? Towards a New Agenda for Latin America." *CEPAL Review* 80: 7–37.

Support Group for the Peasant Committee of the Highlands. 1992. *Canadian CCDA Guatemala Support.* January.

Tarrow, Sidney. 2011. *Power in Movement: Social Movements and Contentious Politics.* 3rd ed. New York: Cambridge University Press. https://doi.org/10.1017/CBO9780511973529.

Thorp, Rosemary. 1998. *Progress, Poverty, and Exclusion: An Economic History of Latin America in the 20th Century.* Washington: Inter-American Development Bank.

Tilly, Charles. 1985. "War Making and State Making as Organized Crime." In *Bringing the State Back,* ed. Theda Skocpol, Peter B. Evens, and Dietrich Rueschemeyer, 169–91. Cambridge: Cambridge University Press. https://doi.org/10.1017/CBO9780511628283.008.

Tiney, Juan. 2015. *Presento mi renuncia irrevocable de CONIC, pero no renuncio de la lucha,* 31 August.

Torres-Rivas, Edelberto. 2012. "The Limits of Peace and Democracy in Guatemala." In *In the Wake of War: Democratization and Internal Armed Conflict in Latin Amerca,* ed. Cynthia J. Arnson, 107–37. Stanford: Stanford University Press.

Tran, Mark. 2013. "Guatemala: One Woman's Campaign against Violent Crime and Corruption." *Guardian,* 8 October. https://www.theguardian.com/global-development/2013/oct/08/guatemala-violent-crime-claudia-paz-y-paz.

UDEFEGUA (Unidad de Protección a Defensoras y Defensores de Derechos Humanos – Guatemala). 2016. *Mi esencia es la resistencia pacífica, soy defensora – soy defensor: informe sobre situación de Defensoras y Defensores de Derechos Humanos – Enero a Diciembre de 2015.* https://www.yumpu.com/es/document/view/55243801/mi-esencia-es-la-resistencia-pacifica-soy-defensora-soy-defensor.

– 2017a. *Exprésate con otro rollo sin odio: informe sobre situación de defensoras y defensores de derechos humanos – enero a diciembre 2016.* http://udefegua.org/wp-content/uploads/2017/05/Informe-Genaral-2016-FINAL6.pdf.

– 2017b. *Informe criminalización en Guatemala. Análisis de situación 2012–2017.* http://udefegua.org/wp-content/uploads/2017/12/Informe-Criminalización-Guatemala-2012-2017-FINAL3.pdf.

Universidad Rafael Landívar. 2009. *Conflicto por el uso de la tierra: Nuevas expresiones de la conflictividad agraria en Guatemala.* Guatemala City: Universidad Rafael Landívar.

Urkidi, Leire. 2011. "The Defence of Community in the Anti-Mining Movement of Guatemala." *Journal of Agrarian Change* 11 (4): 556–80. https://doi.org/10.1111/j.1471-0366.2011.00326.x.

URNG (Unidad Revolucionaria Nacional Guatemalteca). 2008. Meeting minutes of URNG congressional representatives. 30 October.

USAID (United States Agency for International Development). 1982. *Land and Labor in Guatemala: An Assessment.*

UVOC (Unión Verapacense de Organizaciones Campesinas). 2007. *Conflictividad agraria en las Verapaces. Una mirada campesina.* Santa Cruz, Alta Verapaz, Guatemala: UVOC.

van Leeuwen, Mathijs. 2006. *Estratégias y experiencias de Pastoral de la Tierra de San Marcos con el programa de conflictividad 2001–2006.* Pastoral de la Tierra Interdiocesana de San Marcos.

– 2010. "To Conform or to Confront? CSOs and Agrarian Conflict in Post-Conflict Guatemala." *Journal of Latin American Studies* 42 (1): 91–119. https://doi.org/10.1017/S0022216X10000064.

Velásquez Nimatuj, Irma Alicia. 2008. *Pueblos indígenas, estado y lucha por tierra en Guatemala. Estrategias de sobrevivencia y negociación ante la desigualdad globalizada.* Guatemala City: AVANCSO.

– 2010. "Marcos Maa Chaj." *elPeriódico*, 18 January.

Veltmeyer, Henry. 2005. "The Dynamics of Land Occupations in Latin America." In *Reclaiming the Land: The Resurgence of Rural Movements in Africa, Asia and Latin America,* ed. Sam Moyo and Paris Yeros, 285–316. London: Zed Books.

Vieta, Marcelo, and Andrés Ruggeri. 2009. "Worker-Recovered Enterprises as Workers' Co-operatives: The Conjunctures, Challenges, and Innovations of Self-Management in Argentina and Latin America." In *Co-operatives in a Global Economy: The Challenges of Co-operation across Borders,* ed. Darryl Reed and J.J. McMurtry, 178–225. Newcastle upon Tyne: Cambridge Scholars Publishing. https://doi.org/10.5848/CSP.0255.00006.

Vogt, Manuel. 2015. "The Disarticulated Movement: Barriers to Maya Mobilization in Post-Conflict Guatemala." *Latin American Politics and Society* 57 (1): 29–50. https://doi.org/10.1111/j.1548-2456.2015.00260.x.

Wacquant, Loïc. 2012. "Three Steps to a Historical Anthropology of Actually Existing Neoliberalism." *Social Anthropology* 20 (1): 66–79. https://doi .org/10.1111/j.1469-8676.2011.00189.x.

Webber, Jeffery R., and Barry Carr, eds. 2013. *The New Latin American Left: Cracks in the Empire.* Lanham, MD: Rowman & Littlefield.

Weisbrot, Mark, and Rebecca Ray. 2011. "The Scorecard on Development, 1980–2010: Closing the Gap?" United Nations Department of Economic and Social Affairs Working Paper no. 106, June. http://www.un.org/esa/desa/ papers/2011/wp106_2011.pdf

Weld, Kirsten. 2014. *Paper Cadavers: The Archives of Dictatorship in Guatemala.* Durham, NC: Duke University Press. https://doi. org/10.1215/9780822376583.

Williamson, John. 1990. "What Washington Means by Policy Reform." In *Latin American Adjustment: How Much Has Happened?* ed. John Williamson, 7–20. Washington, DC: Institute for International Economics.

Wolford, Wendy. 2003. "Producing Community: The MST and Land Reform Settlements in Brazil." *Journal of Agrarian Change* 3 (4): 500–20. https://doi. org/10.1111/1471-0366.00064.

– 2010a. "Participatory Democracy by Default: Land Reform, Social Movements and the State in Brazil." *Journal of Peasant Studies* 37 (1): 91–109. https://doi.org/10.1080/03066150903498770.

– 2010b. *This Land Is Ours Now: Social Mobilization and the Meanings of Land in Brazil.* Durham, NC: Duke University Press.

World Bank. 1998. *Project Appraisal Document: Guatemala Land Fund Project.* Report 18555. Washington, DC: World Bank.

– 2010. *World Bank Support to Land Administration and Land Redistribution in Central America. An IEG Performance Assessment of Three Projects: El Salvador, Land Administration Project (Loan No. 3982), Guatemala, Land Administration Project (Loan No. 4415), Guatemala, Land Fund Project (Loan No. 4432).* Independent Evaluations Group (World Bank) Performance Assessment 55341. Washington, DC: World Bank.

– 2016. "Guatemala: An Assessment of Poverty." http://web.worldbank.org/ WBSITE/EXTERNAL/TOPICS/EXTPOVERTY/EXTPA/0,,contentMDK:20 207581~menuPK:443285~pagePK:148956~piPK:216618~theSitePK:430367,00. html.

– 2017a. "GINI Index (World Bank Estimate)." https://data.worldbank.org/ indicator/SI.POV.GINI?locations=GT.

– 2017b. "Mortality Rate, Infant (per 1,000 Live Births). https://data. worldbank.org/indicator/SP.DYN.IMRT.IN?locations=GT.

– 2017c. "Poverty and Equity Data Portal: Guatemala" http://povertydata. worldbank.org/poverty/country/GTM.

– 2017d. "World Integrated Trade Solution: Guatemala Trade Summary 2012 Data." https://wits.worldbank.org/CountryProfile/en/Country/GTM/ Year/2012/Summary.

World Food Programme. 2017. "Guatemala." http://www1.wfp.org/ countries/guatemala.

Xunta de Galicia. 2007. *Documento de información y análisis: Comunidad Victorias 3, municipio de Champerico, dept.* Retahuleu.

– 2008. *Programa de desarrollo integral Oxlajuj Tz'ikin Chaperico Retahuleu.*

Yagenova, Simona, and Rodrigo J. Véliz. 2011. "Guatemala: Una década de transición." In *Una década en movimiento: Luchas populares en América Latina en el amanecer del siglo XXI*, ed. Massimo Modonesi and Julián Rebón, 255–74. Buenos Aires: CLACSO and Prometeo Libros.

Yashar, Deborah. 2005. *Contesting Citizenship in Latin America: The Rise of Indigenous Movements and the Postliberal Challenge.* Cambridge: Cambridge University Press. https://doi.org/10.1017/CBO9780511790966.

Ybarra, Megan. 2011. "Privatizing the Tzuultaq'a? Private Property and Spiritual Reproduction in Post-war Guatemala." *Journal of Peasant Studies* 38 (4): 793–810. https://doi.org/10.1080/03066150.2011.607702.

Zibechi, Raúl. 2012. *Territories of Resistance: A Cartography of Latin American Social Movements.* Translated by Ramor Ryan. Oakland: AK.

Index

ACDIP (Petén Campesino
Association), 53–4
ACROX (Rosario Xolhuitz
Campesino Association), 157–66,
237, 238
ACSUR–Las Segovias (Association
for Cooperation with the South–
Las Segovias), 112, 119
activist research, 12–19
ADISC (Santa Cruz Association for
Comprehensive Development),
157–66, 237, 238
ADRI (Alliance for Comprehensive
Rural Development), 53–6, 58, 60,
102, 145, 152, 227
African palm. *See* extractive
industries
agrarian conflict, 8, 37, 43, 57, 63, 69,
77–97, 98–104, 107, 127–30, 136,
155–66, 186, 192–4, 197–8, 204–8,
211–12, 226, 228, 229–30, 232, 236,
237–8, 240; conflictivity, 77–8, 230
agrarian reform, 6–7, 21, 35, 37,
44–6, 48–52, 56, 63, 64, 66–9, 75–6,
90, 95–7, 99, 122, 138, 144–5, 181,
196–7, 227–8, 231, 239
Agrarian Reform Law, 44–5

agrarian regions, 229
agrarian sovereignty, 199–201, 239
Agreement on Socio-Economic
Aspects and the Agrarian Situation
(Socio-Economic Accord), 31–3,
35–6, 50–1, 64, 67, 101, 144,
146, 196–7
agricultural exports, 7–8, 29
agricultural products: bananas, 7,
158, 176; beans, 125, 132–5, 147,
148, 176; cardamom, 89, 133–4, 176;
cattle, 72, 112, 116–20, 122, 171–6,
201; chilli peppers, 133–4; chicken,
148; chipilín, 176, 239; cotton, 47,
71, 110, 118, 120–1; fish, 42, 112, 116,
122, 148, 192, 200–1; macadamia
nut, 156–8, 161; non-traditional
exports, 7, 29, 229; pacaya, 176–7,
239; peanuts, 133–4, 176–7; sesame,
116–20, 134; sugar, 7, 47, 72, 80,
83, 125, 168, 176, 225, 239. *See also*
coffee; corn
Akram-Lodhi, Haroon, 239
alcaldes auxiliares, 113, 115, 124,
135, 172
Alliance for Progress, 45–6
Alonso, Alberto, 70, 232

Alta Verapaz, 8, 15, 17, 55, 72, 74–5,
    80, 81, 83–9, 92, 103, 105–6, 108,
    128–9, 134, 136, 137, 140, 143, 153–
    4, 184, 187, 192, 197, 107, 229–30,
    231, 232, 236, 238, 240
alternative agriculture, 11, 55, 148,
    196, 199–202, 207, 236
alternative economic models, 7, 62,
    126–7, 182–3, 190–1, 198–202, 210–12
Amnesty International, 81, 128
AMR (Alliance of Rural Women), 54
ANC (National Campesino
    Association), 48–9
ANN (Alliance for a New Nation;
    Alternative for a New Nation),
    58, 228
Arbenz, Jacobo, 6, 28–9, 44–5, 67,
    90, 122
Arévalo, Juan José, 44
Argentina, 22, 199
armed conflict, 3, 6–7, 11, 28–31,
    46–51, 59, 69, 80–1, 110–11, 139–41,
    144, 187, 189, 196
armed forces. See state violence
armed groups. See violence
ASOCODE (Central American
    Association of Campesino
    Organizations for Cooperation
    and Development), 227
Atz, Gilberto, 145, 165, 170, 235, 238
autonomy, 4, 6, 22, 39, 63, 126–7, 166,
    180, 201, 203–4, 209–10
AVANCSO (Association for the
    Advancement of the Social
    Sciences in Guatemala), 53, 71, 81,
    91, 229, 232
Aztlán, 107

Baja Verapaz, 53, 55, 86, 89, 103, 108,
    197, 207, 229, 232, 236, 239
Baldetti, Roxanna, 187

banking, 29–30, 34
Bastos, Santiago, 232–3
BC-CASA, 147–8, 236
Berger, Óscar, 81, 225
Bol, César, 105, 194, 232
Bolivia, 22–3
Brazil, 22, 40, 67, 90, 228
Brett, Roddy, 100–1, 227

Caal, Celso, 80, 107
Caal Choc, Mario Tulio, 81
CACIF (Coordinating Committee
    of Agricultural, Commercial,
    Industrial, and Financial
    Associations), 29, 32, 35
Cadastral Law, 52, 144
cadastry. See land title regularization
Café Justicia. See CCDA
CAFTA-DR (Dominican Republic–
    Central America Free Trade
    Agreement), 34
campesinos, 35, 43, 76. See also
    Guatemalan campesino movement
Canada, 147, 150, 168, 196, 198, 236
Canlún, 8, 17, 80–1, 83–5, 185,
    230, 231
capitalism, 23, 25–6, 96, 183,
    190, 198–9
Carchá, 134
Castillo, Federico, 99–100
Catholic Action, 45–6
Catholic Church, 44–6, 49, 77
CCDA (Campesino Committee of the
    Highlands): agrarian conflicts, 91,
    92, 165–6, 182, 205–8; alternative
    economic projects, 11, 62, 139,
    141–2, 148, 150, 199–200; Café
    Justicia, 147–52, 182–3, 195–200,
    202, 207, 210, 239; and campesino
    movement, 53–6, 58–9, 144–5, 152–
    4, 197, 205–6; class, 11, 144, 149, 211;

coffee, 11, 142–4, 147–52, 195–202;
Don Pancho community, 166–83,
200–1; and electoral politics, 58, 187,
198, 208–9; expansion of, 11, 154,
197–8, 205–12; and *Fondo de Tierras*,
59–61, 145–7, 154, 180–3, 196–7;
funding model, 148–9, 151; history
of, 140–4, 235; Indigenous identity,
11, 139–40, 150, 210–11; land access,
142–4, 146–8, 154, 172, 197, 207;
and member communities, 141–3,
146–50, 152–5, 178–83, 207–8, 210;
National Indigenous, Campesino,
and Popular March, 153–4, 197–8,
206–7; National Coordination
Council, 153; negotiation with
government, 148, 153, 197; and
neoliberalism, 195–202; and NGOs,
151, 236; and peace process, 144,
183, 196–7; political activism of,
140–2, 148, 152–3, 197–9; repression
of, 140–2, 154, 185, 206, 239, 240;
and research methods, 10, 13–16;
Salvador Xolhuitz community,
155–66, 181–3, 201–2; and youth,
141, 154, 187, 237
CDN (National Directive Council).
See CONIC
CEH (Historical Clarification
Commission), 111
Cerezo, Vinicio, 48–9, 226
CERLAC (Centre for Research on Latin
America and the Caribbean), 17
Chabil Utzaj, 80, 83, 230, 231
Chahal, 92, 105–6, 127, 135–6, 192, 233
Champerico, 103, 109, 118, 187
Chic, José, 208
Chile, 28
Chimaltenango, 11, 86, 140–3, 146,
168, 181, 198, 200, 211, 226, 229,
232, 236, 238

Chisec, 74, 129, 229
Chitocán, 81, 128–30, 136, 230
Christian Democratic party, 48, 226
Choc Pop, Daniel, 240
Chub Icó, Hermelindo, 15, 92, 106,
128, 136, 193, 232
CIA (Central Intelligence Agency), 6,
28, 45
CICIG (International Commission
against Impunity in Guatemala),
184, 189
civil society, 7, 28, 31–2, 38, 40,
141, 203
clandestinity, 47–50, 140–2, 226, 235
class, 7, 11, 23–7, 43, 46, 99, 140, 144,
149–50, 211, 226; conciousness-
raising, 46
climate change, 9
CLOC (Latin American Coordinator
of Rural Organizations), 227
CNAIC-P (National Indigenous-
Campesino and Popular Council),
53–5, 57–8, 60, 152, 206, 236
CNCG (National Campesino
Confederation of Guatemala), 44
CNOC (National Coordinator of
Campesino Organizations), 50,
52–60, 63, 102, 144–5, 152, 157, 165,
205–6, 227, 228, 235; Proposal for
Comprehensive Agrarian Reform,
52–3, 56, 63, 145
CNP-T (Permanent National
Coordinator on Rights Related to
Land and Indigenous Peoples),
51–2
CNUS (National Committee on
Labour Union Unity), 46–7
Cobán, 81, 105–6, 128, 134, 143, 197,
206–7
COCODE (Community Development
Council), 62–3, 135, 172

CODECA (Campesino Development Committee), 53, 91, 227
coffee, 5–7, 11, 44, 52, 56, 71, 86–7, 89, 91, 107, 110, 142–4, 146–52, 154, 155–9, 161–2, 166–8, 171, 174–7, 179, 182–3, 191, 195–9, 201, 202, 207, 227, 235–6, 238, 239; 1999–2004 price collapse of, 52, 56, 71, 157, 227; direct trade, 107, 139, 142, 147–8, 150, 154, 159, 182, 191, 195–6, 199, 234, 235; fair trade, 147–51, 234, 236
Colom, Álvaro, 81, 102, 145, 152, 184, 193–4, 230
colonato. See mozos colonos
colonialism, 3, 5–6, 22–5
community development, 42, 46, 56, 57, 59, 62–3, 90, 104–8, 110–38, 155–83, 181–3, 191–3, 201–2
community leadership, 63, 108, 113, 115, 123–4, 135–6, 171–2, 237–8
Comprehensive Rural Development Law, 56, 102, 145–6, 152, 154
CONAMPRO (National Coordinator of Small and Medium Producers), 50
CONAP (National Council for Protected Areas), 103
CONATIERRA (National Land Commission), 48–9, 67–9, 226
CONDEG (Guatemalan National Committee of the Displaced), 50, 53, 54, 91
CONGCOOP (Coordinator of NGOs and Cooperatives), 142–4
Congress, Guatemalan, 32, 48, 54, 56, 173, 187, 194, 197, 198, 205, 208, 210, 227, 240
CONIC (National Indigenous and Campesino Coordinator): agrarian conflicts, 11, 80, 83, 88–9, 91–4, 128–30; and campesino movement, 50, 53–5, 59–62, 99–102; CDN

(National Directive Council), 61, 105–8; co-optation of, 11, 102, 193–5, 204–5; and CUC, 50, 99–101; and Fondo de Tierras, 59–61, 101, 125–6; gender, 108, 123–4; Indigenous identity, 11, 99, 211, 232; land access, 102–4, 232; land occupations, 90–4, 101, 129; and member communities, 42–3, 62–3, 83, 104–9, 113–17, 121–7, 128–30, 136–7, 191–3; negotiation with government, 11, 99–102, 193–4; and neoliberalism, 191–5; promotores, 63, 104–5, 191–3; and research methods, 10, 13, 15–16; San José La Pasión community, 127–38, 192–3; tactics of, 100–3; Territorial Collectives, 99, 104–8, 121–2, 136, 191–5, 202, 232–3; Victorias III community, 109–27, 137–8, 191–2
Conquest, Spanish, 4–6, 44; continuing nature of, 6
Consejo Nacional Indígena y Campesino Kut Bal Bey, 237
conservation, 80, 84, 94
consultas. See extractive industries
CONTIERRA (Presidential Office for Land Conflict Legal Assistance and Resolution), 96, 103
cooperatives, 22, 44–6, 83, 95, 128–9, 147, 150, 199, 226, 228, 234
co-optation, 11, 31–3, 40, 51–2, 97, 102, 189, 193–5, 204–5
Copeland, Nicholas, 58–9
corn, 80, 83, 93, 110, 116–21, 125–6, 132–5, 138, 148, 158, 167, 170–2, 176–7, 234, 238
corruption, 61, 68–9, 74, 145, 156, 186–9, 194, 198, 208, 229
counter-insurgency, 29–30, 33–4, 47–8, 225

counter-insurgent state, 29–30, 34, 185–6
CRD (Convergence for the Democratic Revolution), 58, 198, 208
crime, 9, 184–6
criminalization. *See* state violence
CTG (Confederation of Guatemalan Workers), 44
CUC (Committee for Campesino Unity), 11, 43–4, 46–7, 49–50, 53–5, 64, 91, 92, 98–100, 111, 140, 141, 153, 190, 197, 206, 211, 226, 231, 232, 235, 236, 239–40
Cuc Xo, Feliz, 230

dealing, 20
debt, 5, 24, 26, 30, 73, 76, 86, 95, 96, 102, 107–8, 111, 125–6, 135, 137–8, 143, 146–7, 160, 162, 163, 166, 172–3, 178, 192, 197, 200, 204
Decentralization Law, 144, 228
DED (German Development Service), 236, 239
democratization, 26–7; in Guatemala, 30, 34, 69, 90
direct trade. *See* coffee
displacement, 4–7, 47–8, 75, 80–1, 94
Doctors without Borders, 112–13
drug trade. *See* violence

earthquake, 44, 46–7
economic-military-criminal nexus, 185–6, 188–90
Edelman, Marc, 18
EGP (Guerrilla Army of the Poor), 50, 60, 99
El Petén, 8, 53, 67–9, 72, 74, 83, 85–6, 184, 226, 229, 238
El Quiché, 46, 72, 83, 85–6, 140, 229, 232, 236, 239–40

electoral politics, 30–3, 40, 42–3, 48, 58–9, 108–9, 187–9, 198, 205, 208–10, 212, 228, 240
electricity, 8–9, 33–4, 62, 73, 114, 118, 126, 130, 171, 173, 185, 187, 198, 207, 225, 230
elites, 7, 21–34, 37–9, 41, 45, 51, 59, 64, 67, 76, 186, 188, 190, 196–7, 199, 203–4, 212, 225
Escuintla, 86, 90, 143, 168, 232, 236
Esquina, Pedro, 99–100
Estatuto Agrario, 67–8
extractive industries, 6–8, 10, 27, 34, 78; African palm, 76, 78, 225; agro-fuel, 4–5, 7–8, 72, 74, 78, 225, 230; *consultas*, 5, 186–7, 212; geothermal energy, 187; hydroelectric dams, 4–5, 7, 34, 185, 187, 198, 207, 225, 230; iron, 187; mega-projects, 57, 76, 186–7, 197, 212, 225, 230; mining, 7–8, 34, 57, 76–7, 184–7, 197–8, 212, 225; oil, 5, 7, 34

fair trade. *See* coffee
FAR (Rebel Armed Forces), 60, 141, 165, 226
FDYEP (Petén Promotion and Development Agency), 67–9
FEDECOCAGUA (Guatemalan Federation of Coffee Cooperatives), 54, 147, 199
FLACSO (Latin American Faculty of Social Sciences), 54
FNL (National Struggle Front), 53
FOGUAVI (Guatemalan Housing Fund), 173
FONAPAZ (National Peace Fund), 103, 130, 173, 234
Fondo de Tierras, 16, 21, 35–42, 51–2, 54–5, 57, 59–61, 65–7, 69–77, 80–3, 85, 91, 94–7, 101–4, 111–12, 118, 122, 125–6, 137–9, 143–7, 154–8, 160–7,

169–73, 177–8, 180–3, 190–3; and
corruption, 61, 74, 145; Fondo
de Tierras Law, 52; Land Access
Program, 69–70, 72, 75; Land
Administration Project, 67, 74, 76, 96;
Land Fund Project, 67–8, 76; Land
title regularization program, 69, 74
FONTIERRAS. See *Fondo de Tierras*
food security, 73, 112, 144
food sovereignty, 149
Foucault, Michel, 25, 40
Franja Transversal del Norte, 76
Fraser, Nancy, 40
Fundación del Centavo, 69
FUNDAECO (Foundation
for Ecodevelopment and
Conservation), 103
Funes, Sergio, 50, 52

Galicia, Luis, 61, 232
Garoz, Byron, 70, 232
Gauster, Susana, 70, 232
gender, 9, 25, 108, 123–4, 135–6, 172,
198, 200
genocide. *See* state violence
Girón, Andrés, 48–9, 197, 226
Gómez Hernández, Abisaias, 76–7
governance, 22–3, 38–9, 59, 63, 80,
96–7, 209–10
governmentality, 24–5, 39, 67, 204
Gramsci, Antonio, 31–2, 188
Grandia, Liza, 6, 8, 74, 231, 238
Green Revolution, 45
Guatemala, department of, 90
Guatemalan campesino movement:
activities of, 56–63, 187; and
agrarian conflicts, 57, 79–97;
history of, 43–56; internal divisions,
51–6, 59–61, 64; and land access, 57;
and legal support, 87–8, 103; and
member communities, 42–3, 56–8,

61–3, 121–7; national campesino
congress, 50; and neoliberalism,
60–2; and NGOs, 57–8; and peace
process, 50–2, 188; and political
parties, 58; proposals, 50, 52–3,
56, 145; transnational organizing,
227–8. *See also* CNOC
Guatemalan Ministry of the Interior, 63
Guatemalan News and Information
Bureau, 235
Guatemalan peace accords, 7, 21, 31,
33, 36–8, 41, 50–1, 59, 61–5, 96, 101,
142, 144, 154, 183, 188, 190, 197,
204, 209
Guatemalan peace process, 18, 21,
26, 28–33, 37–8, 40, 64, 76, 101, 188,
196, 225, 227

Hale, Charles R., 13–14, 18, 21–2,
38–40, 96, 195, 202–5, 209–10, 239
Handy, Jim, 44–5, 226
Harvey, David, 23
health, 9, 42, 112, 114, 122, 192
hegemony, 26–7, 188–90, 212
historical land claims, 66, 77, 83–6, 240
Homo economicus, 21, 36, 40, 204
Honduras, 9, 39, 242
Huehuetenango, 72, 86, 142, 185, 187,
229, 232, 236
human rights defenders, 12, 19, 34,
186, 239
human rights organizations, 184
Hurricane Stan, 112
Hurtado Paz y Paz, Laura, 8, 74–5, 231

identity, 11, 40, 99–100, 139–40,
149–50, 210–11, 227
ideology, 23, 31
IMF (International Monetary Fund),
24, 32
Incer, Eugenio, 232

Indigenous peoples, 3–5, 22, 31, 37, 43, 51, 56, 208, 211
Indigenous rights, 11, 33, 49, 99–101, 152, 196, 203
Indigenous social movements, 39–40, 43, 58–9, 99–100
indio permitido, 40, 96, 203, 205
inequality, 3–4, 7, 18, 27, 45, 94, 96, 225
INTA (National Institution for Agrarian Transformation), 45–6, 49, 67–71, 74, 84, 102–3, 111, 122, 126, 193, 226
International Coffee Agreement, 86, 227
international solidarity, 18, 58, 142, 144, 147, 150–1, 165, 196, 199, 236
Izabal, 15, 72, 76, 80, 83, 86, 90, 92, 103, 106, 136, 229–30, 232–4, 238

Jonas, Susanne, 31
junta directiva. See community leadership
Juracán, Leocadio, 12, 17, 91, 144–6, 152–4, 167–8, 185, 187–8, 198, 206, 208–10, 239; election to Congress, 154, 187, 198, 205, 208, 210
Just Us! Coffee Roasters Cooperative, 147

Kab'awil, 53–5, 91, 157, 162, 165, 228, 237

labour, 5–6, 24, 35, 44, 46–7, 52–3, 57–8, 77–8, 86–91, 94, 103–4, 110, 120–1, 125, 128–30, 134–5, 143–4, 152, 169, 171–2, 177, 198, 234–5; labour unions, 6, 23, 44–5; minimum wage, 47, 120
labour disputes, rural, 86–90
Laguna Lachuá National Park, 84, 221

land: access, 11, 19, 35, 43, 55, 57–9, 62, 66–7, 69–70, 72, 75–7, 79, 82, 85, 87–91, 93–5, 97–8, 101–4, 107, 126, 128, 136–40, 142, 144–8, 154, 156, 172, 181–2, 191, 193–4, 196–8, 200–1, 205, 209, 226, 228, 231–2; colonization programs, 6, 49, 68–9, 84; concentration, 75; distribution, 6–7, 35, 45, 49, 51, 67–9, 78, 84, 111, 131, 146, 172, 204, 226, 245; evictions, 19, 81; market, 39, 59–61, 75–6, 96, 139, 181, 202–3, 226; occupation, 12, 15, 34, 48–50, 52, 55, 57, 66, 69, 77, 82, 90–2, 101–2, 104, 128, 137, 226; registration, 131, 204, 231; rental, 69, 102; speculation, 75; state-owned, 36, 68, 71; tenure, 95; title, 35–6, 38–9, 46, 56, 67, 69, 74–5, 78, 90, 103, 125–6, 137, 145, 232–3, 237, 240; title regularization, 36, 67, 69, 74–5, 78, 103, 145
land conflicts. *See* agrarian conflict
Land Trust Fund. See *Fondo de Tierras*
landowners, 6, 8, 36–7, 45, 49, 57, 61, 67, 71, 74, 76, 83, 87, 92–5, 97, 101, 110, 159–61, 169, 190, 204
Lanquín, 134
latifundio, 8
Latin America Working Group, 235
Law of Urban and Rural Development Councils, 228
Liberal Revolution, 44
liberation theology, 45
Livingston, 103
López Vásquez, Juventina, 42, 116, 122, 124, 191, 233
Lucas García, General Fernando Romeo, 129

MAGA (Ministry of Agriculture, Cattle, and Food), 37, 86, 103, 112, 234

market-led agrarian reform, 35, 41, 49, 51, 64, 66–77, 81, 83, 94, 145, 156, 201
Martín, Bonifacio, 165
Martínez, Daniel, 142
Martínez Peláez, Severo, 5, 22, 228
Marxism, 11, 23–5, 100, 226
Maya Kaqchikel, 140, 211
Maya K'iche', 83, 140
Maya Mam, 42, 110–11, 121, 237
Maya Q'eqchi', 6, 80, 83, 127, 134, 138, 140, 197, 207, 232–3, 238
Mayan cosmovision, 11
Mazariegos, Juan Carlos, 43, 226
mega-projects. *See* extractive industries
Menchú, Rigoberta, 108
Mexico, 178
Miethbauer, Thomas, 72–3
migration, 73, 166, 178, 180, 182, 198, 200
Milian, Bayron, 8, 74
milpa. See corn
mining. *See* extractive industries
MLAR. *See* market-led agrarian reform
Monteros, Rigoberto, 93–4, 103
Morales, Carlos, 60
Morales, Evo, 22
Morales, Jimmy, 189
Morales, Lesbia, 153, 206–7
Morán, Sandra, 240
mozos colonos, 5–6, 86–9, 105, 109, 128, 156–9, 161, 164, 231
MSICG (Guatemalan Labour, Indigenous, and Campesino Movement), 53, 58, 152
MST (Landless Workers' Movement), 22, 40, 228
Municipal Code, 228
murder. *See* violence

National Indigenous, Campesino, and Popular March. *See* CCDA
neoliberal agrarian institutions, 3, 12, 18–22, 38, 54, 66, 138, 154, 190, 209
neoliberal elites, 32–3, 225
neoliberal multiculturalism, 39–40, 209, 212
neoliberal peace, 28, 33, 38, 40, 212
neoliberal resources, 12, 20, 190–1, 193, 195–6, 198, 200–3, 205, 208–10
neoliberal restructuring, 22–8, 31, 33, 37, 94, 97, 202, 213
neoliberal state, 23, 29–30, 34, 37–9, 41, 67, 188–90
neoliberalism, 4, 19–29, 31, 33, 35, 37–41, 43, 59, 64–5, 67, 96–7, 183, 188, 190, 192–3, 195–7, 199–200, 202, 204–5, 209, 212, 225; in Guatemala, 28–38, 51–6, 64–5, 184–219; history of, 22–8; in Latin America, 22, 26–8; as new economic model, 7, 29; and peace negotiation in Guatemala, 30–8, 51, 64–5; and power, 23, 27, 76; and social movements, 22–3; strategic engagement with, 40–1, 190–213; and violence, 25, 188–90, 212–13
Nicaragua, 39
Nieto, Cristina, 112–13
non-governmental organizations (NGOs), 57–8, 62, 112–15, 117, 119, 121–3, 127, 142, 173–4, 185, 221, 228
Northern Lowlands, 15, 30, 71–2, 84
Nueva Cajolá, 107
Nuevo San Carlos, 143, 157–8, 164, 221, 231, 241

oil, 7, 34, 125
Oqueli, Yolanda, 185
organized crime, 184–6, 188–9

ORPA (Revolutionary Organization of the People in Arms), 60, 165
Oxlajuj Tz'ikin, 122–3, 127, 187, 219

pacification, 3, 12, 18, 39, 195, 203
Palestina Los Altos, 110–11, 121
Panzós, 83, 221–2
passive revolution, 31–3
patriarchy, 9, 108
Paz y Paz Baily, Claudia, 184
peasant leagues, 235
peasant unions, 44
Peña de León, Luis Fernando, 75–6
Pérez Molina, Otto, 34, 153, 185–9, 193–4, 197, 225
plantations, 5–6, 8, 15, 22, 36–7, 44, 47, 67, 71, 74, 90, 110, 120, 123, 134, 137, 156–7, 160, 165, 168–71, 177, 186, 196, 200, 238
Plataforma Agraria, 52–4, 57, 59–61, 65, 76, 143, 183, 190
political imagination, 22
Polochic Valley, 17, 80, 83, 185, 231
"post-conflict" period, 188–90, 212–13, 239
poverty, 4, 8–9, 27, 56, 72, 76, 86, 90
prestaciones laborales, 87, 158, 234, 237
private security. *See* violence
property, communal, 3, 5–6, 21, 42, 56, 62, 64, 66, 77–8, 83, 94–5, 98, 102, 104, 119, 127–8, 135, 137, 142, 156, 166, 197
property, private, 6, 21, 23, 36, 67–8, 74–5, 94–6, 231, 238
Proposal for Comprehensive Agrarian Reform. *See* CNOC
protest, 47–8, 52, 55–6, 63, 107, 125, 152, 154, 178, 185–7, 193–4, 196, 198–200, 206–8, 212
proyectismo, 62–3, 125, 136–7, 180

PTI (Interdiocesan Land Pastoral), 53
PTSM (Interdiocesan Land Pastoral of San Marcos), 77–8, 89, 220
Public Prosecutor's Office, 81
Purulhá, 103, 207

Quetzaltenango, 86, 90, 110, 120–1, 232
Quixayá, 139, 239

racism, 7, 9, 30
remittances, 73, 166, 178, 180, 182, 200
research methods, 12–19
Retalhuleu, 42, 86, 103, 107–8, 113, 118, 121–2, 137, 143, 157–8, 191, 231–3, 236
RIC (Cadastral Information Registry), 52, 196, 237
Río Chixoy, 84

SAA (Secretariat of Agrarian Affairs), 37–8, 77–9, 81–2, 84–6, 88–90, 93–7, 103–4, 122, 127, 129–30, 134, 137–8, 192–3, 230–2, 234, 238
Sabuc, Marcelo, 92, 159, 206, 237
Salacuín, 84, 231
Salvadó, Camilo, 81
Salvador Xolhuitz. *See* CCDA
San Antonio Palopó, 142–3, 149
San José La Pasión. *See* CONIC
San Juan Ostuncalco, 110–11, 121
San Juan Tres Ríos, 240
San Lucas Tolimán, 58, 146, 149, 239
San Marcos, 77, 111, 142, 187, 220, 232, 236
San Martín Jilotepeque, 141, 168–70, 178, 238
San Miguel Tucurú, 89, 103, 109, 231
San Pedro Yepocapa, 142–3
Santa Cruz del Quiché, 46, 239
Santa Cruz Muluá, 156, 165

Santa Rosa, 86, 143, 185, 232, 236–7
school, 33, 62, 112, 114, 122–3, 126,
    130–1, 138, 172–3, 192, 204, 207,
    234, 236
self-governance, 22
Senahú, 81, 103
Serrano, Jorge Elías, 32, 87, 99–100
Short, Nicola, 31–2, 35–6
Sipacapa, 187
social economy, 199
Socio-Economic Accord. *See*
    Agreement on Socio-Economic
    Aspects and the Agrarian Situation
Sololá, 11, 58, 90, 139–40, 142–3, 146,
    149, 159, 198, 211, 226, 232, 236–7, 239
South Coast, 5, 71–2, 110, 120
state formation, 6
state of siege. *See* state violence
state violence, 30–1, 37, 69, 81, 90–1,
    141, 184–9, 212, 235, 247; armed
    forces, 7, 18–19, 29–30, 33–4, 36,
    45–7, 84, 111, 141, 184–6, 188–9, 212,
    230, 239, 242; disappearance, 47,
    89, 111, 141; *estado de sitio* (state of
    siege), 17, 184, 230; genocide, 7, 18,
    30, 43, 59, 141; illegal detention, 19;
    massacres, 7, 30, 34, 47, 141, 185–6,
    242; police, 19, 30, 80, 84, 89, 92–3,
    128–9; remilitarization, 34, 185;
    repression, 5–6, 11, 17, 37, 45, 47–8,
    57, 64, 80–1, 90–2, 94, 96–7, 110, 128,
    140–2, 152–4, 162–4, 166, 184–6, 188,
    192, 194, 197, 203, 206, 235; Spanish
    embassy massacre, 47; state terror,
    7, 30, 90, 227. *See also* violence
structural violence, 9, 248
subjectivity, 21, 24–7, 36, 39–40, 67,
    96, 190, 202–4

Tarrow, Sidney, 43
territory, 3–6, 19, 21–2, 39, 56, 80, 207,
    210–12

Thatcher, Margaret, 25, 40
Tilly, Charles, 189
Tiney, Juan, 31, 61, 99–100, 103–4,
    194–5
Torres-Rivas, Edelberto, 34
Totonicapán, 34, 142, 185
transnational economic activity,
    29, 34
Tzib Quej, Emilio, 89–90

United Fruit Company, 226
United Nations, 32, 189
Universidad Rafael Landívar, 230–1
Urízar, Ingrid, 78, 89
URNG (Guatemalan National
    Revolutionary Unity), 7, 33, 38, 50,
    58, 60, 99, 162, 211
USAID (United States Agency
    for International Development),
    29, 45, 69, 226, 248; Private
    Enterprise Development
    program, 29
UVOC (Verapaz Union of Campesino
    Organizations), 53–5, 91–2, 228

Van Leeuwen, Mathijs, 77–8, 232
Vásquez, Juana, 99
Velásquez, Alvaro, 240
Velásquez, Hélmer, 142–3
Velásquez Nimatuj, Irma Alicia, 52,
    99–100, 107–8, 231–2
Véliz, Rodrigo, 239
Ventura, Marta Cecilia, 62–3,
    107–8, 136
Vía Campesina, 22, 227, 247
Victorias III. *See* CONIC
violence, 3–5, 7–9, 11–12, 17, 19,
    30–1, 45, 47–8, 59, 64, 69, 80–1,
    84–5, 92, 94, 141, 156, 162, 166,
    184–6, 188–9, 212–13, 235, 237;
    death squads, 30, 185, 239; drug
    cartels, 30, 74, 78, 186, 230, 239;

murder, 9, 19, 34, 47, 111, 141, 166, 184–6, 206, 239; paramilitaries, 17, 34, 154, 185–6, 206, 239; private security, 17, 80–1, 93, 185–6; *sicarios*, 186, 239. *See also* state violence

water, 8, 23, 33, 62, 73, 112, 114, 116, 118–19, 125–6, 130, 148, 156, 158, 168–74, 181, 185, 198, 200, 207, 238
Western Highlands, 5–6, 55, 72
Winaq, 58, 108–9
Wolford, Wendy, 18, 40

World Bank, 7, 9, 21, 29, 32, 36, 38–41, 51, 66–70, 72, 74–6, 94–6, 191–3, 196, 200, 202, 210, 237
World Food Programme, 9

Xinka, 43, 53–4, 91
Xunta de Galicia, 111–13, 117, 121–5, 137
Xya'al K'obe', 80–1, 83–5, 92, 221–2, 230–1

Yagenova, Simona, 239
Yashar, Deborah, 58

Zibechi, Raul, 40